CASE MANAGEMENT IN COMMUNITY CARE

CASE MANAGEMENT IN COMMUNITY CARE

An evaluated experiment in the home care of the elderly

David Challis & Bleddyn Davies

Gower

Published by

Gower Publishing Company Limited
Gower House
Croft Road
Aldershot
Hants GU11 3HR
England

Gower Publishing Company
Old Post Road
Brookfield
Vermont 05036
U.S.A.

British Library Cataloguing in Publication Data

Challis David
Case management in community care: an
evaluated experiment in the home care of
the elderly.
1. Aged - Care and hygiene - Great Britain
2. Aged - Home care - Great Britain
I. Title II. Davies, Bleddyn
362.6'1'0941 HV1481.G52

ISBN 0-566-05287-3

Typeset by Parkers Phototypesetting, Canterbury.
Printed and bound in Great Britain by
Blackmore Press, Shaftesbury, Dorset

CONTENTS

PREFACE xv

CHAPTER 1 A NEW APPROACH TO LONG-TERM CARE 1

1. Obstacles to Effective Case Management and Resource Allocation 2
   (a) Problems of coordination: service fragmentation and allocation 2
   (b) Interweaving with informal care 5
   (c) Relative neglect of the elderly 5
   (d) Problems of accountability 7
2. The Community Care Approach, Enhanced Case Management and Efficiency in Social Care 8
   (a) Enhanced case management 8
      (i) Manageable caseload and case responsibility 8
      (ii) Decentralised budget 9
      (iii) Trained and experienced staff 9
      (iv) Coterminous catchment areas 9
      (v) Modified procedures 9
   (b) Improved accountability 10
      (i) Defined caseload 10
      (ii) Budget limit 10
      (iii) Recording system 10
      (iv) Peer review 10
   (c) Better use of resources 11
      (i) Knowledge of unit costs 11
      (ii) Service package costed 11
      (iii) Continuity of responsibility 11
3. Expected Effects 13

Table 1.1 The community care approach, service objectives and aspects of efficiency 12

CHAPTER 2 THE DESIGN AND CONTEXT OF THE STUDY ... 17

1. Cost-effectiveness Issues 18
   (a) Experimental design 18
   (b) Data collection 19
      (i) Differential effects on parties 19
      (ii) Perceptions of client, carer and interviewer 19
      (iii) 'Final' and 'intermediate' outcomes 19
      (iv) General and specific outcomes 20

(v) Positive and negative aspects of ageing 20
(vi) The multiplicity of outcomes in relation to cost 20
2. Social Care Process Issues 21
3. The Selection of Cases 22
(a) Selection criteria 22
(i) Insufficiently needy 22
(ii) External events 23
(iii) Desire for residential care 23
(iv) Unrelinquishing carers 23
(v) Client characteristics 23
(b) The referral process in the experimental area 23
(c) The referral process in the control area 25
(d) Achieving group equivalence: post-selection matching 26
(i) Equivalence of the groups before matching 27
(ii) The matched pairs 29
4. The Characteristics of the Area and the Experimental Cases 30
(a) Characteristics of the area and system of care 30
(b) Characteristics of the elderly people 32
(c) Characteristics of principal carers 36

Table 2.1 Selection of groups for community care and standard provision 24
Table 2.2 Significant differences at the 5 per cent level between the two groups before and after matching 27
Table 2.3 Distribution of the sample on measures of frailty 28
Table 2.4 Private households living at more than 1.5 persons per room in 1971 31
Table 2.5 Private households with the exclusive use of amenities in 1971 31
Table 2.6 Sex and marital status 34
Table 2.7 Living group 34
Table 2.8 Housing circumstances 34
Table 2.9 Help needed with personal and instrumental tasks of daily living. Community care recipients, residents in homes and recipients of domiciliary services in England compared 35
Table 2.10 Activities of daily living 35
Table 2.11 Health problems of clients 36
Table 2.12 Mental health problems of clients 36
Table 2.13 Mental distress of carers 37

CHAPTER 3 KEY WORKERS AND CASE MANAGEMENT 39
1. Raising Referrals: case finding and screening 39
(a) Organisational locus 39
(b) Initial agency contacts 40
(c) Initial procedures and their development 41
(d) Effects on targeting 42
2. Assessment 43
(a) Processes and procedures in assessment 44
(i) Initial contact 44
(ii) Closer involvement of the elderly person and their carers 44
(iii) Collaboration: the influence of other services and helpers 45
(iv) The effect of controlling resources 46
(b) Instrumentation 46
3. Care Planning, Service Arranging, Maintenance and Monitoring 47
(a) Processes and style of practice 47
(i) Making needed help available: enabling 48
(ii) Helping clients cope with loss 49
(iii) Meeting the needs of family and informal carers 50
(iv) Mobilising and coordinating formal services 51
(v) Organising support from the local community 57
(vi) The distribution of social worker time 58
(b) Procedural factors and organisational influences 60
(i) Budgets, costs and care planning 61
(ii) Recording and documentation 61
(iii) Local opportunities and constraints 62
4. Terminating Care at Home 65
5. Conclusions 68

Table 3.1 Seven services most frequently received before enrollment in community care and during subsequent year 52
Table 3.2 Major problem of cases not in receipt of home help at referral ...53
Table 3.3 Use of services over one year 56
Table 3.4 Distribution of social worker time in most representative period 60

CHAPTER 4 RESPONDING TO NEED 71

1. Problems Associated with Physical Frailty 71
   (a) Problems associated with high risk of falling 73
   (b) Elderly people suffering from incontinence 75
   (c) Serious degree of physical frailty 79
2. Problems Associated with Mental Disorder 83
   (a) Problems associated with depressed mood 83
   (b) Problems associated with long-standing personality difficulties 87
   (c) Problems associated with alcohol abuse 90
   (d) Problems associated with functional psychoses 94
   (e) Elderly people suffering from confusional states 95
3. Conclusions 104

Table 4.1 Clients at high risk of falling 72
Table 4.2 Clients with incontinence of urine 74
Table 4.3 Clients with serious physical frailty 80
Table 4.4 Clients with depression 84
Table 4.5 Clients with long-standing personality difficulties 88
Table 4.6 Clients with problems of alcohol abuse 91
Table 4.7 Clients with functional psychoses 93
Table 4.8 Clients suffering from confusional states 97

CHAPTER 5 SUPPORTING THE CARERS 105

1. Elderly People Living with Carers 107
   (a) Elderly people living with a spouse 107
   (b) Elderly people living with other informal carers 110
2. Elderly People Living Apart from Carers 111
   (a) Elderly people supported by family members 113
   (b) Elderly people supported by other informal carers 116
3. Conclusion 117

Table 5.1 Clients living with spouse 106
Table 5.2 Clients living with informal carers other than spouse 109
Table 5.3 Clients with considerable informal help but not living with carer 112

CHAPTER 6 DEVELOPING COMMUNITY SUPPORT 119
1. Social Work and Helpers 119
(a) Recruitment of helpers 119
(b) Selection of helpers 121
(c) Matching carer and care-giver 124
(d) Introducing helpers 125
(e) Payment of helpers 126
(f) Support of helpers 129
(i) Maintaining boundaries 129
(ii) Balancing needs and demands 129
(iii) Ensuring financial payments remain appropriate 130
(iv) Recognition of helpers' own needs and difficulties 130
(v) Group support and informal helper networks 130
(vi) Acceptance of ultimate responsibility for client welfare 131
(g) Turnover among helpers 131
(h) The status of helpers 133
2. Helpers and Clients 134
(a) Tasks undertaken by helpers 134
(i) Night and morning tasks 135
(ii) Personal care activities 136
(iii) Daily household tasks 137
(iv) Weekly or less frequent household care tasks 137
(v) Social and therapeutic tasks 138
(vi) Tasks related to support of informal carers 139
(vii) Other tasks 140
(b) Helper tasks and client dependency 140
(c) Client-helper relationships: the shift towards informal care 142
3. Conclusions 144

Table 6.1 Main source of recruitment of helpers 120
Table 6.2 Age and sex of helpers 124
Table 6.3 Previous relevant work experience of helpers 124
Table 6.4 Rate paid per helper visit, £ at 1977 prices 127
Table 6.5 Turnover of helpers 132
Table 6.6 Helpers leaving project for reasons other than 'natural wastage' 132
Table 6.7 Tasks specified in contracts with helpers 135
Table 6.8 Helpers' activities at night and morning 136
Table 6.9 Helpers' tasks in personal care 136
Table 6.10 Helpers' tasks in daily household care 137
Table 6.11 Helpers' tasks in weekly household care 138

Table 6.12 Social and therapeutic tasks undertaken by helpers 139
Table 6.13 Support to informal carer provided by helpers 140
Table 6.14 Helper activity by dependency level 141

CHAPTER 7 THE OUTCOME OF CARE 145

1. Patterns of Institutionalisation and Survival 145
(a) Location of elderly people after one year 145
(b) Location of elderly people over four years 147
(c) Reasons for admission to residential homes 148
(d) Possible explanations of differences in the probability of death 149
(i) Group similarities and differences 149
(ii) Relocation effects 151
(iii) The effects of service provision 152
2. Changes in Quality of Life of the Elderly Person 153
(a) Cases included in the analysis and the allowance for missing information 154
(b) Effects upon Subjective Well-being and Quality of Care 155
3. Changes in Health Status of Elderly People 157
4. Outcomes for Family and Informal Carers 162
5. The Impact of Community Care on Caring Networks 164
6. Summary and Conclusion 165

Table 7.1 Location of matched pairs of cases over four years 146
Table 7.2 Location of the community care and comparison groups after twelve months 147
Table 7.3 Reasons for entry to long-term institutional care among community care clients 148
Table 7.4 Confiding relationships of clients 153
Table 7.5 Subjective well-being outcomes 156
Table 7.6 Quality of care outcomes 158
Table 7.7 Health care outcomes 161
Table 7.8 Outcomes for principal carers 163
Table 7.9 Effects on informal care over one year 164

CHAPTER 8 THE COSTS OF CARE 167

1. Principles of Costing 167
(a) Opportunity costs 167
(b) Discounting future costs 168
(c) The divergence between private and social costs 168

2. Costs to the Social Services Department 169
(a) Residential care 169
(b) Day care 171
(c) Fieldwork 171
(d) Domiciliary services 172
3. Costs to the National Health Service 173
(a) Hospital services 173
(b) Community health services 175
4. Costs to the Local Authority Housing Department 176
5. Costs to the Social Security Agency 177
6. Costs to Private and Voluntary Welfare Agencies......................................177
7. Costs to Clients 177
8. Costs to Families and Informal Carers 179
9. Public Expenditure Costs 180
10. Social Opportunity Costs 180
11. The Costs of Community Care and Standard Services 181
(a) Costs to the social services department 186
(b) Costs to the National Health Service 186
(c) Costs to elderly people and informal carers 187
(d) Costs to other local authority departments 187
(e) Costs to the public purse and society as a whole......................................187

Table 8.1 Social services department costs, £ at 1977 prices 170
Table 8.2 Total hospital resource costs per inpatient day by discount rate and capital expenditure scenario, £ at 1977 prices 174
Table 8.3 Estimate costs of home nursing, £ at 1977 prices 175
Table 8.4 Unit cost of community health services, £ at 1977 prices 176
Table 8.5 Weekly rates of benefit paid by the Department of Health and Social Security, 1977 178
Table 8.6 Personal income by weekly income level, £ at 1977 prices.........179
Table 8.7 Costs of matched pairs annually and per month of survival, £ at 1977 prices 182
Table 8.8 Cost per case to the social services department for matched cases by Dependency Group (revenue account), £ at 1977 prices 185
Table 8.9 Cost per case to the National Health Service for matched cases by Dependency Group (assuming 7% discount rate) £ at 1977 prices 185
Table 8.10 Social opportunity cost per case for matched cases by Dependency Group (assuming 7% discount rate), £ at 1977 prices ...185

CHAPTER 9 COSTS AND OUTCOMES: THE ISSUE OF COST-EFFECTIVENESS 189

1. The Approach to the Analysis 189
(a) Variables used in the analysis 190
(i) Costs 190
(ii) Outputs 190
(iii) Quasi-inputs 191
(b) The estimation procedure and interpretation of tables 191
2. Costs and Outcomes for the Social Services Department 194
(a) Factors influencing the relationship between costs and outcomes: the process of care 197
(i) Health and dependency 197
(ii) Informal support 198
(iii) Personality and attitude to help 198
(iv) Other factors 199
(b) The costs of outputs for elderly people in different circumstances 199
(i) Costs of ten case types 199
(ii) Effects for informal carers 204
3. Costs and Outcomes for the National Health Service 205
(a) Factors influencing variations in cost 205
(i) Health and dependency 205
(ii) Social support 208
(iii) Personality and attitudinal characteristics 208
(iv) Other factors 208
(b) The costs of outputs for elderly people in different circumstances 208
(c) The interdependence of health and social care 209
4. Costs and Outcomes for Society as a Whole 211
(a) Factors influencing the relationship between costs and outcomes 211
(i) Health and dependency 211
(ii) Social support 213
(iii) Personality and attitudinal characteristics 213
(iv) Other factors 214
(b) The costs of outputs for elderly people in different circumstances 215
(i) Costs of four case types 215
(ii) Effects for informal carers 217
5. Conclusions 217

Table 9.1 Predictor variables used in the cost estimation 192
Table 9.2 Costs of outputs to the social services department in community care, 'outcome by dependency' relationship £ at 1977 prices 195
Table 9.3 Cost of outputs to the social services department in standard provision, 'outcome by dependency' relationship £ at 1977 prices 196
Table 9.4 Characteristics of the ten client types 200
Table 9.5 Annual costs of outcomes to the social services department for different types of case, £ at 1977 prices 202
Table 9.6 Cost of outputs to the National Health Service in community care, £ at 1977 prices 206
Table 9.7 Cost of outputs to the National Health Service in standard provision, £ at 1977 prices 207
Table 9.8 Annual costs to the National Health Service of different levels of output for four Dependency Groups, £ at 1977 prices 210
Table 9.9 Cost of outputs to society in community care, £ at 1977 prices ... 212
Table 9.10 Cost of outputs to society in standard provision £ at 1977 prices 213
Table 9.11 Cost to society of different levels of output for four Dependency Groups, £ at 1977 prices 213

CHAPTER 10 CONCLUSIONS AND FUTURE PROSPECTS ... 219

1. Expectations Reviewed 219
   (a) Admission to institutional care 219
   (b) Cost-effectiveness 219
   (c) Matching resources to needs 220
   (d) Improved benefits 220
   (e) Social work roles and tasks 221
   (f) Variations in responses to different problems 222
   (g) A heightened sensitivity to care networks and informal care 223
   (h) Meeting new needs 224
2. Future Issues for Policy and Practice 224
   (a) Social work and costs 225
   (b) Social work practice and management 226
   (c) Decentralisation and specialisation 227
   (d) Long-term care for other client groups 228
3. Inter-agency Working 230

APPENDIX A
OUTCOME AND DESCRIPTOR INDICATORS 233

Table 1 Distribution of Activities of Daily Living and General Health ratios for matched cases 235
Table 2 Distribution of Subjective Well-being and Quality of care 236

APPENDIX B COMMUNITY CARE RECORDS 241

BIBLIOGRAPHY 268

AUTHOR INDEX 282

SUBJECT INDEX 285

PREFACE

This book is about the first community care project. The Personal Social Services Research Unit (PSSRU) approach to community care decentralises to field workers the responsibility, authority and accountability for performing what we call 'the core tasks of case management', providing them with the opportunity, control over a budget, incentives and knowledge to mobilise and use resources to achieve more equitable and efficient outcomes for clients and carers. This first Kent community care scheme influenced developments by other social services departments and, more recently, health authorities. Some which most closely apply the principles of the PSSRU approach are also being evaluated by us.

This is one of three books about the first PSSRU community care project. One is *Matching Resources to Needs in Community Care* (Davies and Challis, 1986). It shows how the design of the project and the more general PSSRU approach to community care reflect a broader analysis of equity and efficiency in long-term care, how the approach compares with American experimental attempts to develop alternatives to institutional long-term care, and how the approach might be further developed. It provides more technical information about the evaluation, shows the results of analyses in greater detail, and deals with other topics not pursued here. *Matching Resources to Needs* is long. For most, it is a book for reference and for the pursuit of policy, theoretical and methodological argument, not for acquiring a broad understanding of the project and its results. For this reason, we saw the need for *Case Management in Community Care*, a shorter book targeted particularly at field professionals and agency managers. To help the reader to follow up results in more detail, we provide cross-references to *Matching Resources to Needs* in this book. There is also a third book, *Why Help?* (Qureshi, Challis and Davies, 1986). This is a study of the motivations and rewards of the helpers mobilised by the case managers. We expect to publish later studies based on the other community care projects.

Many have helped us, and not all can be mentioned here. The elderly persons and their families allowed themselves to be interviewed at length at least twice. The topics covered included distressing incapacities, stress, fear, and the inability to cope. There would not have been a project without Nicolas Stacey (then director of social services of Kent County Council). Mike Lauerman and Don Brand contributed to the management of the later stages of the implementation; Jack Clark and Roger Morgan had large, frequent and direct impacts on the project. Roger was crucial in the translation of broad principles into precise arrangements and practice policy. Jack was an imaginative and able manager of the implementation. His enthusiasm was contagious. Jack and Roger should be counted as collaborators. The members of the project team -Fred Brown, Jean Donaghay, Jon Holman and Mary Kirk - each made a very personal contribution. Officers of Kent County Council and others contributed data and help with great generosity.

The Monument Trust provided the grant which paid the costs of the evaluation and supported the fieldworker costs. Since 1980 the Department of Health and Social Security has financed the research, and our liaison officers Jack Barnes and Hazel Canter have done much to ensure the success of the work. The Department has also played an important part in the replication and development of the community care approach in other areas. We are particularly grateful to Tilda Goldberg, who not only read an earlier draft with great care and made many invaluable suggestions for its improvement, but also continuously encouraged us throughout. Furthermore, a number of people with particular expertise in this area have made important suggestions which have improved this book. In particular we should like to thank Mr Chris Gostick (Deputy Director of Social Services in the London Borough of Westminster), Professor John Grimley-Evans (Professor of Geriatric Medicine at Oxford) and Professor Olive Stevenson (Professor of Social Work at Nottingham).

Our academic colleagues at the PSSRU have contributed in many ways. In particular, features of the design and the content of the instrumentation reflect the efforts of Andrew Bebbington and Martin Knapp. Su Bellingham and Anne Walker have typed and corrected drafts with great patience; Roger Hampson and Nick Brawn have been invaluable sub-editors; and Jane Dennett has handled the final preparation of the draft and subsequent liaison with the printers and publishers with great zeal and efficiency. The book would have been worse without the efforts of any of them.

CHAPTER 1

A NEW APPROACH TO LONG-TERM CARE

Finding ways of providing effective long-term care in the community has become a central concern in the care of most client groups. In the case of the elderly, the growth in both the size and dependency of the population, in particular those over 75 who are the major consumers of health and social care services, has increasingly directed attention towards the maintenance and extension of community support. In the latter part of the 1970s, when this study commenced, it was expected that by the year 2001 those aged 75 and over would increase by some three-quarters of a million and the number of people aged 85 and over would increase by nearly one-third of a million (Plank, 1978). More recent population projections suggest that the rate of growth, particularly in the over-85 group, will be greater due to changes in mortality patterns. Between 1981 and 2011 the over-85s, who are very heavy users of health and social services, are expected to double in number (Craig, 1983). Despite very real increases in provision up to and following the creation of social services departments - in particular residential care - the level of need among elderly people living at home has increased at a faster rate (Bebbington, 1979). Thus demographic pressure and constrained budgets, a degree of uncertainty about the role of residential care (Townsend, 1962), and the preference of many elderly people to remain in their own homes, underlie the emergence of a significant group of elderly people who require long-term care in the community.

These elderly people and their carers have a wide variety of needs arising from a combination of such factors as the nature and type of physical frailty, mental ill-health, the availability of social support, and the time and duration of the care required. The provision of effective and adequate care at home for such people necessitates a recognition of the 'comprehensive' nature of need (Plank, 1978). The comprehensive nature of need refers to two elements; first complexity - needs cannot be met wholly by the straightforward provision of practical help - and second, extensiveness - the broad span of time over which, and range of tasks with which, an individual may require help during any one day. An appropriate response will require effective identification of cases in need, careful assessment, the organisation and coordination of care from a wide range of different sources (family, friends, intimate social networks, voluntary and statutory agencies) so that the care from each may be interwoven into a total system of care. Such an integrated system of care for a frail elderly person will not happen spontaneously; rather it has to be consciously created. The active building, support and maintenance of a support network requires the development of effective case management with the frail elderly to ensure the coordination and performance of care tasks, in the way that would be expected in the care of vulnerable children (Stevenson and Parsloe, 1978). However, this case management has also to be sufficiently flexible to respond, on the one hand, to the most complicated cases and, on the other, to situations where an existing capable informal network only requires a small addition of support to continue. As Goldberg and Connelly (1982) note in relation to assessment, the aim must be to avoid overcomplication of a relatively straightforward need, and yet to ensure that the signs of wider problems are identified before they reach a crisis.

However, it would seem that at present this case-management function is to a large extent absent in work with elderly people (Stevenson and Parsloe, 1978; Goldberg and Warburton, 1979; Plank, 1979) and there are a number of structural and organisational factors which militate against its development. These we discuss in the next section. The argument is elaborated in *Matching Resources to Needs in Community Care* (Davies and Challis, 1986).

1. Obstacles to Effective Case Management and Resource Allocation

The problems which in the present system of care impede the development of effective case management and improved use of resources in care of the elderly can be summarised under four headings: problems of resource coordination; the difficulty of interweaving statutory and informal care; the relative neglect of the elderly in social work; and problems of accountability.

(a) Problems of coordination: service fragmentation and allocation

Resources for the care of the frail elderly tend often to be used insufficiently flexibly to provide the best possible care for elderly clients, and it is generally rare that domiciliary support is sufficiently focused on those in greatest need so as to prevent admission to long-term care.

A relatively low proportion of the social services budget is devoted to the use of residential homes for short stays or to the provision of domiciliary care (Davies, 1981a). It is difficult to provide home help early in the morning, late at night or at weekends (Dexter and Harbert, 1983), and for some of these tasks, such as checking up, the home help service may not in any case be the most appropriate provider of care. Relatively small amounts are devoted to the personal care tasks required by the very frail and vulnerable (Howell *et al.*, 1979; Hurley and Wolstenholme, 1979; Cheshire County Council, 1981), despite the very substantial increase in disability in the elderly living at home. Indeed, over recent years the home help service appears to have become more thinly spread over a larger number of cases (Cheshire County Council, 1981;

Hedley and Norman, 1982; Dexter and Harbert, 1983). There is some debate as to whether or not small amounts of care provided to relatively less dependent people perform a preventative function or represent a misallocation of resources (Dexter and Harbert, 1983; Audit Commission, 1985). However, one study in London showed that the amounts of help provided were insufficient to prevent the admission to homes of elderly people who were judged capable of continued independent living (Plank, 1977). It concluded that domiciliary care is cheap 'because it often stands for desperately poor levels of care' (p.21). Similarly, a report by the Department of Health and Social Security observed that increases in domiciliary services had not been directed at the provision of alternatives for those liable to enter institutional care (DHSS, 1981). Services such as meals-on-wheels are often provided to an elderly person at a time of need, but are not regularly reviewed so as to reflect changes in the old person's circumstances (Brotherton, 1975; Johnson *et al.*, 1981; Means; 1981). Day centre provision appears similarly often to be mismatched to need (Edwards *et al.*, 1980; Fennell *et al.*, 1981). Some of these criticisms of inappropriate service content were most pertinent at the time the project was developed. Considerable effort has been invested by some authorities in the enhancement of services for frail elderly people (Hedley and Norman, 1982; Ferlie *et al.*, 1984). Examples include the increase in hours of home help provided to the most needy in the Coventry project (Latto, 1980a,b), a greater emphasis on personal care (Hurley and Wolstenholme, 1979); and the development of home care teams (London Borough of Waltham Forest, 1981). Nonetheless, services are still often fragmented and there remains a lack of explicit case management.

Part of the explanation for this mismatch of provision and need seems to lie in separate organisational structures and development. Following the creation of social services departments, a functional mode of organisation was common (Rowbottom *et al.*, 1974). In such a system domiciliary care and social work services are responsible to different managers, the main crossover point being at assistant director level. In departmental reorganisations this has been identified by local authorities as inhibiting lateral linkages between services and thereby making integrated care more difficult (Challis and Ferlie, 1986a,b). Nevertheless, even where this constraint has been removed, at the level of the individual case services are poorly coordinated and rarely systematically organised into a coherent package of care (Goldberg and Connelly, 1982; Hadley and McGrath, 1984). Long-standing patterns of work roles and expectations can be important influences. For example, home help organisers have a large number of home helps and clients to supervise whilst maintaining control of a budget and performing a personnel function to a group of employees, which militates against careful assessment of the help required in each household and sensitive alterations to changes in circumstances (London Borough of Hillingdon, 1975; Gwynne and Fean, 1978; Gwynne, 1980). Regular reassessments of need appear particularly rare (Goldberg and Connelly, 1982). However, it would be unreasonable to expect home help organisers with their current responsibilities to be 'case-accountable' (Hey, 1980) taking broad-ranging responsibility for an individual client. Attempts to restructure these roles, separating the administrative from the social care functions, have met with resistance (Goldberg and Connelly, 1982), despite the benefits observed in the Coventry project when the home help organiser was fully integrated into a social work team (Latto, 1980a,b). Thus, despite the fact that the home help service is the cornerstone of support for the elderly, often the service runs substantially independently of social work teams and local management, replicating the pattern of the service before the Seebohm reorganisation (Cmnd 3703, 1968), policies and objectives are unclear and integrated care is not achieved (London Borough of Merton, 1976; Gwynedd Social Services Department, 1977; Payne, 1977; Howell *et al.*, 1979; Goldberg and Connelly, 1982; Dexter and Harbert, 1983; Audit Commission, 1985).

The involvement of social work staff with elderly people is often only an initial assessment for services such as residential care, and lacks continuity. It could too frequently be described as a 'hit and run' approach (Black *et al.*, 1983). Goldberg and Connelly (1982) conclude their review of research on social care thus:

> *numerous local enquiries have repeatedly thrown up similar issues in many different spheres of social care; the mismatch between needs and resources, the inadequacy of appropriate initial assessment and the lack of monitoring and review procedures (p.247).*

Overall, the picture of resource provision for the frail elderly is one of a series of piecemeal interventions by a range of actors or services, home help organisers, social workers, occupational therapists, each perhaps performing a circumscribed task well. However, none are clearly seen as taking the necessary overview and continuing responsibility required for effective case management, which must include the full range of activities such asassessment, care planning, advising and supporting relatives, interagency negotiation and regular monitoring. There is thus no one to cement together the fragments into an individual care plan. As a result, Plank (1977) could reasonably describe services as 'an uncoordinated set of discrete and relatively autonomous parts'; and therefore 'the care which any individual old person receives is to a major extent fortuitous' (p.12).

(b) Interweaving with informal care

It has long been a criticism of statutory care that it is insufficiently focused on those who provide the bulk of the care in the community, namely friends, family and neighbours (Bayley, 1973; Moroney, 1976; Greengross, 1982; Charlesworth *et al.*, 1984). Indeed, domiciliary services are often less likely to be provided to cases with informal carers, and needs often remain unmet (Family Policy Studies Centre, 1984). Despite the dramatic picture of decline in the number of potential care-givers demonstrated by Moroney (1976), informal care is still substantial (Hunt, 1978; Family Policy Studies Centre, 1984; Wenger, 1984) and effective community care of the frail elderly can only be built upon an equitable sharing and integration of care from a range of sources. If this process of interweaving of care (Bayley, 1973) is to be successfully achieved, carers need help which is responsive to changing needs and circumstances to reduce burden and which is sufficiently sensitive to balance the needs of carers and elderly people (Gilroy, 1982). The stress and difficulty experienced by carers with inadequate support have been well documented (Grad and Sainsbury, 1968; Sanford, 1975; Levin, 1982). However, the relatively few remedies available to a fieldworker to meet the many different and varied problems of caring families and provide them with appropriate support, may render difficult any effective investment in this area of work. Assessments may fail to uncover these problems (Goldberg *et al.*, 1970; Levin, 1982). Even where needs are identified, procedures for resource allocation may be highly inflexible. As a result, there is a danger that statutory help, often provided inappropriately and too late (Wenger, 1984), can substitute for rather than complement informal care and may act as an incentive for carers to give up (Moroney, 1976). Yet a combination of measures, sensitively undertaken, could avoid the distress and guilt experienced when families finally reach the point of giving up and admission to care is seen as the only solution (Allen *et al.*, 1983).

(c) Relative neglect of the elderly

The range of tasks of effective case management, assessment, care planning, monitoring and family support would seem in principle to be part of the repertoire of social work practice. Nonetheless there is considerable evidence that this is not the case. Social work with the elderly has tended to be relegated to the lower end of client priority (Holme and Maizels, 1978; Rees; 1978; Howe; 1980). Students appear to reflect the prevailing values of their departments in their perception of the unattractiveness of work with this group. In one study, only 28 per cent wanted to work with the elderly compared with 88 per cent who wanted to work with children and families (Stevenson and Parsloe, 1978). Relatively large and heterogenous caseloads of the aged tend to be handled by inexperienced or unqualified workers (Black *et al.*, 1983). The large caseloads preclude effective continuity of contact and preventive work to stem the kind of crises which demand immediate rather than satisfactory solutions, all too often leading to a hurried decision to enter residential care in the face of anxiety and pressure from GPs, relatives and neighbours. Frequently the range of interventions considered tends to be narrow and undertaken with relatively low expectations of positive outcome (Goldberg and Warburton, 1979).

It is probable that lack of training and relevant experience, an incomplete knowledge base and large caseloads make adequate assessment unlikely. Indeed, assessments of need tend to be based on criteria of eligibility for service rather than 'problem-oriented' (Goldberg and Connelly, 1982). Service-based assessments will tend to blinker care plans, rendering them insufficiently sensitive to variations in individual need, while inadequate monitoring will mean that changing circumstances of clients and carers are not reflected in service changes. Consequently, important interactions between physical, psychological and social deficits and family stress (Bergmann, 1973, 1979), the very essence of complex cases, are likely to be neglected. Despite a prevailing orthodoxy that the problems of the elderly are unchallenging, they require more than a straightforward response of practical services to reflect the complexity of need (Plank, 1979). The process of balancing different needs, interpreting complicated and often ambiguous evidence, judging appropriate objectives and the consequences of alternative courses of action, are traditional social work skills. Other occupational groups in social services, such as home help organisers, are not expected to be 'case-accountable' in the same way (Hey, 1980), being expected to operate a specific service and decide on allocations of that service, rather than to construct packages from several different sources (Rowbottom *et al.*, 1974).

It is likely that considerable barriers to change exist at the organisational as well as the attitudinal level. At the present time the incentives and pressures of the system at the field level are clear but perverse. First, to invest most thought, effort and personnel into the development of care strategies for the more fashionable client groups, particularly children (Stevenson and Parsloe, 1978; Goldberg and Warburton, 1979). Second, in the care of the elderly, to prescribe a standard package of services in fairly uniform amounts, such as meals-on-wheels or home help. Indeed, since access to resources is limited, and straightforward responses involve relatively little cost in time and negotiation with others, this is a simple if inappropriate solution. Goldberg and Connelly (1982) quote a director of social services who described this as the 'budgerigar response'. For fieldworkers with the demands of a large caseload, such a response appears cheap, the most obviously expensive resource which they must allocate being their own time. On the other hand, the work necessary to enable a frail elderly person to stay at home, reinforcing an existing support network, carefully and sensitively interweaving statutory, voluntary and informal care, is costly to the fieldworker and involves taking risks. Yet these are just the strategies which take account of the complexity of need and are required to provide effective integrated care.

Consequently social workers with the elderly, frequently inexperienced or untrained, are placed in a situation where they can only prescribe a narrow range of remedies to client problems. This cannot enhance the possibility of the interagency collaboration which is essential for effective community care of old people (Stevenson, 1981b). Change requires an enhanced commitment to work with the elderly and an undertaking that departments 'grasp the nettle and ensure that social work time is allocated to the elderly, if needs be by the redesignation of existing posts' (Plank, 1979, p.48). More recently there is some evidence of movement in this direction (Ferlie, 1982) in the growth of specialist posts, although the designation of staff is a necessary but not sufficient condition for the development of case management.

(d) Problems of accountability

There is general acceptance of the legitimacy and appropriateness of the state's role as coordinator both at the individual level and for the system as a whole, and as guarantor of minimum standards. Health and social services are held accountable for the failure to provide adequate support for individuals requiring long-term care and, like any other public agency, they are expected to use their resources to good effect. However, within the social services accountability appears defective in certain respects.

Insufficient clarity about policies and objectives and the lack of systems for routinely monitoring outcomes have been observed. In its pilot study of managing social work, the Audit Commission (1986) found an absence of strategic review of caseloads and caseload mix, with inadequate monitoring and review of resource utilisation. Accountability of fieldwork staff is partly achieved through vertical hierarchies and the operation of defined procedures, often the result of piecemeal development, arising in response to particular situations or difficulties. Consequently, decisions about resource allocation are often made at considerable organisational distance from the individual making the assessment of need. There is a real danger that such systems of accountability may excessively inhibit the freedom of staff and constrain constructive, creative responses to situations of human need by encouraging only a limited range of possible choices. Stevenson and Parsloe (1978), noting vagueness about the precise nature of accountability, suggest that effective practice can only develop where organisational structure and management techniques can provide conditions of 'protection with autonomy'. However, it is only realistically possible for management to facilitate such an environment when staff workloads and responsibilities are clearly known (Bamford, 1984; Audit Commission, 1986). This in turn requires an information system with reliable and comparable documentation which consists of case-records at the individual client level and which can, at a more aggregated level, provide information for policy and resource planning (Goldberg and Warburton, 1979). The possibilities which arise from the development of computer-based information systems make this requirement more explicit (Eason, 1982). Adequate management information and clear parameters to autonomy are prerequisites for decentralising control of resources and giving greater freedom to front-line staff. Under such conditions, achieving a new balance between autonomy and accountability might permit a more effective deployment of resources to meet need.

2. The Community Care Approach, Enhanced Case Management and Efficiency in Social Care

The system of services is therefore fragmented, with no one clearly responsible for coordinating assessment, or arranging and monitoring care plans which tailor resources to the individual needs of elderly people and their families. Indeed, the organisational pressure facing front-line staff may be to avoid risk and the difficulties associated with constructing and maintaining complex packages of care. There is very little in the current service system which provides incentives for front-line staff to use resources more effectively.

The community care approach is a model which provides an organisational framework in which the problems identified in the current service system -difficulties in case-finding and targeting, inadequate assessment, lack of individual care plans, ineffective monitoring and weak accountability - may be tackled, harnessing the norms of good practice to provide more efficient and effective home care of frail elderly people. The approach is designed to modify the work environment to enhance the case-management role and provide social work staff with the means to achieve a more effective use of resources in long-term care. It is detailed below.

(a) Enhanced case management

(i) Manageable caseload and case responsibility

It was expected that dealing with a long-term care population required continuity of commitment by a case manager who could mobilise a range of support systems as an alternative to residential care. This meant that social workers were expected to act as coordinators for the whole care network, acting as key workers with continuing case responsibility.

The expectation was that case managers would undertake more extensive social work activity with elderly people, their relatives and others, and careful ongoing assessment and monitoring, and invest time in raising community resources such as neighbourly help or boarding-out arrangements. Naturally, the resourceful development of packages of care responsive to the individual peculiarities and circumstances of clients is dependent on a manageable caseload. The caseloads were expected to be small by comparison with usual practice (Stevenson and Parsloe, 1978), in the region of twenty-five to thirty cases, similar to those of staff working with vulnerable children.

(ii) Decentralised budget

In order that staff could increase and develop the range of solutions to meet clients' problems, they had direct control of a budget. This could be used on services or developments needed to maintain elderly people in the community and improve their quality of life. It was expected that control of resources by front-line staff would provide an incentive for improved assessment and make possible more creative responses to the individual needs of elderly people and their carers, taking advantage of local circumstances such as the type of neighbourhood, the activity of local voluntary groups and the characteristics of the local service system.

(iii) Trained and experienced staff

It was intended to appoint more highly trained and experienced staff than those who frequently work with the elderly (Stevenson and Parsloe, 1978; Goldberg and Warburton, 1979; Black *et al.*, 1983). Continuity of responsibility and specialisation in care of the elderly were designed to aid learning and the acquisition of knowledge and to improve the ability to judge more accurately appropriate courses of action. Care of the frail elderly at home would involve taking risks, which was seen as more acceptable the greater the experience of the staff.

(iv) Coterminous catchment areas

Catchment areas coterminous with those of other agencies were designed to foster the development of good working relationships based on mutual respect and recognition with other service providers such as geriatricians and community nurses. The additional resources and discretion possessed by the team would add to its capacity to exchange or negotiate and obtain a satisfactory response from others (Huntington, 1981; Whittington, 1983).

(v) Modified procedures

New procedures and operational norms were to be developed so that the team's activity could be monitored and controlled to the necessary degree without conformity to existing procedures inhibiting creative work. For example, most existing systems of budgetary control require modification for flexible budgeting to work effectively.

(b) Improved accountability

Certain features of the approach were designed to improve accountability.

(i) Defined caseload

The target population was clearly defined as the most frail elderly people, those most likely to require admission to institutional care.

(ii) Budget limit

Expenditure on individual cases was limited to two-thirds of the cost of a place in a residential home; expenditure beyond that level required line management sanction. The proportion was chosen to reflect the 'care costs' of residential care.

The expenditure constraint per case/week and the specific targeted caseload were designed to provide clear parameters within which the potential tension between creative autonomy and accountability could be resolved, the expenditure level acting as a 'trigger' for management consultation.

(iii) Recording system

A systematic approach to recording was to be developed covering problem-oriented assessment, regular review of cases and monitoring the resources used. The final version is described in Challis and Chesterman (1985) and is shown as Appendix B. The records could be used to provide feedbacks to the individual worker about their caseload and at a more aggregated level to management about the characteristics of clients receiving care and the cost of the resources used (Challis and Chesterman, 1986).

(iv) Peer review

As the scheme developed it was intended to develop a form of peer review. The objectives of this were to aid the dissemination of good practice, to improve the quality of care by consideration of alternative strategies with individual clients and their families, and to open up individual workers' practice to the scrutiny of their colleagues. Complementing the activities of line management, peer review was intended to provide horizontal rather than vertical professional support and opportunities for continued learning.

Accountability was thus to be achieved more through effective care performance than through rigid procedures, through results rather than process, enhanced by concordance with professional norms, the effects of improved job satisfaction and reduced negative work incentives (Challis, 1985a).

(c) Better use of resources

Enhanced case management is a necessary but not sufficient condition for the better use of resources in long-term care. The approach also provides the information and a basis for staff to consider the costs as well as the effectiveness of care (see *Matching Resources to Needs*, pp.11-13, 75-85).

(i) Knowledge of unit costs

Knowledge of the unit costs of services was expected to enhance the efficiency of resource utilisation. Through its case records, the scheme would be the only sector of the social services department which could readily specify its weekly costs, on either a case by case basis or as a total.

(ii) Service package costed

The whole package of services to each individual case, as well as additional actual expenditure, is nominally charged to the budget. It was intended that workers should be able to consider the likely costs and benefits of alternative courses of action: for example, between five hours home help and attendance at a day centre.

(iii) Continuity of responsibility

Through specialisation and continuing case responsibility, individual workers would have the opportunity for learning the likely outcome of different strategies for different kinds of case. Feedback of caseload information (such as is reported in Challis and Chesterman, 1986) and peer review were to further contribute to this. The overview provided by continued caseload responsibility and costing of the package of care was designed to make it possible for the fieldworker to consider issues of equity: for example, the distribution of resources between different clients, or the biases against carers in the current service system (Charlesworth *et al.*, 1984).

The care objectives which the devices of the community care approach are designed to facilitate - case management, accountability and better use of resources - refer to different aspects of efficiency in long-term care. Table 1.1 indicates how the different features of the approach relate to the objectives of an improved care system and to different aspects of efficiency. For a more detailed discussion of how the performance of the core tasks of case management influences efficiency in social care, the reader is referred to Davies and Challis (1986, Chap. 2) and Knapp (1984). However, a brief discussion is of value here.

Table 1.1.
The community care approach, service objectives and aspects of efficiency

Service Objectives and Efficiency Criteria	Approach
1. Improved uptake and outreach to areas of unmet need (Horizontal Target Efficiency)	(i) Decentralised budget: More flexible and responsive services (ii) Coterminous with other key services/known in locality
2. Improved assessment and screening (Vertical Target Efficiency) (Input Mix Efficiency) (Market Efficiency)	(i) Staff more experienced and qualified (ii) Specialisation: improved knowledge base (iii) Key worker: coordinate contributions of others. (iv) Manageable caseload (v) Respond to elderly person and carers' definition of problems (vi) Targeted caseload - margin of institutional care
3. Improved care planning: overcome fragmentation (Input Mix Efficiency) (Market Efficiency)	(i) Key worker approach (ii) Decentralised budget: more flexible and responsive service (iii) Risk-taking more legitimate (iv) Closer contact with other agencies e.g. NHS (v) Involve elderly person and carers in defining solutions (vi) Gap filling - develop services where none at present (vii) Enhanced status of work with elderly: job satisfaction (viii) Opportunities for continued learning -peer review (ix) Remove negative incentives to staff
4. Continued monitoring and review (Input Mix Efficiency) (Market Efficiency)	(i) Key worker - continuity of contacts in network (ii) Manageable caseload (iii) Recording system - feedback to workers and managers
5. Improved accountability (Vertical Target Efficiency) (Input Mix Efficiency) (Market Efficiency)	(i) Budget limit (ii) Recording system - caseload reviews, and costs (iii) Scheme integrated into SSD (iv) Introduce peer review (v) Targeted caseload - margin of institutional care
6. Make better use of resources (Vertical Target Efficiency) (Input Mix Efficiency) (Market Efficiency)	(i) Targeted caseload - margin of institutional care (ii) Knowledge of costs (iii) Services normally charged to budget

Five different aspects of efficiency can be distinguished. Two of these are concerned with efficiency in targeting services on those in need. *Horizontal target efficiency* refers to the extent to which those deemed to need a particular service actually receive it. Activities to enhance this would include a concern with improved outreach and service uptake. *Vertical target efficiency* refers to the extent to which available resources or services are received by those deemed to need them. This would include activities such as screening applications for residential care. *Input mix efficiency* refers to the degree to which the mix of care inputs are adjusted to reflect their costs and constraints in supply. An example of an attempt to improve input mix efficiency might be the substitution of domiciliary services for residential care for people inappropriately placed there. *Market efficiency* (also called output mix efficiency) refers to the degree to which the outputs of services reflect consumer preferences. An example of enhanced market efficiency might involve achieving a better balance between the needs of an elderly person on the one hand and their family carers on the other. Finally, *technical efficiency* refers to the production of maximum output from a given set of inputs. As we can see, technical efficiency is the only factor not noted in Table 1.1. This is because effects on technical efficiency in the provision of individual services arising from case management and the other developments are likely to be less direct, operating initially through the other mechanisms listed.

These criteria of efficiency are helpful in that they break down a complex concept into different aspects which may be influenced by the choice of different courses of action. For instance, misplacement of elderly people in residential homes may reflect a lack of vertical target efficiency in admissions policy, or a lack of horizontal target efficiency of domiciliary services in failure to ensure uptake, or a lack of market efficiency in domiciliary services - for instance, that home care is not available to provide the necessary assistance at appropriate times. It follows then that service systems which perform well on different tasks of case management may well appear efficient by some critria and not by others and require different forms of remedial action.

3. Expected Effects

What then were the expected benefits of this new approach to care? *Matching Resources to Needs* (pp.13-17) presents the community care scheme as a model in which changes in work environment trigger certain processes which result in the desired outcomes. Briefly, they amount to the proposition that changes in work environment, resource control, specialisation in work with a particular client group, a greater degree of case responsibility and the opportunity for closer assessment, individual care planning and monitoring of need would lead to more creative and resourceful responses by fieldwork staff. These possible responses can usefully be formulated as predictions of a fairly high level of generality to be tested against the experience of the scheme.

(a) A lower proportion of elderly people should enter institutional care.
(b) At least for some cases, the new scheme should be more cost-effective than the usual range of services.
(c) A closer relationship between levels of need and levels of resource provision should be evident than in the usual range of services.
(d) There should be evidence of greater benefits to elderly people and their informal carers than in the usual range of services.
(e) The assumption of responsibility for the long-term care of frail elderly clients should differentiate a more distinct role for social work with the elderly than is at present evident.
(f) Substantial variation in packages of care should occur reflecting the nature of different types and combinations of problems.
(g) The use of resources should show greater sensitivity to the care network as a whole. This would mean that care from a wide range of sources would be interwoven, closer support given to informal carers and new elements of community support introduced.
(h) Attention should be given to needs which are not usually met. This refers both to certain groups of elderly clients, such as those with mental impairment, or to higher order levels of need, such as loneliness and depression, as well as to more basic care needs.

The extent to which these expectations were fulfilled is the subject of our research. This is the first evaluation of a series of studies of the community care approach to long-term care. In the first application of this approach a team of two social workers, increased after six months to three, was appointed to work in the same district as a generic area social service team to develop care at home for frail elderly people who would otherwise require admission to residential care. In this initial project most of the features described above as comprised by the community care model were included from the beginning, although as will be seen from Chapter 3, others (such as the recording system) were developed greatly during that project, and peer review was feasible only after the extension of the approach across the local authority. Subsequent developments have taken place in both rural and urban settings (Challis *et al.*, 1983; Dimond *et al.*, 1987), in one area with a joint team of both health and social service staff, and these are also being evaluated in detail.

The remainder of this book divides into three main sections. The first of these - Chapter 2 - describes the way in which the evaluation was undertaken and the setting in which it took place. The second section - Chapters 3, 4, 5 and 6 - is concerned with the process of care, the way in which case-management tasks were performed and the responses made to clients with very different patterns of needs. The third section - Chapters 7, 8 and 9 - deals with the analysis of the outcome of the project for clients and their families, the costs of care, and with identifying those types of case for whom the scheme is most appropriate. Finally, in Chapter 10 we discuss our conclusions and the future development of this approach to long term care.

CHAPTER 2

THE DESIGN AND CONTEXT OF THE STUDY

The overarching framework for the evaluation of this new approach to care of the elderly, which links together the set of questions posed at the end of Chapter 1, was provided by the production of welfare model taken from the economic theory of production (Davies and Knapp, 1981; Knapp, 1984; Davies, 1986). It provides a structure for comprehending the complex relationships between resource inputs (such as home care services), non-resource inputs (such as dependency, health and social networks) and outputs or effectiveness. It therefore provides a theoretical underpinning to the collection and analysis of data in a cost-effectiveness evaluation (Davies and Challis, 1981; Challis *et al.*, 1984). The research question which is posed by the production of welfare approach is: 'What were the costs to different parties of the outcomes of care for elderly people in various circumstances, and how were these outcomes achieved?'

When this is broken down into its component parts we can see that it was necessary to attempt to provide answers to questions in two broad areas: the first relating to issues of efficiency in social care and the second relating to changes and improvements in social work practice. These two areas, which are the central concerns of the study, may be summarised as follows.

1. Cost-effectiveness issues. These included the following questions. What was the effect of the new scheme for elderly people and their carers compared with the usual range of services? What were the costs of care? For what kind of elderly person was this type of provision the most appropriate use of resources?

2. Social care process issues. These included the following questions. How did the team respond to the opportunity of greater flexibility and control of resources? What did the scheme indicate about the roles and tasks of fieldworkers in long-term care? What kinds of care strategies were appropriate for elderly people in different circumstances? Why was the care of certain types of case more or less effective or costly?

In this chapter we delineate our approach to tackling these issues and explain the procedure for selecting cases to compare with those receiving the scheme. Finally, we describe the nature of the local service system and the characteristics of the elderly people and their informal carers.

1. Cost-effectiveness Issues

(a) Experimental design

In order to make a judgement of the relative effectiveness of the new scheme we needed to compare two groups of elderly people who were similar in most respects save that one group received community care and the other did not. This required a comparison group who received the realistic alternative mode of care to the new scheme; that is, the standard range of services provided in the locality. It was considered important that the comparison should be with 'the realistic alternative'. A number of studies have compared the costs of residential or hospital care for elderly people with the actual cost of care at home (examples are Wager, 1972; Dunnachie, 1979; Gibbins *et al.*, 1982) Since in practice only a proportion of those at risk of institutionalisation actually enter institutional care, the effect of such comparisons will be to exaggerate any apparent advantage of the community alternative.

In many evaluation studies the two groups are found by randomly allocating the chosen population to experimental and control groups. In such a design, extreme care is taken to ensure that every person in a target population has the same chance as any other to be selected for the experimental or control group, by random processes and therefore, in the long run, any systematic difference between the groups will be averaged out. In certain situations, however, randomisation may not be the most appropriate solution (Goldberg and Connelly, 1982).

(i) Service providers may argue that the allocation of cases to services on a random basis is unethical, and offends against principles of social justice since they believe one service to be preferable to another. A degree of sabotage may occur, for example, by deliberate shifts in referral behaviour to try and ensure that certain cases receive one kind of service rather than another (Applebaum *et al.*, 1980).

(ii) A public agency such as a local authority may experience political difficulty in denying a service to some clients, living in close proximity, on apparently arbitrary and irrational grounds. Allocation of scarce services by geographical criteria can appear more acceptable.

(iii) Randomisation in a scheme concerned with community care within an area office might cause 'contamination'. For example, where the experimental scheme was receiving cases from an area team, a randomised design would mean that their workload would be reduced and therefore control cases might receive an improved service, thereby distorting the comparison.

(iv) Where the concern is to detect not only the effect of a single treatment, but also the effects of a programme on the system of care, for example demand for other services, then separate areas are required.

The alternative approach which was adopted to tackle these difficulties was the 'quasi-experimental' design (Campbell and Stanley, 1966). In our study, experimental and control groups were selected from adjacent but demographically similar areas. These areas, being a single district council, were part of the same health and social services system, which reduced the risk of possible service-related differences such as hospital admission policies. Following identification of cases by similar processes, individuals were matched by criteria likely to influence the outcome of care such as age, sex and degree of disability. One obvious potential source of bias in this design is a change in the behaviour of referral agents in response to a new scheme, occurring in only that area, which would certainly make the acquisition of comparison cases more difficult. However, one of the purposes of the evaluation was to identify such system effects. These are more readily detectable in the quasi-experimental approach by comparing not just two groups of elderly people but also two service systems, similar in most respects except for the presence of community care.

(b) Data collection

The production of welfare model required the collection of data on resource inputs or costs, the circumstances and characteristics of elderly people, and outcomes. A number of important principles underlay our approach to data collection and analysis (Davies and Challis, 1981, 1986). These were:

(i) Differential effects on parties

Outcome and cost information should reflect the varying incidence of costs and benefits to different parties and permit us to examine the effects of the scheme from different viewpoints such as those of the elderly person, informal carers, service agencies and society as a whole.

(ii) Perceptions of client, carer and interviewer

Indicators of outcome or effectiveness should be of a wide range, reflecting the perceptions of both the interviewees and external assessors.

(iii) 'Final' and 'intermediate' outcomes

Indicators of outcome should include both effects valued in their own right (final outcomes, such as improved morale) and also intermediate effects likely to be of value (intermediate outcomes, such as receipt of welfare benefits) (Davies, 1977a).

(iv) General and specific outcomes

Indicators of final outcome should include both highly general criteria (such as subjective well-being) and more specific needs (such as adequacy of care).

(v) Positive and negative aspects of ageing

Outcome indicators should include developmental aspects as well as the absence of negative features. Hence in assessing subjective well-being we were concerned not only to include indicators of the presence or absence of psychopathology, such as anxiety and depression, but also indicators of morale.

(vi) The multiplicity of outcomes in relation to cost

The likely outcomes of care are multiple and therefore their relationship with one another is complex. For instance, a service which provides a meal to meet nutritional needs may also check up on someone and meet safety requirements and perhaps provide companionship as well. Our analyses were therefore designed to examine the relationship between the cost of a care service and its several consequences.

Outputs or outcomes were defined as changes in circumstances as a result of care inputs. Their measurement therefore required a 'before-after' design with at least two interviews with elderly people and their carers. In order to allow for seasonal variation and to allow the effects of care to become evident, the assessments were conducted at an interval of one year. These interviews were relatively lengthy, about one-and-a-half hours with the elderly people and, where applicable, about one hour with their principal carers, usually family members. The range of information covered both descriptive information and indicators of outcome or effectiveness. The descriptive indicators included aspects of housing, social support, physical disability and symptomatic health. Outcome indicators included morale, depression, loneliness, shortfalls of help with activities of daily living, and carer stress and burden. They are described in more detail in Appendix A and the outcome indicators are discussed in Challis (1981). All the interviews were conducted by one researcher, a trained social worker (one of the authors). A shortened follow-up interview was conducted with elderly people in residential care and none at all where they had entered long-term hospital care, since the hospital setting and the old person's health would not be conducive to it. Where the old person had died, no follow-up interview was conducted with relatives, to avoid causing distress. In view of the relatively small scale of the experiment, and the likely wastage of cases as a result of the matching process, an excess of control group cases was collected to ensure minimal loss of crucial experimental cases for analysis.

Cost data were collected retrospectively over the one-year period of monitoring for each case. Much of the relevant cost information could be established from records, such as those of hospital or residential care admissions, or those used by the scheme. Some cost information such as welfare benefits was gathered from the interviews with the elderly people and their carers. In general, the principle adopted was that the higher the weighting of a given resource in the cost of care, the greater the effort made to ensure reliability. Thus, for example, inaccuracy in assessing the use of residential beds or hospital facilities would offset costs more seriously than in the use of meals-on-wheels. However, even the relatively unproblematic data extraction, such as for hospital admissions, could prove extremely onerous in terms of time.

2. Social Care Process Issues

This aspect of the study was important to explain how the new approach to care operated in practice and why it was more or less effective or costly with some clients than others. Lacking this detail an evaluation can only be like a 'black box', where we learn *what* happened but have little understanding of *how* it occurred. Such research findings cannot be expected to influence practice since without understanding the link between process and outcome it would be difficult to reproduce the effect to benefit clients elsewhere.

There were two concerns. One was to analyse the performance of the core tasks of case management in long-term care. Whereas a reasonably well-defined repertoire of approaches has been developed based on task-centred, short-term interventions (Reid and Epstein, 1972; Goldberg *et al.*, 1985) no such clarity exists about long-term intervention for those cases for whom the short-term approach is unsuitable. It was therefore particularly important to examine how case management was undertaken in the scheme. The second was to identify the variety of responses to a range of care problems and the extent to which certain patterns of response are associated with desired outcomes. This is a crucial area for the development of social work practice. As Smale (1983) has argued, given the relatively poor knowledge base of much social work intervention there is a need to adopt a far more experimental or developmental approach. The lack of adequate practice theory makes the relationship between process and outcome appear as necessarily unclear. The development of a more 'clinical' perspective in social work could reduce this indeterminacy, linking research and practice through the identification of patterns of effective intervention couched in the form of probability statements or norms. These 'clinical generalisations' would take the form that a given care strategy, with given likely resource commitments, has a reasonable probability of being effective in certain situations (Challis, 1985b). Such a knowledge base has already begun to develop in areas such as child abuse (Porter, 1984) and child psychiatry (Lask and Lask, 1981), but is less evident in care of the elderly. The extent to which this knowledge could be developed from the study was therefore important.

Information on care processes came from several different sources. Interviews with elderly people and their carers provided important insights into the ways in which the scheme responded to needs. Other sources of information were also important: observation of the social workers in their day-to-day activities through long periods of time spent in their office, reading casenotes, attending meetings, interviews and discussions with the members of the social work team, and collecting data on resources provided to individual clients, including 'contracts' given to helpers. It was not possible, however, to use systematic case-recording information (Challis and Chesterman, 1985) since this was a development from the original scheme.

The comparison of care processes, activities and strategies was with 'the usual response to the elderly', the nature of social work activity documented in recent British research (Stevenson and Parsloe, 1978; Goldberg and Warburton, 1979; Levin, 1982; Black *et al.*, 1983). Observation of the practice of control group teams suggested that they did not differ significantly from that described in those studies. Furthermore, given our limited resources, it was considered most important to identify ways in which the new scheme departed from more traditional approaches.

3. The Selection of Cases

It is helpful to conceive of the processes by which referrals were acquired as a funnelling procedure through which at various stages cases could be excluded and the targeting criteria fulfilled for both experimental and control groups. Exclusion of potentially eligible cases could occur at several points: (i) on referral, at the evaluation interview or the initial assessment by the social work team; or (ii) clients could be removed by events beyond the control of the scheme, such as death or sudden admission to hospital before initial assessment.

Five criteria for excluding cases emerged during the progress of the scheme, the relative importance of each changing through time. For example, a higher proportion of 'insufficiently needy' cases were referred in the early stages. The five criteria were as follows.

(a) Selection criteria

(i) Insufficiently needy

The case referred did not seem to meet the target criteria of the scheme. This is extremely difficult to define, 'need for residential care' reflecting lack of adequate coping arising from a combination of physical, mental and social stress. An attempt was made to provide broad guidelines which reflected a concept of 'inadequate social functioning sufficient to consider a move away from independent living'.

(ii) External events
Factors which led to case exclusion independent of the scheme. These were defined as death or permanent admission to institutional care occurring between referral and first visit, or within two weeks of the assessment visit by the evaluator.

(iii) Desire for residential care
Where the elderly person had a clear preference for residential care at the earliest possible opportunity.

(iv) Unrelinquishing carers
Where the elderly person was receiving all or nearly all their care and support from informal sources, who despite difficulty were unwilling to cede part of this caring activity to others.

(v) Client characteristics
Where aspects of the client's physical or mental condition led to a decision by the scheme not to provide support.

To minimise selection bias it was attempted to apply these criteria in as similar fashion as possible in both experimental and control areas. This is summarised in Table 2.1.

(b) The referral process in the experimental area
Referrals came predominantly from the area social work team, particularly in the early stages. There were 202 potential cases considered. Initial clarification of eligibility and possible exclusion could occur where a case was already known to the department. For example, one person was excluded due to difficult personality and attitude to help on the basis of casenote material and discussion. External events could also occur prior to interview by either evaluator or scheme social worker. There were thirty-one such cases of whom seven were admitted to a residential home and fourteen to hospital and ten died. A further forty-two cases were assessed as insufficiently needy and four expressed a positive desire for residential care. Altogether 129 cases were seen by the evaluator of whom six, already mentioned, were lost through external events, insufficient need and stubborn independence. Thus 123 cases were seen by the community care team.

Table 2.1
Selection of groups for community care and standard provision

	Community care N	Standard provision N
Potential cases	202	291
Insufficiently needy	42	74
Clients lost to external events	31	34
Clients wanted residential care	4	2
Unrelinquishing carers	0	2
Unsuitable for community care	2	14
Seen by research worker	129*	165
Seen by SSD team	123	165
Insufficiently needy	12	33
Clients lost to external events	4	1
Clients wanted residential care	2	1
Unrelinquishing carers	3	
Unsuitable for community care	10	11
Final groups	92	116

* includes six cases not seen by the team due to external events, insufficient needs and client characteristics.

Of the 123 cases seen by the team, ninety-two were helped by the scheme and thirty-one cases were not. Two made positive decisions to enter residential care, one to a home run by her son, the other to a home in another district close to her friends. External events removed four cases within two weeks of the evaluation interview, one admitted to residential care under family pressure, another moving to live with her daughter and two being admitted to hospital care. Another three cases were excluded because carers were unwilling to share the care with others despite the difficulty they experienced. Indeed, it appeared as if the very existence of the scheme contributed to their willingness to carry on, knowing where to turn for help. Fourteen cases were assessed as insufficiently needy, and often the demand for additional care for these elderly people came not from the clients, who were reasonably content, but other professionals. Two of these cases deteriorated over the year subsequent to their referral and were later accepted into the scheme, leaving the figure of twelve in Table 2.1.

Finally there were ten cases whom the team decided they were unable to help due to the circumstances of the elderly person. These cases should be considered further since they revealed perceptions by team members of the boundaries of the possible. One old person suffered from a chronic anxiety state and rejected help, three suffered from dementia with associated behaviour that did not at the time appear amenable to intervention, one old person was chronically depressed and would not accept help, three were stubbornly independent and two appeared inaccessible through extreme deafness. The subsequent experience of the scheme suggests that probably all except the stubbornly independent would have been successfully helped.

(c) The referral process in the control area

It was attempted to make the selection processes as similar as possible in the control area. This was made more complicated by the fact that there were two area offices covering the control area. In one district the researcher regularly attended case allocation meetings in order to identify new referrals who might be appropriate, and in addition met regularly with the social work staff dealing with the elderly and home help organisers. In the second district, which had a different allocation system, regular visits were made to the office at 'strategic' times such as coffee and tea breaks when staff were most likely to be available, thus ensuring the opportunity of regular discussion with those staff most concerned with elderly cases.

There were two difficulties in identifying comparable cases of sufficient frailty. The first was that the researcher lacked a 'permanent' presence in the control area, such as office accommodation. Thus, whereas a difficult and vulnerable case would be referred quickly to the scheme in order to obtain service for the elderly person, in the control area swift alternative action had to be taken, which was often admission to a residential home. The second problem arose as the scheme became known within the locality. Elderly people with substantial health care needs were likely to be referred to the scheme by caring professionals such as general practitioners, but similar cases were less likely to be identified in the control area since no new scheme was available there.

Recruiting suitable control cases became progressively easier as staff became more aware of the type of case required and the number of inappropriate cases became less frequent. As in the experimental area, potentially suitable cases were discussed with social work or home help staff, and any available casenotes were read carefully. When processes of case exclusion occurred in the experimental area, then a similar process was for that time adopted in the control area. Thus cases who appeared to exhibit a stubborn independence and were clearly unreceptive to help were excluded if similar exclusions took place in the experimental area. Similarly, during the earlier phase of the scheme there appeared to be a reluctance to tackle certain types of cases with dementia and for that period similar cases were excluded in the control area.

In the control area, as Table 2.1 shows, 291 cases were considered as potentially suitable referrals. Decisions about marginal cases in the control area were discussed with the scheme team leader wherever there was doubt to ensure that comparable judgements were made. Seventy-four cases were identified as inappropriate following further consideration and two wished to enter residential care. The thirty-four cases which were excluded due to exogenous events reveal the different processes operating in experimental and control areas. Whereas the reaction to a crisis in an elderly person's life in the experimental area was a visit from both evaluator and scheme social worker in a short time, in the control area no such additional community support was available and other forms of action were taken. In seventeen of these thirty-four cases, the researcher actually visited and only then found that action had been taken: seven people had entered residential care, eight had been admitted to hospital and two had died. Of the remaining seventeen cases lost due to external factors, nine entered residential care, seven entered hospital and one died. The apparently higher death rate in the 'exogenous' cases for the experimental group can probably be explained by the influence of admission to long-term hospital care. In the control area when a case was admitted to long-term hospital care it was no longer eligible, whilst in the experimental area the scheme was considered as a possibility for client rehabilitation. This longer period of 'case consideration' made it likely that a higher proportion would die, since those entering hospital were extremely frail.

Fourteen cases were rejected due to client characteristics similar to cases not proceeded with in the experimental area. Of these, six were dementing and had behaviour characteristics making them unlikely to be receptive to help, five were stubbornly independent or unwilling to accept help and the remaining three suffered from chronic depression, anxiety and profound deafness respectively.

One hundred and sixty-five cases were actually interviewed, of whom thirty-three were identified as inappropriate, three appeared to have 'unrelinquishing carers', one had a positive desire for residential care and one was lost due to an external event, having died a week after the interview. Eleven were excluded due to client characteristics similar to those excluded in the experimental area: four had extremely unreceptive attitudes to help, three were chronically depressed and anxious, rendering them unwilling to accept help, two were stubbornly independent, one was extremely confused and one exhibited a mixed pattern of depression and confusion. This left 116 suitable control group cases.

(d) Achieving group equivalence: post-selection matching

Every effort had been made to ensure that referral and exclusion procedures in the two areas were as similar as possible. In addition, post-selection matching was used to minimise group differences. The benefits of matching are illustrated by the results of the reanalysis of data collected by Miss E.M. Goldberg and her colleagues for *Helping the Aged* (1970) and reported in *Matching Resources to Needs* (Appendix 5.1, pp.213-15).

(i) Equivalence of the groups before matching

In order to assess the equivalence of the two groups of elderly people, they were compared by one-way analysis of variance on seventy-eight variables which consisted of basic descriptions of status and intial assessments of outcome measures. The significant differences are listed in Table 2.2, which notes in which group the lack of similarity increased the level of need.

Table 2.2
Significant differences at the 5 per cent level between the two groups before and after matching[1]

	Before Matching		After Matching	
Variable name	**Community care**	**Standard provision**	**Community care**	**Standard provision**
Loneliness		*		*
Morale	*		*	
Dissatisfaction with life	*		*	
Boredom		*		*
Contact with neighbours	*		*	
Need for help with home care	*		-	-
Adequacy of personal care	*		-	-
Coping with coal fire		*		*
Going out of the home		*	-	-
Need for additional services		*		*
Physical disability (ADL)	*		-	-
Incontinence of faeces	-	-	*	
Age (mean value)	80.2	82.7	-	-
Dependency Group 4 (Number of cases)[2]	19	11	14	9

Notes
1. * indicates in which group the level of need was greatest.
2. This category was only constructed after the matching process to assist further analyses.

It was clear that these differences were spread between the two groups, however the three most striking differences were the slightly greater age of the control group and the greater psychological needs and physical disability in the experimental group. We used two measures of disability. The first was a count of the number of activities of daily living (ADL) with which a person required help (Katz *et al.*, 1963). The second was a composite measure of four categories of dependency based on the work of Isaacs and Neville (1976). 'High disability' or 'critical interval need' defined those persons who were unable to rise from the bed or chair, walk to the toilet unassisted, use it and return safely without danger of falling, or who were incontinent of urine or faeces, or who were suffering from mental abnormality presenting a hazard to themselves or their environment. The second group, 'short interval need', were those whose needs were not as intense as those above, but who required help with such tasks as meal preparation occurring at short intervals once or more daily. The third group correspond to the 'long interval need' category of Isaacs and Neville (1976) whose needs were at more predictable intervals. The fourth group, 'moderate disability', fell into none of these categories and were frequently characterised by low morale, apathy and a tendency to neglect themselves. Whereas 41 per cent of the scheme cases were in the high disability category, only 30 per cent of the control group were. These four categories were used in the matching process.

Following the matching process, in later analyses to investigate the difference in survival rates a more sensitive measure of frailty was constructed which divided the original 'high disability' group into two: the upper band of this (Dependency Group (DG) 4) consisted of those individuals who were bedridden, chairbound or suffering from faecal incontinence; and the lower

Table 2.3
Distribution of the sample on measures of frailty

Disability group	Community care		Standard provision	
	N	%	N	%
High disability	37	41	35	30
Short interval need	40	43	67	58
Long interval need	5	5	7	6
Moderate disability	10	11	7	6
DG4	19	21	11	9
DG3	18	20	24	21
DG2	40	43	67	58
DG1	15	16	14	12
Totals	92	100	116	110

band (DG3) consisted of the remainder of the 'high disability' group. At the same time the original groupings of 'long interval' and 'moderate disability' were joined together because of their relatively small numbers, to form group DG1. These categories of dependency have been used throughout the rest of the work. The distribution of the two samples on these composite measures of frailty is shown in Table 2.3. There is a greater degree of frailty evident in the experimental group.

(ii) The matched pairs

Multivariate procedures as described by Sherwood *et al.* (1975) proved unhelpful. Six variables were identified which were likely to be strong predictors of survival in the community for matching individuals. These were sex, age above or below 75, 'living group' in the sense of household composition, disability (using the four groups of 'high disability', 'short interval need', 'long interval need' and 'moderate disability' described earlier), a three-point rating of apparent confusion and a four-point rating of apparent attitude to help. Other information such as the known presence of particular health conditions was used to assist the choice of pairs where relevant. Thirty matched pairs were obtained using these six variables. Simplification of the attitude to help measure so that it only discriminated between those elderly people who were particularly difficult and resistant to help and others provided a further thirty-one pairs. Relaxation of the age criterion alone produced a further six pairs, and relaxation of the sex criterion whilst holding the other five variables comparable produced another four pairs. These four pairs were similar in other important aspects, respectively confusion, drinking problems and in two cascs severe disability whilst being cared for by another family member. On two occasions both age and sex criteria were relaxed to match two pairs living with others, of whom one pair was living with a younger family in a stressful situation and in the other was living with an even more frail elderly person. There was no distortion in the overall balance between experimental and control group arising from the relaxation of either age or sex in all these cases. Finally, a pair was obtained by the relaxation of the living group criterion, where the relatively independent wife of a frail husband was matched with a woman living alone, since for a relatively independent person it was considered that living group was a less important predictor of outcome. By these processes it was possible to derive seventy-four matched pairs from the two samples. These seventy-four matched pairs were compared, as were the two whole samples, on a wide range of variables, using a one-way analysis of variance. The significant remaining differences between the groups are listed in Table 2.2.

It can be seen that fewer variables showed differences between the groups, although greater frailty was still evident in the experimental group. The different distribution of cases in Dependency Group 4 arises because the construction of this category was for later analyses after the process of matching was completed, and probably reflects the difficulties of obtaining extremely frail control cases, which was noted earlier. Differences which had been evident between the groups in terms of activities of daily living, age and shortfall of personal and household care were eliminated as a result of the matching process and the remaining factors could to some extent be interpreted as random differences.

4. The Characteristics of the Area and the Experimental Cases

(a) Characteristics of the area and system of care

The district from which both the experimental and control cases were drawn consisted of three distinct towns surrounded by flat arable land. One of these towns received community care, the other two comprised the comparison areas. The overall population of the district was approximately 110,000. The population distribution reflected the retirement orientation of the area. In 1971 the proportion of people over 60 was 32.3 per cent, which can be compared with 24.6 per cent in England and Wales. However, perhaps reflecting the more recent tendency towards in-migration, the over-80 group constituted only 4.4 per cent of the population compared with 8.2 per cent in England and Wales. There were some population differences between the three towns, whose populations were 40,000, 50,000 and 20,000 respectively. Town A, the experimental area, had a population aged over 60 of 27.7 per cent, whereas towns B and C, which were the comparison areas, had populations over 60 of 35.8 per cent and 34.6 per cent respectively. Those aged 80 and over were 3.7, 4.7 and 5.2 per cent of the population. It was hoped that this difference in eligible populations would facilitate the study by providing a higher number of possible control group cases for matching. In terms of the proportion of the population over pensionable age in different sized households, the experimental town fell midway between the two control towns.

All three towns possessed relatively good housing. Nevertheless, it was apparent that a slightly higher proportion of households were overcrowded in the experimental area, and a lower proportion possessed exclusive use of key amenities, as can be seen in Tables 2.4 and 2.5. However, it is unlikely that such differences would significantly influence the experiment. Of greater importance was likely to be the range of services provided.

Table 2.4
Private households living at more than 1.5 persons per room in 1971

Area	%
Town A	1.6
Town B	1.3
Town C	1.0

Source: OPCS, 1971, Table 24.

Table 2.5 Private households with the exclusive use of amenities in 1971

Amenities	Area (%)		
	Town A	Town B	Town C
Hot water supply	87.3	92.4	94.3
Fixed bath	84.9	89.8	93.4
Inside water closet	86.8	90.6	93.3
All three amenities	80.5	86.3	90.5

Source: OPCS, 1971, Table 25.

The same system of health and social care covered the whole area, therefore differences in outcome were unlikely to arise due to this factor. There were three social services area teams, one located in each town, and each team had the home help service based within it. At the start of the scheme no basic grade social work staff were trained and there was a tendency for the elderly to be dealt with by the least experienced members of staff. However, by the time the scheme had been running for three years, there were several qualified staff in each team, some of whom were dealing with the elderly. The home help service in each area provided a basic domiciliary service, there being very little out-of-hours and weekend provision. In part this reflected the relative level of provision within the authority as a whole, home help expenditure per thousand elderly being £14.50 compared with £18.41 in all counties and £26.74 in metropolitan districts (CIPFA, 1978). The meals-on-wheels service was provided by the Women's Royal Voluntary Service (WRVS) in all the three towns, the maximum level of provision ranging from two meals per week in the smallest town to three or four in the two larger towns. Day care was provided in residential homes until the scheme had been in the field for about two and a half years when a purpose-built day centre, to serve all three towns, was provided. There were four local authority residential homes, three of which were modern and purpose-built and the fourth, with nineteen beds, was an older converted dwelling. The total number of local authority residential home places was 158.

The health service resources were common to all three towns. There was a geriatric assessment ward at the district general hospital and long-stay provision of about 200 beds in two other hospitals. There was one geriatric day hospital which in the first year of the scheme had 12,176 attendances. The district health authority had a below-average provision of established posts in geriatrics, being 73.8 per cent of the national level. The psychiatric service was based in a hospital twenty miles away, with two consultants responsible for the three towns. There was no special psychiatric service for the elderly.

There was the expected range of local and national voluntary agencies active in the area, although only two of the ninety-two cases who received community care were in contact with a voluntary agency. Indeed, it appeared as if the prime focus of much voluntary activity was on the less frail elderly for whom a range of clubs and day centres were provided. Voluntary agencies provided a substantial level of residential provision, although not all of this was for local residents, and there were 161 registered voluntary agency residential beds. Perhaps most striking was the level of private residential provision, of which there were 1,157 registered beds. This feature was the most atypical aspect of the area where the experiment was undertaken and reflects the particular nature of certain retirement resorts.

(b) Characteristics of the elderly people

Ninety-two elderly people were helped by the community care scheme during the period of monitoring. The average age of the group was 80, ranging from 66-94 and as would be expected the majority were female.

Most, 70 per cent, were living alone, and as found by Goldberg *et al.* (1970) this reflected the preponderance of single, divorced and widowed people, which is vastly different from a national picture of 30 per cent (Hunt, 1978). Not only was a very high proportion of this group living alone, but they were also very isolated, which is a characteristic of retirement areas (Karn, 1977). Using a composite measure of isolation devised by Tunstall (1966), 51 per cent were socially isolated. Fifty-nine per cent complained of loneliness (probably an underestimate as people appeared sometimes unwilling to admit this). Furthermore, 52 per cent had no living children. Retirement to a new district had played a part in the level of support available; 73 per cent received no help from their children, compared with 58.5 per cent in a national survey (Hunt, 1978). Nearly half had moved to the area on retirement.

The level of owner-occupation was below that for retirement areas as a whole: 51 per cent compared with 66 per cent in a national survey (Hunt, 1978), reflecting the lower status of the area as a retirement resort compared with the Sussex or Hampshire coast (Karn, 1977). The average length of time that people had lived in the area was only twenty years and in their present home fifteen years. The housing stock was generally of a relatively high standard, although in 7 per cent of the cases there was no running hot water, in 12 per cent no fixed bath and 4 per cent no indoor toilet. A relatively low level of dissatisfaction with housing, 20 per cent, was noted. The accommodation difficulties which were most commonly noted concerned either the area or difficulties about the property itself. Complaints about the area reflected a dissatisfaction with the move by people who had retired, particularly the distance from family. For instance, the complaint of a widow who had moved to please her husband, and was now very isolated, was that she had lost all contact with her friends. Aspects of housing itself which led to complaint were difficulties with stairs, with access and the sheer problem of managing a large house, which was very difficult to keep adequately warm. Twenty-three per cent complained of difficulty in keeping warm and 12 per cent had inadequate means of heating, such as a dangerous paraffin heater.

The elderly people experienced considerable difficulty in managing the crucial activities of daily living and home care, many retaining their independence only by painful perseverance. They were more fragile than in a London sample of welfare clients (Goldberg *et al.*, 1970) and very disabled compared to the elderly as a whole (Hunt, 1978). From Table 2.9 it can be seen that they are similar to a residential care group. The average score of the group on a composite measure of Activities of Daily Living (Katz *et al.*, 1963), which represents a count of the number of key activities of daily living with which help is required, was 1.77. These activities are bathing, dressing, toileting, feeding, transfer and maintaining continence, and the index yields a score with a range from 0 for the least disabled to 6 for the most disabled. Physical ill-health was widespread, and there was also a high prevalence of anxiety and depressed mood amongst the group, which might be expected in view of the high level in the elderly population as a whole (Kay *et al.*, 1964). In seven cases there were problems of alcohol abuse, sufficient to make management in the community extremely difficult. Paranoid psychosis had been diagnosed in four cases. The circumstances of the elderly people are shown in Tables 2.6 to 2.12.

Table 2.6 Sex and marital status

	N	%
Sex		
Male	21	23
Female	71	77
Marital status		
Married	19	21
Single	13	14
Widow/divorced	60	65

Table 2.7 Living group

	N	%
Living alone	64	70
With spouse	19	21
Family	3	3
Friends	6	6

Table 2.8 Housing circumstances

	N	%
Tenure of Dwelling		
Owner occupier	47	51
Council rented	29	32
Private rented	16	17
Accommodation		
House	38	41
Bungalow	23	25
Flat	30	33
Bedsitting room	1	1
Totals	92	100

Table 2.9
Help needed with personal and instrumental tasks of daily living. Community care recipients, residents in homes and recipients of domiciliary services in England compared

Activity	Persons receiving			
	Community care		Residential care	Domiciliary services
	N	%	%	%
Personal				
Washing self	18	20	13[1]	5[1]
Get up from bed	21	23	22	11
Dressing	21	23	28	16
Using toilet	12	13	20	7
Mobility in home	10	11	13[2]	6[2]
Going outside	80	87	47[3]	62[3]
Transfer - rise from chair	13	14	15	8
Bathing	67	73	74	52
Managing toenails	75	81	n.a.	n.a.
Instrumental				
Light housework	40	44		
Making drinks/snacks	29	32		
Preparing meals	68	74		
Heavy housework	87	95		
Shopping	90	98		
Laundry	84	91		
Soiled linen	19	21		

Notes
1. Wash hands and face
2. Get around the room
3. Walk outdoors
Source: Wright *et al.* (1982)

Table 2.10 Activities of daily living

Number of daily activities with which help is required	N	%
0	22	24
1	27	29
2	18	20
3	11	12
4	6	7
5	5	5
6	3	3
Total	92	100

Table 2.11 Health problems of clients[1]

Condition	Moderate %	Severe %	Present %
Physical health			
Eyesight difficulty	35	17	
Hearing difficulty	29	3	
Breathlessness	27	22	
Giddiness	25	49	
Risk of falling	22	69	
Urinary incontinence			35
Faecal incontinence			7

Note
1. Percentage of clients with the health problems and at the degree of severity specified. The analysis for incontinence is of the presence of the problem, not of its severity.

Table 2.12 Mental health problems of clients

	Moderate %	Severe %
Depressed mood	40	8
Anxiety	46	15
Confusion or disorientation	23	3

In general the greatest need shortfalls were in the areas of rising and retiring, personal care involving actual care and the supervision and safety of those at risk of falling, and low morale. There was considerable need for help with regular household activities such as making hot drinks and meals, although the less regular household activities such as home cleaning and shopping were reasonably well catered for by existing services and levels of support.

(c) Characteristics of principal carers

The study was also concerned with the problems and difficulties experienced by principal carers, who were likely to be family members, but who could be neighbours or friends. A principal carer was defined as a person providing a substantial amount of regular care and the primary person in the care network. They would be undertaking several essential caring tasks or taking day-to-day responsibility for the elderly person. A number of principal carers were themselves clients and interviewed as such, for example, a frail elderly couple or two sisters living together. In other cases the principal carer was interviewed to identify the difficulties and problems experienced in coping. The relative isolation of the group of elderly people compared with the elderly population as a whole has already been noted, and this isolation was apparent in the low number of readily identifiable principal carers.

Twenty-one carers were interviewed, eighteen of whom were female. Most (ten) were daughters, daughters-in-law or a stepdaughter (Jones *et al.*, 1983), three were wives, five were neighbours, two were sons - one of whom appeared responsible for coordinating a considerable degree of care from different members of the family - and one was a nephew who shared care of his aunt with his wife. The major difficulties experienced by carers were disruption of the household routine in two-thirds of the cases; more than half experienced disruption of their social life and nearly half experienced tiredness, strain and exhaustion. All but one suffered a sense of burden to some extent, whilst a high proportion suffered a degree of mental distress. The main problems with the elderly person which were complained of were uncooperativeness, the need for physical or nursing care, and the demand for companionship. In 60 per cent of the cases the level of strain appeared to create considerable difficulty for the carer. In spite of this there was real warmth and concern for the elderly person in all cases, and in only one case was there evidence of any hostile feelings towards the elderly person. Carers' difficulties are shown in Table 2.13.

Table 2.13 Mental distress of carers

	N	%
Feelings of depression	11	52
Loss of sleep	8	38
Unable to relax or tense	15	71
Worried or anxious most of the time	16	76
Receiving psychotropic medication	5	24

Despite the clear evidence of 'psychic costs' incurred by the carers, readily observable financial costs were less evident. In two cases daughters were foregoing employment - one a full-time teaching job, the other a part-time job -but in most others it was difficult to discern whether gifts or costs of travelling would be significantly less if the old person were in residential care.

CHAPTER 3

KEY WORKERS AND CASE MANAGEMENT

The community care approach was intended to concentrate responsibility for case management so as to enable and encourage social workers to organise more effective care. In this chapter we examine the ways in which the five stages of case management - case finding, assessment, care planning and service arrangement, monitoring and review, and closure - were performed. In so doing, we shall consider the roles and tasks of fieldworkers in long-term community care and examine the ways in which these may contribute to the effectiveness and efficiency of care. For the sake of simplicity and economy, the third and fourth stages - care planning and monitoring and review - are treated as a single section in this chapter.

1. Raising Referrals: case finding and screening

As for any new service being established, both 'case finding' and 'screening' were important tasks. Case finding is intended to ensure that a high proportion of those for whom the service is the most appropriate mode of care actually receive community care - subject to their right to refuse it if they so wish (horizontal target efficiency). Screening is intended to ensure that a high proportion of users have the appropriate characteristics for a particular service (vertical target efficiency). A number of factors were relevant to targeting: organisational locus, initial agency contacts and procedures.

(a) Organisational locus

The community care team was fully integrated into the organisation of the social services department, working from the same building, and covering the same territory as a generic area team. The team leader's role differed from that of others only in that the team had resources of its own to deploy, was smaller than other teams and that there was research involvement. In addition, the project had its own management team consisting of both local authority and university personnel.

It is helpful to contrast this integrated model with a 'detached' model in which case managers were organisationally separated from the main providers of resources such as in a voluntary agency. In such a model the team would depend for its effectiveness on influencing the policy and practice of others. One example is the Resource Worker Project (Glendenning, 1984). 'Detached' status may on the one hand confer disadvantages such as a lack of an official identity or credentials to establish relationships with agencies or families, but on the other may enable staff to be more partisan on behalf of their clients in pressurising agencies. However, there were no substantial visible improvements in access to and uptake of services (horizontal target efficiency). On the other hand, screening (vertical target efficiency) would not be demanded of a detached team lacking control of service resources. Indeed, their very existence could make targeting poorer if the pressure which they applied on behalf of one group of clients was not countervailed by that of others acting for other groups. The community care scheme was designed to provide additional or alternative care for those elderly people who were likely to require admission to residential homes, and therefore was dependent on vertical target efficiency. Integration into the local authority structure was crucial for effective screening and also for ensuring uptake of services at the critical moment.

More importantly, an integrated structure was crucial in determining the locus of case responsibility which was central to the project. At first, the social workers in the area team were ambivalent about allowing the community care workers to take full responsibility for 'their' cases, particularly those staff who spent most of their time working with elderly clients. This attitude was the more understandable because the first members of the team lacked appropriate social work qualifications and experience. Transfer of responsibility was made easier by personnel changes when two qualified and experienced social workers were appointed to the project and after the community care team had begun to establish credibility through work with individual clients, although staff of the area team retained involvement in one or two cases with whom they had developed particularly close relationships. Transfer would not have been so readily possible for a 'detached' team.

Later the scheme was relocated in an elderly persons' home having a high proportion of its beds allocated to short-stay residents. It was also made responsible for the allocation of residential and day care places. Placing the scheme at the doorway to residential care was more likely to ensure that the alternatives were automatically considered when application was made for a residential bed, and thereby to improve efficiency in referral procedures. Furthermore, the new location made it easier to use residential care as part of a package of care in which residential staff could be more closely involved. But however logical this arrangement may seem, it would probably have been unacceptable initially because of the greater disruption to existing systems.

(b) Initial agency contacts

Before the scheme entered the field, preparatory discussions were held with social workers in area teams and hospitals, home help organisers, community nurses, voluntary organisations, some general practitioners and other physicians to establish links and extend awareness of the scheme.

At the end of the preparatory period of five months the fieldworkers felt that there had been insufficient time for all the groundwork essential for successful implementation, particularly developing contacts with nursing and medical staff. However, such contacts are often more effectively developed through work with individual cases, as was reflected in the growth of referrals from health service personnel. Consequently, developmental and promotional activity continued after the scheme moved into the field, as can be seen from analysis of staff use of time. Even in the period when the scheme was operating fully, developmental activities consumed on average about 28 per cent of the social workers' time. In the first quarter after the scheme entered the field, such activities consumed about 60 per cent of their time. This is probably an underestimate, since in the early phase much of the work attributed to clients was developmental because procedures were being tested involving such activities as joint visits.

(c) Initial procedures and their development

Sources such as case files and the waiting list for residential care were expected to provide a poor guide to suitable cases, and the original intention was that social workers from the area team would be a source of screening and selecting appropriate referrals for the the scheme. Referral was to be made by a standard form developed by the team in the planning period. It covered functional disability, physical and psychological state, material environment, financial circumstances, social contacts, family relationships and recent emotional traumas. In addition a team member attended meetings when referrals were allocated to identify suitable cases.

After an initial group of thirty suitable cases had been referred during the first six months, the number of new cases declined and there was some anxiety whether sufficient suitable cases could be found. Of the thirty cases, twenty-one had received support from the scheme.

Three factors appeared to have contributed to the apparent scarcity of cases:

(i) Both of the original members of the community care team lacked basic social work qualifications and substantial experience of social work with the elderly, which accounted for some difficulty in the uptake of more complex cases.

(ii) There was some degree of uncertainty about what constituted appropriate referrals and vagueness about the meaning of 'a high probability of needing residential care'. The pathways and decisions by which elderly people are channelled in the direction of residential care are complex, reflecting such local and historical factors as staff perceptions and experience, the level of domiciliary care, and the balance between hospital and local authority provision, as well as explicit policy criteria (Neill, 1982). In an attempt to

anchor the concept of 'need for residential care' in identifiable characteristics, the team circulated guidelines for admission to residential care which had been developed elsewhere (Davies and Duncan, 1975). However, these criteria were perhaps too general to provide specific guidance.
(iii) The process of referral was elaborate. Completing a form which was excessively detailed and longer than that required for application to residential care was a deterrent for busy staff.

After the project had been operating for six months the problem of uptake was tackled afresh under pressure from the management team, facilitated by staff turnover. New staff who were qualified and experienced were appointed, and approached the problem by considering additional sources of referrals, particularly the home help service, occupational therapists and the intake of new cases to the area team. The referral process was made more informal, individual social workers being encouraged to discuss possible cases and then provide only basic details and a case summary. This served to clarify criteria for referral by concrete example. Once these processes were instituted the number of referrals rose substantially, and the proportion of inappropriate cases fell greatly. Thus, of the fifty-four cases who after consideration were identified as below the threshold of need, thirty-nine were referred during the first year of the scheme.

A second issue considered by the management team during the first year of the scheme was the dependency level of cases. The scheme had been originally conceived as an alternative to residential care. However, a few cases were substantially more frail than this. Their health status was such that they would benefit from both medical and nursing assessment. It was recognised that a significant number of cases requiring more complex packages of support would be likely to reduce the overall number that could be managed at any one time. Nonetheless it was decided to treat the criterion of 'need for residential care' as only a minimal requirement.

(d) Effects on targeting

After the early period of slow uptake, the procedures appeared to work adequately to ensure that the right people were referred (vertical target efficiency). The evidence of this is the high degree of frailty of the elderly people, who were more dependent than originally envisaged.

Increased uptake (horizontal target efficiency) is more difficult to evaluate. However, since the team's resources were limited, any increase in the number of new cases tended to lead to an improvement in horizontal target efficiency. There appeared to be two areas where new needs were being met. One group, referred by general practitioners and community nurses, required a level of care greater than that provided in residential homes and were usually supported by spouses and daughters. They were often previously unknown to the social services department. Of these cases with overburdened carers, seven were not receiving other services from the social services department. It was difficult to find equivalent cases in the comparison area, since without the additional service offered by the community care scheme they were not coming to the notice of the department. The second group of cases for whom new needs were met was where serious depression, anxiety or confusion were the major components of their dependency. There were twenty-seven such cases. Of these, eleven were not in receipt of other services, and in another five cases the community care workers managed to introduce home help to those who had previously been reluctant to receive it.

However, the effort which was devoted to raising referrals from within the social services department in the early stages must have distracted attention from raising referrals from other agencies. There was an almost complete lack of referrals from the hospital service despite close contact with the geriatric physician who was mainly responsible for day hospital services, and few referrals from hospital social workers. The use of the scheme to facilitate early discharge or rehabilitation, with the possible benefits to elderly people and lower costs to the health service, was mainly confined to episodes of hospital care for existing clients of the community care scheme. Only two cases were directly referred from hospital. However, after the evaluation period, discharge from long-stay hospital care and residential homes was organised.

2. Assessment

Improved assessment was an important objective of the community care approach. Whilst case-finding and screening go far towards determining that appropriate people receive services, assessment and care planning determine how effective an intervention is in achieving its objectives. 'Assessment' has been heuristically separated from 'care planning', the former being focused on the identification of the objectives of care and the problems which are to be tackled, and the latter being focused on the actual selection of appropriate means to meet these needs, such as negotiating and coordinating services. The blurring of this distinction between ends and means in social work is likely to be great in the care of the elderly where ends themselves are often poorly defined (Goldberg and Warburton, 1979).

Assessment, designed to ensure that needs and preferences are clearly identified, is a prerequisite of two aspects of efficiency described in Chapter 1 (market efficiency and input mix efficiency). In the design of the scheme, the economic theory of need as a cost-benefit judgement (Culyer, 1976; Davies, 1977a) provided a valuable framework for the separation of ends and means and enabling the team to consider important issues in the development of a new service for the elderly: 'what should constitute acceptable levels of client well-being?'; 'what balance should be struck between one client and another, or the elderly person and their carers?'; 'what alternative combinations of resources would produce well-being?' and 'what are the relative costs of alternative forms of provision?'

(a) Processes and procedures in assessment.

Smaller caseloads permitted the workers to devote more time to assessment, which underlay the whole process of case management in the scheme, being the basis for the social worker 'to set both long and short-term goals, to reach a decision about how or whether to intervene, and to recognise when to transfer or terminate a case' (British Association of Social Workers, 1977, p.10). Assessment was conceived of both as an 'event' in the initial phase of early contact betwen the social worker and elderly person, and also a 'process' whereby there was continual reassessment and monitoring.

Adequate assessment had to consider not only the nature of particular problems experienced by each individual but also the peculiar interaction of these multiple hazards and their likely impact on these difficulties of any additional help. Thus assessment was concerned not only with the *needs* of the elderly person but also their *strengths* and the identification of *obstacles* to achieving change.

(i) Initial contact

Where referring social workers knew the elderly person well and had established a good relationship, the initial visit was a joint one, especially when it was felt there might be a degree of reluctance on the part of the client to receive help. This could be particularly important in gaining access to and making realistic assessments of people who appeared confused, since it would help to determine whether or not the confused behaviour was of recent onset and to ascertain the reliability of information. A brief explanation of the scheme, formulated in a way that was relevant to the elderly person, was followed by an exploration of current difficulties and ways of coping. This involved careful enquiry into crucial aspects of the elderly person's life: physical limitations, mental health, personality and attitudes to help, housing, financial needs, family and social network, and existing services. Although it was not deliberate policy to ask a disabled person to perform difficult tasks to assist assessment, elderly people had frequently developed coping strategies to deal with a particular disability, which was indicative of personal strengths.

(ii) Closer involvement of the elderly person and their carers

Smaller caseloads also enabled the social workers to involve the elderly people and carers themselves more closely in the definition of their needs, and the ways in which help might be provided. They had the resources to respond to the elderly person's particular wishes about simple things such as times of meal, or retiring to bed or type of diet. The exercise of choice, within the limits set by disability, could be a great morale booster. Target problems were jointly selected and agreed as in task-centred work (Reid and Epstein, 1972; Goldberg *et al.*, 1985). The approach was of course more complicated in cases of high dependency, particularly where the elderly person suffered from mental impairment and their capacity for defining their needs was thereby limited. In such cases a more directive approach was required, which usually involved the provision of services apparently suited to the elderly person's needs, unless there was explicit rejection, a procedure described by Wasser (1971) as 'protective services'.

A balance had to be struck between what might appear to an anxious elderly person as intrusion and the need for responsible intervention based on accurate knowledge. This required a sensitive appreciation of the elderly person's attitude to help and ways in which help could be provided to avoid undermining their independence (Goldberg *et al.*, 1970). Consequently, a level of care less than the ideal might be introduced in the hope of developing in the longer term a more comprehensive package for a doubtful elderly person.

(iii) Collaboration: the influence of other services and helpers

It was important to clarify precisely what was being provided by other services and their perception of the clients' problems. The knowledge of other professionals was seen as essential for a full assessment. Sometimes an occupational therapist was involved in making decisions about the appropriateness of suggested activities or aids. The close working relationship which developed with a geriatric physician meant that medical assessment was available where the effects of illness were unclear. The value of this informal process suggests that there can be considerable future gain in a more formalised arrangement.

Continuing assessment, or access to places where assessment could be undertaken, was at times devised as part of a package of care, particularly where the extent of need was unclear due to confusion in the elderly person or the complications of an associated physical illness. In one case, the team arranged for a woman to enter a residential home for an assessment of her mobility difficulties, particularly at night and morning.

Where clients were socially isolated, and information was hard to glean, helpers were sometimes used to uncover the real extent of need, and to gain cooperation. This was made explicit in their contracts. Information would then be fed back to the social workers enabling them to establish a package of care based on more complete knowledge, with the helper already established and known to the elderly person. In one case where both husband and wife exhibited symptoms of confusion and were ambivalent about the receipt of help, the initial contract given to the helper specified assessment and finding ways of making help acceptable. It stated: 'To visit and initially assess the extent of problems of daily living ... and to be prepared to give assistance in those areas Mrs W. finds acceptable'.

(iv) The effect of controlling resources

Control of a budget appeared to give the workers a real incentive to undertake careful assessments since it was possible to devise individual solutions to the problems identified. The assessment approach was a 'problem-oriented' one, rather than one of identifying eligibility for the receipt of a standard service. This explicitly separated the means from the ends of intervention. Thus the function of assessment was not to ask the question all too commonly formulated in the care of the elderly - namely, 'what service does this elderly person require?', but rather to pose two separate questions: first 'what difficulties are this elderly person and their carers experiencing?' and secondly 'what is the most appropriate means of dealing with these difficulties?'

Budgetary control meant that the team had to consider not only the extent of unmet need, but also the level of need at which help was appropriate. In many care settings, the resources which can be allocated are much less than would be required to meet need, thereby reducing the incentive to make accurate assessments. However, in the community care scheme the workers were able to mobilise and develop care resources, so this constraint was removed. This created a danger that workers might be uncertain about what would be appropriate upper limits of provision. There were no clearly defined boundaries for cases other than those at the financial ceiling of the scheme. In practice, the limits were set by an implicit concept of 'what was reasonable', based on experience of elderly people in general and a concept of diminishing returns, intervention appearing justifiable as long as the improvement in quality of life expected was relatively substantial.

(b) Instrumentation

Since the provision of appropriate care is predicated on adequate assessment, it was felt to be essential for the team to codify norms of good practice in procedures and recording instruments. Therefore considerable emphasis was placed on this set of activities in the early period, although the development of procedures continued after the scheme had begun to provide services to clients.

Effective intervention requires that assessments should make the objectives of care explicit. Outcome was defined as the reduction of a shortfall in well-being compared with a state considered to be acceptable. Different outcomes may be observed at different stages in the process of producing welfare (Davies, 1977a). Thus an outcome at the early stages such as the receipt of a service for which the person is eligible, i.e. an attendance allowance, is not direct evidence of improved well-being; for example, the money may be mislaid or simply stored. Keeping the house warm and clean, or providing nutritious and appetising meals - activities valued in their own right - represent outcomes at a subsequent stage. The most general effects on welfare, such as subjective well-being, can be seen as outcomes at a much later stage in a hierarchy of needs (Davies and Knapp, 1981). The schedules which were developed by the team attempted to embody these principles.

The original assessment document was highly structured, requiring the collection of a considerable amount of information, largely in precoded form, with insufficient space for explaining individual variations. It covered the range of needs described earlier, including aspects of physical and mental health and the adequacy of services. The detail was too highly structured to be helpful, and with changes in personnel the team saw that it required simpler documentation. However, the process of constructing schedules led to the internalisation of a range of dimensions of need for assessment. A shorter and more flexible assessment document was developed and forms a component of the record system still in use (Challis and Chesterman, 1985). The layout was designed to cover the main aspects of need in a precoded format and to provide space for recording other significant material. In this way, it attempted to strike a balance between standard, structured information and the individuality of each case.

3. Care Planning, Service Arranging, Maintenance and Monitoring

These activities, bringing together the stages of care planning and monitoring in case management, describe the main experience of the scheme for most elderly people since along with regular reassessment they are repeatedly performed throughout the care process. It will be remembered from Chapter 1 that effective performance of these tasks was designed to ensure that individuals received a more appropriate mix of services (input mix efficiency) and that these services were responsive to consumer preferences (market efficiency). It is helpful to consider two interrelated sets of issues: first, the processes and style of practice in the context provided by the project; and second, the influences of a procedural and contextual nature on that practice.

(a) Processes and style of practice

One distinctive feature of the approach to long-term care was the continuity of fieldworkers' involvement with clients, leading to established relationships and a knowledge of cases, which made support more effective than if a worker came anew to a case in response to a crisis. Continuous involvement meant that making necessary help acceptable, dealing with the ambivalences and anxieties of family and informal carers, and establishing and maintaining a care network could be handled more effectively.

(i) Making needed help available: enabling

Reluctance or ambivalence is familiar to those in helping professions. Goldberg *et al.* noted the importance in work with the elderly of 'the social worker's role as an enabler, making needs explicit and helping clients to accept services which they need and to which they are entitled' (1970, p.197).

Assessment at times revealed anxieties about receiving help, perhaps reflecting a fear that it would undermine independence or be the first step towards institutional care. Underlying this could be a variety of factors, including residual stigma attached to the receipt of services, the expectation of loss of autonomy associated with receipt of help (Williamson, 1981) or a denial of the extent of their difficulties. In such cases, it was frequently necessary for the social worker to make an initial investment in gaining the confidence and trust of the elderly person, and exploring their particular fears and anxieties. For these reluctant cases, the general approach was to focus the immediate aims on those problems identified by the elderly people themselves, in order gradually to construct a comprehensive package of care.

Where the elderly person was initially reluctant to receive help, it was important for the scheme to be seen as competent through an immediate response. Actions as simple as ensuring an aid worked more effectively helped to gain confidence, and provided a key to fuller involvement and subsequent development of a package of care. As an example, one lady protested that she had no need of help in a regular fashion, and yet it was clear that small problems became almost insurmountable to her. The initial help was simply transport to an optician and help with the repair of her husband's electric shaver. This small beginning evoked trust and paved the way for a very substantial level of support to a woman caring for her dying husband. From this apparently trivial and straightforward intervention, it was possible to build a more extensive level of support.

To commence with the client's own definition of the problem and to proceed only at the pace which the old person can tolerate have for long been seen as central principles of social casework (Biestek, 1961; Reid and Epstein, 1972). However, they are easy although costly to neglect in the context of a large caseload with many competing demands. The point is aptly made by Rowlings who argues that for many elderly clients 'the apparently simple nature of the help being offered should not obscure the sensitivity and the skill required of the worker who may be faced by a client whose apathy or sense of hopelessness is a major obstacle to the introduction of any kind of change' (1981, p.48).

Equally influential in determining the acceptability of help, and therefore the task of the worker, was the elderly person's attitude to their own disability. In some, a sense of helplessness and loss of control over their own life produced a range of responses from demandingness for care on the one hand to criticism of the adequacy of what was offered on the other. A particularly difficult task was trying to keep in balance clients' ambivalent feelings of need for care and drive for autonomy. One way in which help could be made acceptable was by re-establishing the elderly person's sense of esteem, thereby balancing the caring exchange. A number of elderly people would describe their previous levels of activity in helping in the community, a process which appeared to increase their sense of self-worth and establish a basis for mutual respect. This use of previous experience has been described by Cormican (1977) as 'functional reminiscence'.

The process of 'enabling' is concerned with what Goldfarb (1968) has described as 'pseudo independent' behaviour, which renders the person unmanageable because of their failure to accept help, advice or relief. He suggests that in such cases help can only be given by establishing 'even in a disguised form ... some dependence in a protective relationship'. The pace at which an effective support network can be constructed will depend on this early process.

(ii) Helping clients cope with loss

As Brearley (1975) argues, dealing with loss is a central activity in social work with the elderly. Thirteen (14 per cent) people suffered bereavement, defined as the loss of a close carer or spouse, within the year preceding help by the scheme or during the first year of care.

> *Mrs M. was a determined, but physically weak, woman with a heart condition. She cared for her husband who had suffered a severe stroke. Following a period of increasingly difficult care at home, during which time considerable support had been provided, he was admitted to hospital where he subsequently died. Whereas in the initial phase Mr M. had been administratively defined as the 'client', while he was in hospital the focus of the social worker increasingly became his wife, to assist her with her feelings of guilt about whether he should be at home. Following her bereavement, the aim became to support Mrs M., helping her to plan for the future while she came to terms with her altered life. As her own health was also deteriorating, Mrs M. became a client of the scheme in her own right.*

Immediate involvement with death proved to be a very demanding aspect of the work. Of those cases who died, twice as many did so in their own homes, or after they had been in institutional care for less than a week, than in the comparison group.

Mr B., a widower living alone, suffered from a heart condition and cancer of the bowel. For this he had to attend hospital regularly. He adamantly refused long-term care in hospital. During the period of the scheme's involvement his health declined further, and he became increasingly aware that he would soon die. It was essential for the social worker to support him and those helpers who were closely involved through his feelings of isolation, anger and depression.

As well as bereavement, impending death, chronic isolation and loneliness, there were other significant loss experiences. Considerable distress was experienced by two elderly women who were aware that their mental faculties were declining and who developed secondary depression. Sensitive handling was essential in such circumstances, since distress at loss of competence could easily increase the extent of the person's difficulties.

(iii) Meeting the needs of family and informal carers

Some of the more complicated and demanding cases were those where considerable family or neighbourly care was available. The cause for concern was often less the inadequacy of care being received by the elderly person than the carer's need for relief. Lacking help, carers would find themselves excessively committed as the old person's frailty increased, faced with the competing demands of the old person and their own needs. They were often unable to perceive any alternative to the routine they had constructed. In these cases, the social worker had to assist them in reaching difficult decisions, considering and evaluating the risks of alternatives, and subsequently to support them, ensuring that the burden of care did not become too great. In other cases the social worker had to find ways of reducing carers' anxiety about an elderly person's decision to remain at home and tolerate a reasonable level of risk.

On three occasions it was decided to incorporate members of the family into the scheme as helpers to enable them to cope more adequately. Contracts were used to determine realistic boundaries to any one person's involvement in care and relieve them of the feeling of sole responsibility. Continuing support was usually necessary to maintain equilibrium.

Mrs G., who suffered from dementia, was extremely forgetful and unable to perform usual daily activities such as preparing meals or getting up and going to bed. She lived in a large terraced house less than a mile away from her two sons, both of whom were retired and in relatively poor health. However, the family were very concerned to support Mrs G. The demands of care, which included fairly frequent supervision, were a source of difficulty and anxiety for the family, and there was some friction as to who should be responsible on which days. Careful planning, with the social worker acting as broker between the different family members, led to the construction of a more explicit rota of care and supervision between the family members, a neighbour, and regular relief at a day centre. This system of support, with the social worker maintaining oversight, avoided the 'polarisation of care' (Ratna and Davis, 1984) *and proved adequate without the need to introduce additional care at home.*

As might be expected, in nearly half of those cases where the elderly person had a clearly identified principal carer, they were experiencing disrupted household routine and chronic tiredness. Over half had disrupted social lives, whilst most suffered a degree of mental distress and all but one experienced a sense of burden in caring (Sainsbury and Grad, 1971; Levin, 1982). The feeling of sole responsibility weighed heavily on carers, whose attitudes were crucial in planning care. People under considerable stress found it difficult to conceive of relinquishing care, often experiencing guilt in so doing (Allen *et al.*, 1983). At this juncture the social worker had to agree realistic limits to the carer's commitment, perhaps by focusing discussion on the extent to which their horizons had been narrowed over time. Where it was planned to involve a helper to support the carer, consideration was given to the implications of this for the relationship between the elderly person and their informal network. In most cases the elderly person welcomed the change and was glad to see relief provided for the carers. On occasions they could, for a variety of reasons, be more cooperative with an 'outsider' than with an existing carer, and anticipation and preparation for this could avoid tension and possible competition. It was clear that factors such as patterns of communication, dependence and power in the relationship could be relevant (Bergmann *et al.*, 1984). Failure to identify the possibilities of 'manipulation', and prepare carers for the likely effects would have run the risk of fission of support networks.

(iv) Mobilising and coordinating formal services

The case-management role explicitly made the social worker responsible for the whole pattern of care and attempting to restructure or modify it to provide more adequate support. As found by Goldberg *et al.*, 'collaboration with a host of other statutory and voluntary agencies on behalf of the elderly client, acting as coordinator of these services, ensuring they function smoothly and appropriately, emerged as a central task in the present fragmented personal social services for the aged' (1970, p.197). The high degree of frailty of elderly clients required the close coordination of the efforts of many different services in conjunction with the activities of informal carers. In some cases it was possible to renegotiate the patterns of visiting of several people to provide greatly improved cover.

On average, people were receiving three domiciliary services before admission to the scheme. In the subsequent year, the average number of domiciliary health and social services received was 5.37. The main services used before receipt of the scheme and over the following year are shown in Table 3.1. The services which were increased most were the introduction of community care helpers, the day hospital and chiropody. The increased social work involvement was a direct consequence of case-management responsibility. It is certainly possible that the use of the day hospital and chiropody services may have helped to reduce the decline in mobility which is discussed in Chapter 7. There was a slight increase in most other services such as home help, the exception being meals-on-wheels, which was seen by clients and the social work team alike as a less than satisfactory means of improving diet.

Table 3.1
Seven services most frequently received before enrollment in community care and during subsequent year

Before scheme		In subsequent year	
Service	**% receiving**	**Service**	**% receiving**
Home help	72	Social work	100
Aids[1]	44	Helpers	99
District nursing	41	Home help	80
Social work	37	Aids[1]	48
Chiropody	27	District nursing	44
Meals on wheels	16	Chiropody	41
Geriatric day hospital	16	Geriatric day hospital	32

Note
1. Refers to such major aids as for bathing, for walking and special beds.

Home help and other SSD services. Most cases - sixty-six out of ninety-two - were already receiving the main domiciliary resource, the home help service, before they were referred for community care. In another five cases the service was arranged where there was none before. The other common services were meals-on-wheels, day care and aids. The major problem of those cases not in receipt of home help at referral is noted in Table 3.2. With the exception of the few who had experienced a recent crisis, these were cases where home help was not provided because of the presence of other carers; because clients were suffering from depression, but were often not identified as needy by the home help service; or because they suffered major psychiatric disorder such as dementia or paranoid psychosis, and the home help service found it difficult to respond appropriately.

Table 3.2
Major problem of cases not in receipt of home help at referral

	N
Recent major crises	4
Problems of family or informal carers	7
Depression or low morale	7
Major psychiatric disorder	8
Number of clients	26

If it had been feasible to do so, it might have been thought efficient to reconstruct care plans from scratch for all cases at the point of entry to community care. However, this was not possible for a variety of reasons. First, like any providers of a new service, community care workers were anxious to establish for themselves a role which would be valued by other carers, and so encourage referrals. To threaten the domain of an established service would have been likely to deter referrals. Second, an existing service might well have become greatly valued by a client, such as when a close relationship had developed with a home help. To disrupt the existing pattern would have been inefficient and have had negative effects on the client. No attempt was therefore made to replace home helps by community care helpers, and a formal agreement was made to this effect, although inevitably some degree of rearrangement of time and tasks was negotiated to provide a more comprehensive service package. Such rearrangement was carried out as opportunities presented themselves, and was not forced on the home help service. This was possible as the scheme could vary the service it provided to fill whatever gaps were left by the policies and practice of the local home help service. Unsurprisingly, therefore, the effect of community care was to increase demand for other domiciliary services and not to reduce it, by revealing needs which required additional inputs of home care as well as prolonging survival in the community.

In theory, such an acceptance of existing service inputs could threaten the ability of a scheme to achieve the best use of resources. First, tasks performed by home helps may not always be those which are most important. The best use of resources might involve less household care and more personal care at more varied times. Second, the home help and client might be inappropriately matched and this might interfere with an overall care plan although, of course, in practice a long-established home help would more usually be a significant and valued person in an elderly person's network. Third, the home help might conceivably resent the intrusion in 'her' case by others and seek to undermine the position of a new helper. Fourth, since the influence of the fieldworkers was negotiated, they had relatively little power to secure more effective services in situations where an employee of another service was thought to perform inadequately. There might, therefore, be a series of disadvantages arising from an inability to substitute services. However, in practice it appeared for a number of cases that the effectiveness of the scheme in building care packages required a baseline of care provided by the home help service.

It is interesting to consider whether the acceptance of existing service levels is a necessary price to pay for the survival of a new development (Simons and Warburton, 1980). This need not necessarily be the case. One solution might be to increase the power of the case manager by manipulating financial allocations so that they could make the equivalent of direct purchases of services. An alternative, and less disruptive, approach would be organisational change giving increased prescriptive authority to case managers, thereby reducing the danger of independent service allocation by parallel hierarchies.

As time passed, the complementarity of community care and the home help service was increasingly evident. As a result, assessment was often followed by discussion with the appropriate staff and adjustments of service allocations. At times it was necessary to negotiate extra provision where assessment had revealed gaps or where work with a reluctant elderly person had resulted in their willingness to accept services. Decisions about who would perform which care tasks were made in regular discussion with the home help service and difficulties were usually readily resolved. On occasions community care helpers would be brought in to help alongside home helps. For example, in the case of Mr Q., a partially sighted man with a long-standing alcohol problem, it had proved impossible for the home help to accomplish many of the tasks considered essential because he was so lonely that he would spend most of the time following her around seeking attention. It was arranged for a helper to visit at the same time, and to distract him by providing stimulation and company, so the home help could get on with her tasks.

Health and other services. Contacts with health personnel were necessary to identify possible unmet medical needs and to incorporate day hospital treatment into the package of care to tackle the problems of mobility. This was easier because community care workers were specialists working with a particular group of clients and had regular contact with others with similar concerns. It was therefore possible over time to reap the benefits which can come from more personal contact and exchange of favours to advance shared goals.

Regular contact was maintained with the district nursing service, which attended 44 per cent of the elderly people. The indeterminacy of the responsibilities of domiciliary and home nursing services caused problems, particularly about bathing. The team avoided a wholesale colonisation of areas of unmet need which were not obviously the province of either agency, decisions being made on a case by case basis. Yet adequate care was always the overriding priority and could lead to exchanges of favours. On one occasion it emerged that a district nurse was visiting an elderly person for predominantly social reasons, and it was possible to relieve her of this by ensuring that these visits were undertaken by helpers. Subsequently, and probably as a consequence, it was possible to obtain increased nursing care for another person who needed it. The number of unnecessary 'check-up' visits by nursing staff was reduced. On occasions, when a domestic crisis prevented a helper from visiting an elderly person at the last minute, a district nurse did so in return for help received in the past. Collaboration with the district nursing service grew and, although it did not result in the regular and formal review of cases, informal contacts and shared case planning increased. They included frequent visits by nurses to the team office.

Sometimes it was feasible to discharge elderly people from hospital earlier because community care provided additional support at home. This may have helped workers to obtain improved health care for other clients. Six months after the scheme commenced, the workers arranged a regular monthly review of elderly people with a clinical assistant in geriatrics at the local day hospital. This led to closer coordination of activity and improved access to geriatric assessment. Use of the day hospital increased from 16 to 32 per cent of clients. Again, these improvements in liaison and coordination were achieved to a considerable degree because of the workers' specialisation in the care of one client group.

It might have been expected that the Attendance Allowance would be a valuable element in care and applications were made for this benefit. However, few clients were in receipt of this (Levin, 1982), and there was a real problem in its inclusion in a package of care due to the considerable time-lag between application, assessment and receipt of benefit. Contact with the housing department was made on behalf of three cases who required sheltered housing after they became involved with the scheme. Surprisingly, only two of the elderly people were in contact with a formal voluntary group, such as Age Concern, and both of these received occasional visits from the same volunteer. Private residential care also was used for short-term and permanent care on occasions.

The components of care. The average combinations of services which were used over one year are listed in Table 3.3.

Table 3.3 Use of services over one year

Service	Units
Local authority residential care (days)	10.92
Private residential care (days)	6.38
Day care (days)	6.24
Home help (hours)	100.31
Meals on wheels	21.13
Community care helpers (£)	180.20
Voluntary visits by helpers (visits)	17.70
General hospital care (acute/mainly acute) (days)	13.20
Geriatric hospital (days)	8.38
Psychiatric hospital (days)	1.20
Geriatric day hospital (days)	7.19
Psychiatric day hospital (days)	1.24
District nursing (visits)	28.10
Chiropody (visits)	1.24

Although these figures indicate the extent of usage of different services, they do not represent typical weekly averages, since not all services were used by all clients. The actual packages of care varied considerably in their cost and the proportion of costs accounted for by the community care scheme. That quarter of elderly people who were the most expensive to the social services department were extremely frail and chronically sick and likely to enter residential care. They therefore required substantial domiciliary services. They tended to survive the full year, since the longer a person stayed at home, the greater the tendency for average costs to increase. Conversely, those cases least costly to the social services department included those surviving a shorter time, and those suffering from mental disorder and family stress.

There were distinct differences too, between the cases for which the costs of community care helpers were a low proportion of the costs, and the cases for which they constituted a high proportion of costs. Those cases for whom helper costs were a low proportion of costs (less than 10 per cent) tended to enter institutional care and to need a substantial amount of domiciliary support, such as meals and home help, at times when such services were readily provided. Conversely, those cases for whom community care helpers constituted a high proportion of costs (above 50 per cent) tended to suffer from mental disorder, need care out of hours and care tasks lying outside the usual domiciliary service remit, such as check-up visits, companionship and stimulation, or support for families.

The greater the degree of case complexity, the greater tended to be the need to coordinate care. The average number of services, including hospital and residential care, received by community care clients over one year was 6.23, the range extending between 2 and 10. If this is seen as a measure of case complexity, then clearly most cases required a considerable degree of activity on the part of the social worker, particularly since this measure tends to underestimate service usage, taking no account of multiple hospital or short-term care admissions. Coordination of services at times also required the social worker to sort out conflicts between different members of the care network; for example between a home help and a helper. These could arise through misunderstandings about one another's role. This coordinating role in social care was central to effective case management. It can be distinguished 'from administrative competence and resourcefulness' since it requires 'continuous appraisal, before and during the arranging of services, of the effects this may have on the elderly person ... practical activity on behalf of clients is integral to the social work task; yet the need to formulate the plans with the person concerned and, in so doing, to relate sensitively to the feelings of others (relatives, volunteers, etc.) is crucial' (Stevenson, 1981a, pp.160-61).

(v) Organising support from the local community

The community care workers assessed need, supported and advised clients and carers, and undertook brokerage and advocacy. In addition they mobilised new resources directly to provide care. The budget was used to provide both human and material resources. The latter included purchase of aids, heating appliances for loan to elderly people in cold weather, large manageable flasks for providing hot drinks for the chair- or bed-bound and automatic kettles for people suffering from dementia. However, it was found necessary to provide additional support from 'helpers' paid by the scheme for nearly all cases. They were recruited from the locality by the team, as people interested in caring for the elderly. Helpers were sought both from within an elderly person's existing range of social contacts and from people who were 'strangers' brought in to care for the elderly person.

Helpers were matched with elderly people with the kind of care more usually associated with foster placements for children. In matching clients and helpers attention was paid not just to proximity and availability but also to attitudes and personality. Important too was the potential helper's previous experience, their capacity to deal with the more unpleasant circumstances encountered and to tolerate uncertainty. In certain situations, such as an elderly person at risk, a tendency towards anxiety or overprotectiveness could militate against effective help. Attention was also paid to factors which were related more to the potential chemistry of the relationship between helper and client than to the performance of caring activities: for instance shared cultural interests. Again, as well as matching the helper to the client on the basis of individual characteristics, the fit between the helper and the elderly person's existing social network was also important.

Introduction of client and helper usually followed a discussion with the social worker of the needs of the particular client, possible difficulties and ways of tackling them. A personal introduction by the social worker was designed to legitimise and clarify the role of the helper. This was reinforced by the use of a 'contract' or letter of agreement which specified the tasks which helpers were to undertake and the agreed fee.

Following this introduction support was provided by the team which varied according to the needs and circumstances of both elderly person and helper. Usually this was provided on an individual basis, although on occasions where several helpers were involved with one client small group meetings were held to share ideas and discuss approaches to care. Coffee mornings were held on a monthly basis for all helpers, to provide a forum for passing on information, general support and as a social gathering. The process of work with helpers is discussed in more detail in Chapter 6.

At a later stage, one social worker involved several helpers in developing a luncheon and social club in a sheltered housing unit for both community care clients and the residents. This further broadened the social worker's role from the construction and maintenance of networks around individual frail clients to facilitating the development of support services for a wider group.

The maintenance of a package of care was not simply a process of creating a stable network which once established was relatively self-sustaining. The circumstances of the elderly people, their families and informal carers were subject to change, as were their attitudes and feelings about continued living at home. For example, the average number of 'movements' of the elderly people from home to hospital or residential care was 1.27, the range being from 0 to 8. Changes also occurred due to events in the lives and commitments of helpers. Therefore there were frequent changes in the support network and the social worker had to react accordingly.

(vi) The distribution of social worker time

It was possible to differentiate five broad categories of the use of staff time:

Running (client) time. Activities clearly associated with the care of specific individuals. These included visiting, supporting family members and arranging services.

Running (overhead administrative) time. Activities essential to the day-to-day running of the scheme but not readily attributable to any one client, such as supporting and recruiting helpers or attending departmental or interagency meetings.

Development time. Time spent on activities in any new approach but which would only be a small part of an ongoing service. It includes developing procedures, systems and interagency arrangements. This time should be discounted over an appropriate period, since it is in effect an investment yielding a stream of benefits over a period.

Miscellaneous time. Time spent on activities such as education and publicity.

Research time. Time spent in attending meetings, writing, or record keeping beyond the time required for the running of an established system.

The division of social worker activities into these very broad categories made it possible to assess the time spent on each activity. From the launch of the project in May 1977 to the beginning of 1980, a sample of time distribution was reconstructed from workers' diaries and casenotes. Staff had wherever possible noted the time certain activities had taken them to complete. The sample days chosen were every fifteenth day, so that the assessment was regular but on different days of the week. Over a period of 138 weeks this meant that there were sixty-four observations.

The best basis for generalisation about time use is during the period when the scheme was operating with full caseloads, but before the advent of new developments. The average distribution of time during this period is shown in Table 3.4.

Developmental activity accounted for a substantial proportion of time. In part this was inevitable, since procedures for payment of helpers, ensuring appropriate referrals and recording of information were important concerns during the project, and new procedures were developed and updated through the whole period. However, certain overhead costs were extremely difficult to differentiate from development activities. For example, activities to improve methods of recruiting and supporting helpers were difficult to separate from recruitment activities themselves, the latter being an overhead cost, the former a developmental activity. Again, project team meetings, interagency liaison and the planning of alternative approaches to care involve both developmental and overhead activities. Time not readily allocatable to overhead costs tended to be defined as development activities. It would, however, require a specific study to discriminate precisely between developmental and overhead activities.

Table 3.4.
Distribution of social worker time in most representative period

Time activity	%
Client time	34.8
Overhead time	19.2
Development time	28.3
Miscellaneous time	4.8
Research time	12.9

On the other hand, the proportion of time spent on client-related activities was not dissimilar to that of studies of social workers in area teams. Given the importance of mobilising community resources in community care, much of the 'overhead' activities consisted of recruitment and support of helpers, raising the client and resource-centred components of social work time to over 50 per cent. This corresponds more closely to patterns of time use in hospital social work (Carver and Edwards, 1972; Chernesky and Lurie, 1976; Law, 1982), where a smaller proportion of time is spent in administrative activities.

In conclusion, a high proportion of time was spent on client-related activity in the community care scheme, requiring continuing contact with the elderly people and their carers after packages of care had been established, as well as considerable activity with helpers not attributable to individual clients.

(b) Procedural factors and organisational influences

The processes which we have just described in part simply reflect features of good practice but these were made possible by the procedural devices of the scheme: the deployment of a decentralised budget with expenditure limits by specialised fieldworkers with lower caseloads. In this section we discuss this and a second procedural device of the scheme - the recording system - before moving on to consider the extent to which the greater flexibility afforded by the budget enabled fieldworkers to respond more sensitively to local variations.

(i) Budgets, costs and care planning

The potential costs of packages of care were calculated as part of care planning and the actual costs of care were recorded on a weekly basis. The initial budget limit of two-thirds of the ('marginal') cost of a place in a new residential home was not inflexible. It was set at a level which ignored most of the hotel costs of residential care and attempted to ensure that the costs of the new scheme would not be much greater than standard provision. Where the cost of care of an individual case was expected to exceed this budget limit, the issue was considered by local management. Few cases were expected to exceed the limit over a substantial period of time, and the policy was not to declare cases ineligible for the scheme simply because their care packages exceeded the cost limits.

In practice only five cases exceeded the limit, considering their average cost over the year, and one of these only exceeded it by 50 pence per week. In three of these five cases, the high cost was caused by entry to residential care. The other two cases required hospital care. One was an elderly man with terminal cancer who refused to remain in hospital, and the other a dementing man living in an outlying village. He suffered from double incontinence but refused to enter hospital. Other cases exceeded the limit for brief periods; such as a patient discharged from hospital requiring intensive support for a short period followed by a package of lower cost for an indefinite period.

There was no evidence that taking account of costs caused either ethical or practical difficulties to fieldworkers. No doubt the relative rarity with which packages exceeded the limit helped to avoid such problems. Indeed, the evidence we have discussed indicates that command over a budget, taking account of costs as well as welfare objectives, enabled staff to enhance the quality of services to elderly people.

(ii) Recording and documentation

One of the principles of the scheme approach was that there should be a system of documentation to make accountability more effective, to record information needed for case-management activities and to provide the basis for retrospective accountability. The early development of assessment documents has been described previously. A care-planning schedule was also developed in the early phase, recording possible alternative forms of care, the effects of existing care and the expected costs. However, it was later replaced as part of the simplification of records. A monitoring chart was developed as a simple operational tool to summarise on one sheet the regular pattern of care for each individual. The costs of care were recorded on a weekly basis using quarterly sheets so that a running total of the cost of care was always readily available. These latter two items were incorporated into the recording system which was developed subsequently and has been used across a range of schemes.

The recording system has been described in detail elsewhere (Challis and Chesterman, 1985) and is shown in Appendix B. It consists of four elements:

1. *An Assessment Document* completed within two weeks of initial visit. It covered the main aspects of social needs and physical and mental health in a precoded format, with ample space to record significant features for which precoded material was insufficient.

2. *A Case Review Form* which was first completed within three weeks of assessment and thereafter on a quarterly basis or at time of significant change or closure. It was based on the generic form developed by Goldberg and Warburton (1979) but was adapted to work with the elderly. Hence sections about problem categories and resource utilisation were more highly detailed.

3. *A Monitoring Sheet*: a matrix with the seven days of the week on the vertical axis and critical periods of the day (such as getting up, breakfast and lunch) along the horizontal axis. Completing this sheet by filling in the visits and activities of different carers made it easy to identify periods of solitude and risk and modify care plans accordingly. It was also a helpful summary whenever the key worker was absent.

4. *A Costing Sheet* recorded expenditure by the social worker from the budget to pay helpers, plus the cost of other services such as home help, day care or residential care. The information was divided into thirteen weekly units, each sheet covering the costing of a case over one quarter.

The system has been proved to be acceptable in operation across a number of different areas and routine feedbacks are given to fieldworkers and managers of caseload profiles, activities and cost information. It has also been used to examine patterns of fieldworker activity through time and compare the care of elderly people receiving the scheme with those receiving standard provision.

(iii) Local opportunities and constraints

It has been argued that decentralisation of authority will lead to greater knowledge about local needs and resources, permitting more appropriate forms of intervention (Hadley and McGrath, 1984) and contributing to efficiency through a better mix of inputs in a care package. Local factors may also influence the nature of the target group served by the scheme, such as the presence of industrial disease in the population or opportunities arising from the local care system such as the existence of a psychogeriatric service.

Mobilising community resources: helpers and volunteers. The direct recruitment of helpers by the community care team, local people receiving relatively small payments and sometimes only expenses, was one of the keys to the flexibility of the community care scheme. Among the different community care schemes, however, there has been considerable variation in modes of recruitment and the extent to which payment covers the tasks undertaken or just the expenses of the helpers.

In the original scheme discussions were held with voluntary organisations for the aged, but it emerged that they were not sufficiently active in the field to be a source of help or competition. This is at first sight odd. The district is a retirement area, with seasonal employment and a relatively low proportion of women of working age in paid work, so that voluntary activity might have been more highly developed. However, of the ninety-two cases, only two were in touch with one formal voluntary organisation for the elderly, and they both received once-weekly visits from the same volunteer. Hence, there seemed little scope for an agreement with formal voluntary organisations to supply potential helpers as later proved possible in another area. Nonetheless, thirty-eight cases, 41 per cent of the group, received some of their formally arranged visits from helpers on a voluntary basis, only expenses being paid. Of course, many helpers visited their clients at times in addition to those which had been arranged by the social workers so that the extent of voluntary input by the helpers would have tended to have been underestimated. Nonetheless, it was noticeable that whether or not a helper involved with an individual elderly person received fees depended more on the circumstances of the helper than the characteristics of the client. This has proved to be the case in other developments of the scheme. Elsewhere in Kent and in North East England -areas with a high level of unemployment - it appears that the payment of fees to helpers has been important in order to augment household incomes, and nearly all receive fees.

Responses appear to have been influenced by different local conditions. In a relatively poor part of Kent with little public transport and where relatively few helpers have cars, the degree of precision in the matching of helpers to elderly people was limited by geographical factors. In a rural area of North Wales this was regarded as a factor of such importance that matching was seen as more a 'negative' than a 'positive' process; that is, identifying those who would definitely not relate well to one another. This was based on the notion that 'most people can get on with one another'. These considerations were only significant in the two outlying villages of the original project.

Local factors may also influence the outcome of care. In one area where recruitment of helpers appears more difficult and a high proportion of men undertake shift work, it seems difficult to guarantee the continuity of helpers required to manage the care of a dementing or suspicious mentally frail elderly person in their own home. It is therefore likely that local variations in the availability of helpers may set different limits on those who can be effectively cared for by such a community care scheme.

Other local care. It was at first sight both surprising and disappointing that the team did not use local resources other than helpers, such as the commercial sector. For instance, the provision of meals for individuals by arrangement with a cafe was a possibility. Ironically, one woman in the comparison group was found to have made such an arrangement with her neighbour, but this did not occur for scheme clients. No doubt this reflected in part the fact that every new development had a cost in terms of time, which conflicted with the pressure to recruit new cases. However, it was also a recognition that many elderly people did not simply need a meal. For example, food alone was insufficient to meet care objectives for people who were mildly depressed with a tendency to neglect themselves. These people needed the stimulation of company and encouragement to eat the food, whilst involvement in meal preparation with a helper was a valuable means of promoting independence. Other clients benefitted from being taken out on a one-to-one basis, which was most easily achieved by recruiting a helper.

The extent of local care services. Patterns of response were undoubtedly influenced by the local level of service provision. As noted in Chapter 2, the area had relatively low provision of both health and social care services, despite the in-migration on retirement, which is not uncommon in such areas (Karn, 1977).

The development of meal provision by helpers was partly a response of the scheme to the lack of available services, although justified also by care objectives other than nutrition. Again, localised day care in the homes of helpers was both a response to shortfalls in service provision and preferable to day centres for some elderly people, since it avoided the need to travel and mix in large groups. Care in helpers' homes seemed particularly beneficial for the mildly confused and depressed, giving continuity of attention by one or two familiar people. This simple approach was suggested some years ago, but has rarely been used (Rosin, 1965), perhaps because it requires a decentralised budget to establish such an initiative.

The role of community care and of the helpers was influenced not only by the level of provision but also by the policy of other services. In the original district, the home help service was not supplemented by domiciliary care assistants or 'home carers' providing personal care and, relatively speaking, tended not to be allocated in large quantities and at difficult times to those in the greatest need.

Conversely, in another area of the same authority, the scheme has been introduced into a system with a home help service which at times provided personal as well as household care. The response was to identify gaps in care; to undertake activities inappropriate for the home help service, such as improving the client's safety by visiting regularly to check up on a vulnerable person, and to focus on clienteles less easily catered for by existing provision, such as the dementing elderly or those receiving substantial informal care. Again, the development of regular consultation and liaison meetings with the local geriatric services represents a response to opportunity rather than constraint.

Environmental influences of the area. Morbidity patterns and the social, economic and housing environments of frail elderly people might be expected to influence care. Neither housing problems nor particular patterns of morbidity influenced the response of the scheme, as might have been expected in an area where industrial diseases were prevalent. The major environmental factor which influenced the response of the scheme was that the area was a retirement resort. Many elderly people had left behind their networks of social contacts, and their sense of social isolation was exacerbated by their own frailty or that of their partner. The lack of social support influenced the strategy of care since for many cases whole support networks had to be constructed and not merely reinforced.

4. Terminating Care at Home

This is a crucial issue for any scheme which attempts to offer an alternative to institutional care, since the parameters of normal practice are no longer useful and new guidelines have to be negotiated. Residential care was seen as one among many possible services to improve the quality of life. Therefore admission was not necessarily a sign of failure of community care. However, for many elderly people wishing to retain their own homes, it could prove very difficult to decide that community support was no longer viable. The social worker had to strike a balance between the wishes of the elderly person, a tolerable level of risk, and the difficulties experienced by carers. The latter is particularly significant since Carter and Evans (1978) found that admissions to residential care were determined less by changes in circumstances than by changes in the ability of elderly people or their carers to tolerate the situation.

During the period in which the project was evaluated, decisions to terminate care at home were relatively rare. These difficulties would, however, prove greater the longer a scheme was in operation since elderly people would become too frail for residential care and require increasingly scarce hospital beds. Of the fifteen cases who entered long-term care, twelve did so as a result of events beyond the control of the scheme such as declining health, a fall, or death of a carer. One entered care following family discord, and two made a positive decision to enter a home. Five elderly people entered residential care following help in making their decision of a kind which would not have been possible without the scheme. On follow-up after twelve months, all five cases were comfortably settled in old people's homes. For some, the extension of community support had provided a real choice whether or not to enter residential care.

Mrs J., an anxious and depressed lady, lived alone in a purpose-built bungalow for the elderly. Her main anxiety was that she was likely to fall on retiring to bed, with consequent insecurity, and she suffered debilitating loneliness. Support from a network of helpers who visited regularly provided companionship, helped her to bed and secured the house. This relieved her anxiety, and improved her morale for some months. Mrs J. commented to the social worker: 'Before you came, weekends were like a rehearsal for death'. However, on one occasion a helper was unable to visit at the last minute and could not contact anyone to back her up. Mrs J. found it difficult to tolerate this one incident of uncertainty and her anxiety increased again. Fortunately, at this time, a period of short-term residential care over Christmas had been arranged and Mrs J. found the experience very comforting. After careful discusson with the social worker she decided to remain in the home. The outcome was an acceptable one since the opportunity to stay on in her own home provided her with months of pleasure until finally she was able to make a realistic decision about her future in the light of experience.

A more positive and protective decision-making role was required in those cases where the elderly person was mentally impaired. One elderly woman, living in a high-rise block of flats and suffering from dementia, was unable to manage her hygiene adequately and was unhappy in her home and liable to wander. She did not respond to extensive support, and the anxieties of neighbours increased. In the light of what appeared to be an insoluble difficulty, the social worker decided to place her in a residential home where she settled comfortably.

Sometimes an elderly person would adamantly refuse admission to care, despite the belief of all concerned that this was the only realistic option.

Mr G. was a physically frail, moderately confused man living alone in an outlying village. He was supported adequately by an intensive network of care involving home help, district nurse and community care helpers. These arrangements worked well until the onset of faecal incontinence. This made great demands on the helpers, one of whom decided to discontinue her involvement. In the light of Mr G.'s adamant refusal to enter hospital, as proposed by his family practitioner, a meeting of the helpers was convened. They decided to continue mainly as a result of a personal commitment which they had developed towards the old gentleman. A boarding-out arrangement in one helper's home who had managed to retrain him in toileting with some success proved acceptable as an interim measure. After eighteen months in the scheme, the same helper opened a private residential home and the arrangement was made permanent. The crucial factor in this case appeared to be the willingness of helpers to persist with a difficult case. This gave time to work towards a solution.

In only two cases did it prove necessary to refuse continued care in the community.

Two elderly sisters were admitted to hospital for treatment having been helped by the scheme for some months, although posing a considerable management problem. The more active partner required the amputation of the lower part of one leg, while the other was virtually chairbound and incontinent of urine following a stroke. The couple had been difficult to help because of their demanding attitudes, a hostile-dependent relationship, physical frailty and the rate of attrition of carers. The social worker was faced with the contradictory pressures of different medical staff. The consultant in charge of the medical wards considered them fit for discharge whereas the rehabilitation unit saw them as 'beyond rehabilitation'. The sisters strongly desired to return home although the active partner had lost her leg, and it was virtually impossible to provide adequate community support without undue strain on the helpers. In these circumstances it was reluctantly decided that the project could no longer continue to offer support, and that the elderly couple should enter residential care. The community care workers had to balance the feelings of helpers and other carers against the unrealistic desires of the two sisters. However, some two years later, following the death of one sister, it was arranged for the other to live in a flat supported by the scheme.

In considering terminating care it was important for the social worker to plan in a way that would minimise the risk of damage to the elderly person or their carers, and prepare them for such a change. On occasions, helpers' personal commitment to an elderly person was sufficiently great to overcome extremely difficult circumstances, but the social worker had to ensure that this did not lead to their exploitation. In other cases, helpers were enlisted to help prepare an elderly person for admission to residential care, providing continuity and making the transition less abrupt. Crucial in the decision whether or not to terminate care was the responsibility of the community care social worker to assess and balance the tolerance of all those concerned.

5. Conclusions

At the beginning of the chapter the importance of the integration of the scheme into the social services department was noted. This 'integrated model' of case management is likely to become even more crucial as the sources of care multiply with the growth of private and voluntary services. The devolution of resources and information about their costliness to the individual fieldworker, as developed in the scheme, combined in one person a wide range of roles and provided continuity of care in a fashion hitherto rare in social work with the elderly (Stevenson and Parsloe, 1978; Goldberg and Warburton, 1979). This broader perception of roles could be usefully transferred to work with other groups requiring long-term care, such as the chronically mentally ill and the mentally handicapped.

Goldberg and Connelly (1982) identified six social work roles in the care of the elderly. These were *(i)* assessing need, *(ii)* mobilising resources, *(iii)* direct casework, *(iv)* coordinating/monitoring, *(v)* resource person/consultant to other helpers in direct contact with the client, and *(vi)* community work. The first three of these roles are probably those most usually defined as normal practice in the care of the elderly. However, in the community care scheme, assessment was more fully performed, direct casework was more integrated with other activities and in general there was a more systematic approach than is usual (Levin, 1982) and greater continuity. In the fourth and fifth activities -'monitoring' and 'resource person' - the scheme appears also to have extended the nature of usual practice by combining these with the other roles in a coherent whole. This could be seen in the acceptance of responsibility for coordinating a whole care network, providing support and direction to helpers in contact with a client and a concern for the interweaving of formal and informal networks, even creating such networks where they were deficient. In this the scheme appeared to offer certain of the advantages of the more locally-based approaches to the organisation of social care (Hadley and McGrath, 1980, 1984). However, an important difference lies in the community care scheme's focus on a defined caseload of individuals within a particular client group, providing the opportunity for closer interprofessional collaboration. Clearly, specialisation is not incompatible with a sensitivity to the needs of informal carers and responding to local needs. The sixth role - community work - was less easily performed within a scheme targeted on a narrowly defined population. However, some developments of this kind could be seen in the creation of a luncheon and social club in a sheltered housing unit.

Elsewhere a carers' support group has been established under the auspices of the scheme. In addition community care staff were responsible for developing mechanisms to identify the appropriate cases more effectively and were therefore less 'reactive' (Black *et al.*, 1983) in their approach to meeting need.

The evidence suggests that the activities of case management described in this chapter are compatible with the kinds of improvements in effectiveness and efficiency of care set out in Chapter 1. However, what is important is not just that the community care approach provided an environment conducive to good social work practice, but rather that for the scheme to achieve its objectives these aspects of good practice were central to its operation.

CHAPTER 4

RESPONDING TO NEED

Here we consider the responses made to the care of elderly people with different kinds of problems. Of special interest is how particular characteristics influenced the ways in which the team devised and managed packages of care for elderly people. The chapter is structured in terms of problem categories since the presence of particular problems led to different caring responses. These 'clinically' relevant factors provide a basis for making generalisations about responses to particular kinds of situation so that a more coherent practice knowledge base may develop in social care. This detail also enables us to understand more clearly the relationships between the costs and outcomes of care discussed in Chapter 9.

There are two main sections in this chapter. The first covers problems associated with physical frailty and deals with the risk of falling, incontinence and serious incapacity. The second covers problems associated with mental frailty and deals with depressed mood states, difficulties of personality, alcohol abuse, functional psychoses and confusional states. Despite this division, it is important to remember that, in practice, nearly every individual experienced 'multiple pathology' or clusters of problems, so that individuals will overlap the categories identified. In each section concerned with a particular type of problem, a table shows the number of cases in that particular category, the extent of particular outcomes and disabilities, the use of key domiciliary resources and the average monthly cost over one year. For some of the groups the number of cases is very small, but for consistency the tables are all presented in the same format. The corresponding figures for the whole community care group are shown for comparison. For the destinational outcomes - such as whether or not a person entered long-term care, the provision of home help, and total costs for the social services and National Health Service - the figures for cases with similar problems in the control group are shown in brackets. The resources, being an average for one year which includes periods in hospital or residential care, will of course understate the amount of, say, home help received whilst at home in any one month. Furthermore, comparisons between experimental and control groups in this chapter must be treated with great caution since the cases are only matched by a single problem category, such as confusional state.

1. Problems Associated with Physical Frailty

Some degree of physical frailty was evident in all the elderly people, as might be expected (Brocklehurst *et al.*, 1978), but for many this constituted the primary

Table 4.1 Clients at high risk of falling

	Risk of falling		All cases	
	Community care	**Standard provision**	**Community care**	**Standard provision**
Number of cases	63	83	92	116
Average age (years)	81		80	
Male	25%		23%	
Female	75%		77%	
Outcomes				
At home	60%	47%	67%	45%
Died	19%	27%	16%	28%
Local authority	5%	16%	4%	16%
Private residential care	10%	5%	8%	5%
Moved away	1%	2%	2%	2%
Hospital care	5%	3%	3%	4%
Resources per month				
Average cost to SSD (£)	49.86	51.67	48.55	49.23
Home help (hours)	8.70	7.58	8.20	6.71
Community care helpers (£)	15.44	-	14.92	-
Community care voluntary help (visits)	1.44	-	1.50	-
Home help as percentage of SSD cost	33	-	30	-
Community care helper as percentage of SSD cost	32	-	31	-
District nursing (visits)	2.5	-	2.5	-
Average cost to NHS (£)	95.55	76.80	80.82	81.16
Problem prevalence				
Incontinence of urine	40%		35%	
Giddiness	81%		74%	
Breathlessness	52%		49%	
Depressed mood (moderate or severe)	51%		49%	
Anxiety moderate or severe	62%		61%	
Confusion or disorientation	24%		26%	
Needing help with activities				
Rising and retiring	29%		23%	
Toileting	17%		13%	
Getting in and out of chair	19%		14%	
Bathing	76%		72%	
Making hot drinks	38%		32%	
Making meals	78%		74%	
ADL score[1]	2.06		1.77	
Level of informal care				
Low	22%		21%	
Moderate	59%		60%	
High	19%		19%	
Weekly social contacts[2]	18.6		19.2	

Notes
1. ADL refers to six Activities of Daily Living (Katz *et al.*, 1963).
2. Social contacts score as used by Tunstall (1966).

problem. The particular need of these individuals was for a regular, reliable network of help. It is helpful to examine the care provided for the physically frail in terms of responses to the risk of falling, problems of incontinence and care of the severely frail both in crises and on a long-term basis.

(a) Problems associated with high risk of falling

The risk of falling was experienced by two-thirds of the community care group, as can be seen from Table 4.1. Indeed, it was in many cases the prime fear of both elderly persons and associated professionals. In a number of these cases, arrangements were made for them to attend the geriatric day hospital for assessment and, where possible, treatment to improve their mobility. Indeed, the higher NHS costs for community care cases reflected greater use of day hospital and acute facilities.

Since risk of falling by its nature is unpredictable, it is a cause of anxiety to both elderly persons and carers, and often the provision of an alarm system is not an appropriate solution. The concern of both elderly persons and carers about possible falls may lead to an intolerable level of anxiety only resolved by admission to care. However, it was clear that the problem of falling could be tackled by focusing separately on its constituent parts: the subjective and the objective, or the 'fear' and the 'event'. The 'event' refers to the fall itself, the crisis and any associated injury which may remove the power to decide from the old person and precipitate entry to care. The likelihood of the 'event' leading to this is reduced when the elderly person does not run the risk of the secondary effects of the 'long lie' (Hall, 1982) associated with falls. However when an elderly person is being considered for discharge from hospital or when they are 'at risk' in their own homes, then it is not the 'event' but the 'fear' which is predominant. If the old person's fear or the anxieties of significant others become intolerable, entry to a residential home may be seen as the only solution.

Where an elderly person had decided to take a reasonable risk in being at home, intervention was tailored to the reduction of the threshold of fear of the elderly person and their carers. It involved the recognition that often visitors are unpredictable and call at infrequent intervals and therefore, should an elderly person fall, they might remain where they lay for an indefinite period. A regular, predictable pattern of visiting organised on a local basis combining helpers and statutory workers could reduce this level of uncertainty and provide reassurance, thus making the fear and risk acceptable to the old person, who would know that should they fall a visitor would be coming at a certain time. Also the likelihood of the 'event' itself could be reduced by the provision of aids, the removal of obvious hazards such as unstable furniture or frayed carpets, ensuring the elderly person sleeps downstairs and providing a

Table 4.2 Clients with incontinence of urine

	Incontinence of urine		All cases	
	Community care	Standard provision	Community care	Standard provision
Number of cases	32	33	92	116
Average age (years)	80		80	
Male	25%		23%	
Female	75%		77%	
Outcomes				
At home	63%	43%	67%	45%
Died	25%	24%	16%	28%
Local authority	3%	15%	4%	16%
Private residential care	3%	3%	8%	5%
Moved away	0%	0%	2%	2%
Hospital care	6%	15%	3%	4%
Resources per month				
Average cost to SSD (£)	47.16	52.79	48.55	49.23
Home help (hours)	8.90	7.09	8.20	6.71
Community care helpers (£)	11.92	-	14.92	-
Community care voluntary help (visits)	1.40	-	1.50	-
Home help as percentage of SSD cost	36	-	30	-
Community care helper as percentage of SSD cost	26	-	31	-
District nursing (visits)	3.5	-	2.5	-
Average cost to NHS (£)	107.81	101.96	80.82	81.16
Problem prevalence				
Incontinence of urine	100%		35%	
Giddiness	69%		74%	
Breathlessness	47%		49%	
Depressed mood (moderate or severe)	47%		49%	
Anxiety moderate or severe	62%		61%	
Confusion or disorientation	34%		26%	
Needing help with activities				
Rising and retiring	41%		23%	
Toileting	28%		13%	
Getting in and out of chair	28%		14%	
Bathing	97%		72%	
Making hot drinks	47%		32%	
Making meals	91%		74%	
ADL score[1]	3.25		1.77	
Level of informal care				
Low	22%		21%	
Moderate	53%		60%	
High	25%		19%	
Weekly social contacts[2]	19.2		19.2	

Notes
1. ADL refers to six Activities of Daily Living (Katz *et al.*, 1963).
2. Social contacts score as used by Tunstall (1966).

commode to reduce the need to go to less accessible parts of the house.

Mrs S. lived alone in a purpose-built bungalow in a village. She had retired to the area, having worked in an old people's home in the North of England. She was determined not to enter a home herself, although she suffered from arthritis and was unstable on her feet. She refused to use a walking aid, preferring to lean on furniture, and had a poor diet, tending to have food fads and never eating fresh meat, vegetables or fruit. She tended to be hypochondriac and at times abused her medication. She had no family in the area and had little support from neighbours, having alienated them by not always eating the meals which they provided. Her GP exerted pressure for her to enter residential care because of risk of falling. Her only support was her home help living in the village, who visited six days a week, and was as much a friend as a helper, visiting at other times informally when Mrs S. was unwell. It was possible to construct a package of support which involved the home help visiting in the morning, and one helper visiting at lunchtime with the objective of checking her well-being, and encouraging her to eat more adequately. In the early evening another helper visited with the same objectives. On Wednesdays it was arranged for her to attend the geriatric day hospital. A difficult task for the social worker was to reassure the helpers regarding the risk that Mrs S. was taking, as some of them expressed considerable anxiety about leaving her overnight. The helpers were given copies of the 'chart' describing her support network. Knowing who helped the old lady at different times, they were able to stand in for one another to ensure that visits were made and security provided. On several occasions the home help stood in on an informal basis at weekends to cover for a helper who was sick. These arrangements maintained her at home for over a year.

There was a considerable degree of success in reducing risk and making continued living at home possible for people liable to fall who otherwise would have entered residential care.

(b) Elderly people suffering from incontinence

Over one-third of the cases suffered from incontinence of urine and 7 per cent suffered from incontinence of faeces. The estimates of the prevalence of incontinence from the first assessments will tend to understate the condition, and therefore the extent of need which the team faced; partly due to shame and unwillingness to admit the problem, since only in some cases would it be evident from factors such as smell, and partly due to the development of the condition some time later than the initial assessment.

Table 4.2 shows that the cases suffering from incontinence of urine tended to be more physically frail, more likely to die, more likely to receive district nursing and as might be expected more likely to exhibit symptoms of confusion and disorientation (Isaacs and Walkley, 1964). People receiving community care appeared less likely to enter long-stay hospital care and were less costly to the social services department. These cases tended to use above-average amounts of health service resources. Again, for community care clients this consisted mainly of acute treatment and day hospital assessment.

Incontinence could arouse very negative responses in previously very supportive carers, not only due to the physical aspects of the problem but also because of the need for speedy washing of soiled laundry. There were three factors which influenced the scheme's capacity to manage the care of incontinent elderly people adequately. First, within the local area there was no provision for a soiled linen service. Second, the official remit of the home help service was to deal with the washing of light articles of personal clothing only. Third, even if it were possible to ensure that the washing itself were undertaken, the drying of large amounts of washing was feasible in only a few of the clients' houses. Ordinary commercial laundrettes did not welcome this sort of washing, and helpers were understandably reluctant to take it into their own homes and had difficulty in transporting it.

Because the condition was extensive and no other services were available, the team had to respond on an *ad hoc* basis. When the problem was identified, the first task for the team was to ensure that investigation and treatment was provided where this might be appropriate and to secure such aids as incontinence pads or rubberised sheets. Gaining access to treatment for clients was not always easy. Some general practitioners had fatalistic attitudes to incontinence, despite the emergence of more positive attitudes in recent years (Brocklehurst, 1978; Hamdy, 1980) and the geriatric service was relatively understaffed.

In cases where periodic incontinence occurred due to difficulties of access to the toilet, it was sometimes possible to provide a commode and regular assistance in emptying it. At one stage the team considered whether a small part of the budget should be used to provide a washing machine of commercial specification in a day centre, and to organise a collection and delivery service. However this was not pursued. In the absence of any other service, it was arranged that the washing and drying of elderly people's bedding be undertaken by helpers, often on a shared basis.

Mrs M. was only able to walk very short distances, was frequently incontinent of urine during the night, and she was socially isolated and depressed. She lived in a first-floor flat which was reached by steep stairs. She was referred as requiring immediate long-term care. Particular concern was expressed by her landlady. However, she did not wish to leave her flat. The initial aim was to provide her with encouragement and stimulation, raise her morale and tackle the difficulties associated with incontinence. Services were arranged which consisted of home help three times a week, meals-on-wheels, day care, a helper to launder the bedding, visits to a helper's home and provision of incontinence pads. It was also arranged for her to spend some weekends with a helper, who had coped with her incontinent husband until his death.

After about four months it was evident that additional care was necessary because of her depressed mood, increasing forgetfulness, problems of incontinence and inadequate nutrition. Meals-on-wheels proved ineffective since she required encouragement to eat. Further help with the laundry, nursing care and incontinence garments was arranged. A helper visited each day to encourage Mrs M. to get up and have breakfast and at lunchtimes the home help or a helper would provide her with a meal and encourage her to eat. Visits were also made in the evening. Friends visited during the week and a daughter who had recently moved into the area visited regularly and managed her finances. It was possible to stabilise the situation for a further two years until her daughter had to leave the area. The old lady began to drink quite heavily, which exacerbated her incontinence. Her mobility declined further. Eventually she was admitted to hospital for long-term care, but she had lived in her own home for two years longer than had been expected. This she had greatly valued. It had proved possible to manage the problem of incontinence, albeit with difficulty, until the difficulties increased in association with depression, forgetfulness and frailty.

Underlying all the work with elderly people suffering from incontinence was the knowledge that this could constitute a 'breaking point' for carers, especially when faecal incontinence became evident (Sanford, 1975).

Mr G. had retired to the area having run a grocer's shop in Essex. His only relative living nearby, a sister, had died some five years previously, and he lived in an elderly person's bungalow on the edge of a village. He appeared lonely, forgetful and not to be receiving adequate food. The home help visited three times each week and meals-on-wheels were delivered twice. Other meals were provided on the remaining days and the home help undertook to split her session and to provide both encouragement to eat and stimulation. Helpers were also involved in attempting to maximise his mobility. The emergence of urinary incontinence after a few months marked a new phase. Attempts to arrange for the investigation of a possible treatable infection were unsuccessful, and it became necessary to adapt the programme of support. It was arranged for a helper to collect and wash soiled clothing, which was then dried at a local laundrette. One helper felt unable to continue to help Mr G. because of the need to cope with the incontinence. The pattern of care provided involved frequent contact.

Early morning: home help or community care helper to provide breakfast and to help out of bed.
Lunch time: home help or community care helper either to cook meal or to encourage him to eat meals-on-wheels.
Afternoon: district nurse visits; on four or five days community care helper visits to collect and deliver washing.
Evening: community care helper provides meal and companionship.

The development of faecal incontinence, however, led to greater difficulties. Efforts to persuade Mr G. to go into hospital were unsuccessful. The social worker convened a conference of helpers involved with Mr G. to decide how and whether it was possible to continue. Clearly, the care for such a highly dependent person, whose mobility was deteriorating, was taking a toll of the home help and helpers. One helper, an ex-district nurse, who had had some success in training him to use the commode and thereby reduce soiling, agreed to board him for short-term care in her own home. This proved successful in managing him, and when the same lady opened a private residential home he stayed there permanently. It was very clear in this case that incontinence defined the boundaries to social care.

It was sometimes necessary to respond when aids or appliances were inappropriately supplied. Castledene and Duffin (1981) suggest that in many cases catheterisation of an elderly person is unnecessary, and that simple measures are more effective. This was the case for one confused woman, living alone. She had been catheterised in hospital, but was quite unable to manage in her own home where basic care was more appropriate. However it did appear that use of a catheter at home could be effective where there was regular supervision.

Mr and Mrs C. lived in a dark basement flat. Mrs C. was a registered blind diabetic lady undertaking the care of her husband on an almost full-time basis. He was incontinent of urine and almost chairbound, following a stroke some three years previously. Initially, help was provided in terms of a range of aids, home help and a helper who would assist with the laundry. Shortly after the first visit, Mr C. was admitted to hospital where he was fitted with a self-retaining catheter and urine bag. Mrs C. was very anxious and unsure about her capacity to cope with changing the bag at night and morning as required, and sufficient nursing support was not available. The helper, who was a trained nurse, gradually taught Mrs C. to manage this process. This gave her a real sense of achievement in caring for her husband.

The team necessarily responded to individual needs using simple measures such as assistance with laundry, encouraging evening fluid restriction, toileting regimes and the use of incontinence garments, which can play an important part in increasing self-respect and making management at home more feasible (Castledene and Duffin, 1981). Changes in the service system were not possible in the short run. Consequently, the management of incontinence at home faced the social workers with real difficulties because certain key resources were lacking: in particular laundry facilities and access to appropriate health care. First, the lack of an incontinence laundry service meant that the scheme had to respond at an individual level for each client, often using helpers' own washing machines or laundrette facilities. As found by Sanford (1975), faecal incontinence appeared substantially more difficult for carers to tolerate, and made a laundry service even more crucial. The prevalence of incontinence has been estimated to be 17 per cent in women aged 65 and over (Yarnell and St Leger, 1979) and would be much higher in a frail population. In view of this high prevalence and the drudgery of the continual washing, an incontinence laundry service is probably a prerequisite for effective care at home of the very frail (Levin, 1982). Second, closer working arrangments between health and social services staff could be beneficial in managing incontinence since the presence of urinary tract problems is often unknown to general practitioners (Williamson *et al.*, 1964; Yarnell and St Leger, 1979). This could help to develop therapeutic optimism and increase knowledge (Brocklehurst, 1978), as well as improve access to both assessment and treatment. However, where the services do not collaborate well together, medical problems tend to be obscured among elderly people suffering a gradual decline (Boyd, 1981). The problem is all too frequently perceived as 'social', and medical help is not provided.

(c) Serious degree of physical frailty

Table 4.3 shows that more than one-third of clients were physically very frail (defined as those who were bedridden or chairbound, incontinent of faeces or unable to walk to the toilet unassisted, use it and return safely). A higher proportion of these died or entered hospital over one year than in the group as a whole. They received more district nursing, home help and helper resources. It is notable that they also tended to receive more than the average amounts of voluntary helper visits. This reflected the concern of the workers that the

Table 4.3 Clients with serious physical frailty

	Serious physical frailty		All cases	
	Community care	Standard provision	Community care	Standard provision
Number of cases	33	22	92	116
Average age (years)	79		80	
Male	30%		23%	
Female	70%		77%	
Outcomes				
At home	55%	36%	67%	45%
Died	30%	36%	16%	28%
Local authority	3%	14%	4%	16%
Private residential care	3%	0%	8%	5%
Moved away	0%	0%	2%	2%
Hospital care	9%	14%	3%	4%
Resources per month				
Average cost to SSD (£)	54.79	55.86	48.55	49.23
Home help (hours)	9.40	6.38	8.20	6.71
Community care helpers (£)	17.68	-	14.92	-
Community care voluntary help (visits)	1.80	-	1.50	-
Home help as percentage of SSD cost	29	-	30	-
Community care helper as percentage of SSD cost	31	-	31	-
District nursing (visits)	4.4	-	2.5	-
Average cost to NHS (£)	133.89	113.72	80.82	81.16
Problem prevalence				
Incontinence of urine	61%		35%	
Giddiness	64%		74%	
Breathlessness	33%		49%	
Depressed mood (moderate or severe)	36%		49%	
Anxiety moderate or severe	48%		61%	
Confusion or disorientation	39%		26%	
Needing help with activities				
Rising and retiring	46%		23%	
Toileting	33%		13%	
Getting in and out of chair	33%		14%	
Bathing	94%		72%	
Making hot drinks	54%		32%	
Making meals	94%		74%	
ADL score[1]	2.98		1.77	
Level of informal care				
Low	18%		21%	
Moderate	61%		60%	
High	21%		19%	
Weekly social contacts[2]	21.8		19.2	

Notes
1. ADL refers to six Activities of Daily Living (Katz *et al.*, 1963).
2. Social contacts score as used by Tunstall (1966).

quality of their social life as well as quality of care should be improved, with some of the visits aimed at providing companionship and the regeneration of old interests. Unsurprisingly, the costs for these people were higher than average. Those receiving community care were less likely to enter long-stay hospital care, but used more day hospital and acute facilities than the comparison group.

In some cases, there was need for intensive help following sickness or an accident, and discharge from hospital care.

Mrs S., aged 68, had been crippled with arthritis for a number of years. She lived in a terraced cottage with outside toilet, steps up to the front door, and different floor levels between the front room and kitchen. These features made mobility extremely difficult. She fell in the home and broke her left leg, and this was encased in plaster up to the hip. As a result she was virtually immobile, being confined to her chair during the day. A very alert person, she was very distressed at the prospect of being in hospital for a long period, and it proved possible to arrange an early discharge for her with an extensive package of support. A rota of helpers was arranged to assist her in getting up and going to bed, to prepare meals and to make regular check up visits. These were undertaken in conjunction with the home help, district nurse and a circle of friends. Indeed, one of the helpers was several years older than Mrs S. Mrs S. was closely involved in planning the rota and determining what was done when, and her morale improved visibly in hospital as the planning proceeded. The care which was provided involved only short periods of solitude.

Early morning: community care helper got her up and dressed and provided breakfast; different helpers at weekends.
Morning: district nurse visited and assisted with washing and dressing her leg.
Lunch time: home help provided a meal and did other household jobs on weekdays; community care helper did the same at weekends.
During day: community care helper living nearby provided tea, social visits and check ups as required on a flexible basis. Friends and neighbours visited to provide support.
Night time: at about 10 p.m. community care helper assisted Mrs S. to bed.

As Mrs S.'s mobility slowly improved, it was possible gradually to reduce the level of support. It is interesting to speculate how often a crisis, such as a fracture, can lead to a series of irrevocable decisions such as a long period in hospital followed by transfer to residential care. In this case not only was early discharge made possible, but also the provision of help at an early stage in the crisis contributed to the maintenance of her morale and determination to remain at home, and her continued contact with friends and neighbours.

For many cases the task of the community care scheme was to build a network of support for extremely disabled people when the available support was either insufficient or under excessive strain.

Mrs W. lived in an elderly person's bungalow at the edge of a housing estate. She suffered from arthritis and syringomyelia, a defect of the spinal cord, and was confined to a wheelchair. She was just able to lever herself from the wheelchair to the toilet and back, although this effort soon proved beyond her. Even smoking a cigarette was an almost impossible operation due to her twisted arthritic joints. Although she was under considerable pressure to enter a residential home, her determination and refusal aroused both admiration and anxiety in those who met her. It proved necessary to construct a virtually complete network of care, her informal support being limited to a visit from her cousin once a fortnight. The home help and a community care helper lived in the same street. In the morning both visited together, helped her get up and organised breakfast. This would have been too much for one person alone. The pattern of care consisted of eight different visitors plus a visit to the day hospital.

Early morning: community care helper and home help assisted her to get up, dress and have breakfast; district nurse visited one morning.
Late morning: home help and community care helper visited, prepared lunch and helped Mrs W. to the toilet, and provided companionship. One day each week she attended a geriatric day hospital.
Afternoon/tea time: community care helper visited and prepared meal, checked she was safe and helped with toileting.
Evening: community care helper, usually the one who lived in the same street, helped Mrs W. to bed and ensured that she was safe and secure.

In such cases where safety and basic human care needs were prominent, regular and reliable care was essential in order to minimise risk and periods of solitude. The 'monitoring charts' showing who visited at what times were provided to all involved. On occasions, the social worker would convene meetings of all the carers involved with an elderly person to exchange ideas about helping that person, ensure a common approach, identify difficulties experienced, and ensure that the helpers knew one another. Care was taken to avoid placing any person who might tend to become excessively possessive towards a client in such a group. A 'back-up' system would frequently be organised which was partly dependent on the informal contact between the helpers themselves.

Care of the severely disabled could often involve intimate physical care. For example, one contract for Mrs W. read: 'to help Mrs W at bedtime, including help her use the toilet. Leave her comfortable and secure for the night'.

While some helpers had felt there were certain personal care activities which they could not undertake, few experienced any difficulty when faced with the need in a person with whom they had developed a personal relationship. However, it was an important part of the social worker's responsibility to keep a close track of the changing demands of care on helpers to prevent them from becoming excessive and formally to recognise extra care by revising the contracts.

In dealing with people who had been severely restricted by physical impairments, it seemed particularly important to try to improve their quality of life and to enable the elderly person to extend their capabilities. This could mean providing an opportunity to get out of the house, or arranging for people to take up an old interest, such as playing Scrabble. One example was the case of an arthritic lady who, although unable to write, could again take an interest in doing crosswords, memorising answers for a helper to write down later (Challis *et al.*, 1983). Another example was the provision of a television remote control for someone who was bedridden. By imaginative attention to detail, it was possible to contribute both to the quality of care and the quality of life of this very frail group. However, given the high degree of personal care needs of these clients, it seemed that the stability and effectiveness of the service would have been enhanced had the team also been able to deploy 'home care' staff as well as helpers.

2. Problems Associated with Mental Disorder

In this section we consider the influence of mental disorder on the work of the scheme. Consideration is given both to the effects of minor mental disorders (in particular depression, personality difficulties and problems associated with alcohol abuse) and also to major mental disorders (in particular functional psychoses and confusional states). It appeared that the management of most of these conditions could have been improved by closer working relationships with appropriate health service personnel.

(a) Problems associated with depressed mood

Those clients were categorised as suffering from depressed mood who had symptoms of moderate or severe mood disturbance: a frequent tendency to weep, a considerable degree of pessimism or extreme symptoms of depression (Hamilton, 1960); or a formally diagnosed depressive disorder. By this criterion, 49 per cent of the community care group were suffering from depressed mood and of these 87 per cent suffered also from a considerable degree of anxiety. From Table 4.4 it can be seen that these cases tended to be

Table 4.4 Clients with depression

	Depression		All cases	
	Community care	**Standard provision**	**Community care**	**Standard provision**
Number of cases	45	51	92	116
Average age (years)	79		80	
Male	20%		23%	
Female	80%		77%	
Outcomes				
At home	80%	45%	67%	45%
Died	7%	26%	16%	28%
Local authority	2%	20%	4%	16%
Private residential care	9%	4%	8%	5%
Moved away	2%	2%	2%	2%
Hospital care	0%	3%	3%	4%
Resources per month				
Average cost to SSD (£)	45.91	54.29	48.55	49.23
Home help (hours)	8.40	6.92	8.20	6.71
Community care helpers (£)	15.08	-	14.92	-
Community care voluntary help (visits)	1.90	-	1.50	-
Home help as percentage of SSD cost	33	-	30	-
Community care helper as percentage of SSD cost	29	-	31	-
District nursing (visits)	2.4	-	2.5	-
Average cost to NHS (£)	80.43	73.14	80.82	81.16
Problem prevalence				
Incontinence of urine	33%		35%	
Giddiness	71%		74%	
Breathlessness	56%		49%	
Depressed mood (moderate or severe)	100%		49%	
Anxiety moderate or severe	87%		61%	
Confusion or disorientation	15%		26%	
Needing help with activities				
Rising and retiring	18%		23%	
Toileting	9%		13%	
Getting in and out of chair	16%		14%	
Bathing	69%		72%	
Making hot drinks	27%		32%	
Making meals	78%		74%	
ADL score[1]	1.58		1.77	
Level of informal care				
Low	27%		21%	
Moderate	60%		60%	
High	13%		19%	
Weekly social contacts[2]	16.9		19.2	

Notes
1. ADL refers to six Activities of Daily Living (Katz *et al.*, 1963).
2. Social contacts score as used by Tunstall (1966).

less expensive than the community care group as a whole, but more likely to receive support from volunteer or unpaid community care helpers. This is interesting, as other studies have also suggested that elderly people with diagnosed functional psychiatric disorder are not likely to be heavy consumers of services (Foster *et al.*, 1976). They tended to be substantially more socially isolated and less physically frail than the group as a whole, although breathlessness was more evident. It is noteworthy that in the comparison group those with depressed mood were particularly likely to enter residential care, whereas for those receiving community care it was very unlikely that they would.

It was not altogether surprising to note that depression and anxiety could be observed in a substantial proportion of the cases helped by the community care scheme. The expected prevalance of these conditions in the elderly is high (Kay *et al.*, 1964). Physical ill-health and affective disorder are frequently associated in the elderly (Roth and Kay, 1956) and the community care population was already identified as substantially more vulnerable than average. However, the association between physical ill-health and affective disorder in the elderly makes it likely that where medical attention is provided, it is concentrated on the physical condition, especially as the elderly person will probably present this as their complaint. Goldberg and Huxley (1980) noted that two factors - the presence of physical illness and old age - predisposed GPs to fail to identify psychiatric disorder, and Bergmann (1978) has observed that 61 per cent of neurotic and 71 per cent of depressive disorders were unknown to the general practitioner.

Whenever depression was suspected in elderly people, the social work team was in contact with the family practitioner about the possibility of treatment. In certain cases it was made part of a helper's task to ensure that medication was taken appropriately by the elderly person. Making help acceptable proved to be one of the most daunting tasks with withdrawn and apathetic old people. Nevertheless, in some cases it did appear that the scheme was able to reduce depression and hopelessness.

Mr H. lived alone in a small terraced house. He suffered from chronic bronchitis, appeared lonely and depressed, and received relatively little help from a daughter living nearby. He was on the point of giving up his home to enter residential care. After some considerable effort, the social worker was able to persuade him to accept a combination of support from the home help service, a helper, and visits to a day centre. The helper provided him with companionship, prepared meals, encouraged him to eat them, and did those odd jobs he found particularly daunting such as sewing buttons onto his shirts. It seemed that in many ways she became a substitute for the attention which he felt was lacking from his daughter. His interest in life revived considerably. He asked that he should no longer be considered for residential care, and began to show interest in his home, organising repairs and arranging for the installation of a new gas fire. He commented 'I'm far better off here than in one of those homes ... you have more freedom here'.

Mrs J. was a frail woman living in a council bungalow; she was liable to fall and was intensely worried about her security. She had little appetite and frequently expressed her indifference to living or dying, although her moods tended to fluctuate. She felt that her family practitioner paid little attention to her complaints, ascribing them to old age. She was, however, determined not to enter residential care. She was reluctant to consider help but at an early stage responded warmly to the social worker's approach of carefully examinining her difficulties and immediately providing for needs such as chiropody. She commented: 'All this time I've been waiting. Now you've come, everything seems to be happening'. A combination of home help and community care helpers gave her assistance with meal preparation, settling at night, companionship, and personal care tasks such as hair-washing. There was a marked improvement in her spirits, she was more cheerful and less anxious, saying 'before you came the weekends were a rehearsal for death'.

While some cases seemed to respond extremely well, and a carefully planned approach could transform what appeared to be a hopeless situation, there were others where the depressed mood appeared to be chronic and the elderly person unresponsive to intervention. This possibly reflects what Post (1962) found, that in about 20 per cent of cases depression in the elderly does not seem to respond to treatment and pursues a steady course of deterioration.

Mr H. lived alone in a large house following the death of his wife, on whom he had been very dependent. He was depressed and apathetic. His main source of help was a neighbour who provided a great deal of support for him, including meals, which made considerable demands on her. Despite antidepressant medication and attempts to provide him with stimulation, Mr H. increasingly neglected himself, often remaining in his dressing gown during the day. It did not prove possible to motivate him and help was increasingly focused on providing support for the neighbour. Despite the efforts of all concerned, a gradual decline was observed.

It is interesting to consider whether closer working relationships with psychiatric services could have improved the care of these elderly people. Whilst readier access to psychiatric consultation and care would probably not have reduced the need for other support services, it is likely that more psychiatric help would have benefited the elderly people. However, in the area where the scheme was established, such collaboration would have been difficult because of the distance of the local psychiatric hospital, some twenty miles.

(b) Problems associated with long-standing personality difficulties

It was possible to distinguish two clusters of difficult attitudes and behaviour towards the receipt of help which reflected long-standing personality traits. These can be conceived of as the 'hostile-rejecting' on the one hand, and the 'dependent-demanding' on the other. To varying degrees these attitudes and characteristics were present in a substantial number of cases. For example there was a large group of people - 27 per cent of cases - whose sense of independence and reluctance to receive help meant that the social workers had to make considerable efforts to make help acceptable. However, only a small proportion of these could be regarded as displaying a 'hostile-rejecting' attitude. Similarly, in 14 per cent of cases, some aspects of 'dependent-demanding' attitudes were present, although only a small proportion could be seen as conforming to the 'ideal type'. Consequently in Table 4.5 only those few cases of the two groups showing these pronounced characteristics have been included. It was notable that those cases with extreme personality difficulties tended to be less expensive, to receive less help on a voluntary basis, to be younger, and to be slightly more frail and socially isolated than the cases helped by the scheme as a whole.

Bergmann has described how the attitudes of the 'hostile-rejecting' group can be at times adaptive: 'the fighting stance of the hostile paranoid personalities keeps them intact, failure is never their own, ill-health could be remedied if only the doctor gave adequate treatment ... The world at large has to be taken on in single combat; life presents a very busy and diverting struggle against the dangerous and hostile forces from without and there is little time for despair, depression, fear and anxiety' (Bergmann, 1978, p.62). This group is similar to the 'active-paranoid' described by Gray and Isaacs (1979). However, such behaviour may become maladaptive when continued effective coping requires regular support from others. Dealing with such a person was very demanding, requiring determination and perseverance before help was accepted.

Mrs A. was a large woman who lived alone. She had suffered a stroke six years previously and was crippled with osteoarthritis. Her movements were slow, painful and laborious. She disliked her home, blaming her GP and solicitor for the move from London. She had a reputation for causing home helps to

Table 4.5 Clients with long-standing personality difficulties

	Personality difficulties		All cases	
	Community care	Standard provision	Community care	Standard provision
Number of cases	4	5	92	116
Average age (years)	75		80	
Male	0%		23%	
Female	100%		77%	
Outcomes				
At home	100%	40%	67%	45%
Died	0%	29%	16%	28%
Local authority	0%	20%	4%	16%
Private residential care	0%	0%	8%	5%
Moved away	0%	0%	2%	2%
Hospital care	0%	20%	3%	4%
Resources per month				
Average cost to SSD (£)	37.00	62.41	48.55	49.23
Home help (hours)	9.60	4.20	8.20	6.71
Community care helpers (£)	11.03	-	14.92	-
Community care voluntary help (visits)	0.80	-	1.50	-
Home help as percentage of SSD cost	46	-	30	-
Community care helper as percentage of SSD cost	25	-	31	-
District nursing (visits)	0	-	2.5	-
Average cost to NHS (£)	60.90	52.84	80.82	81.16
Problem prevalence				
Incontinence of urine	50%		35%	
Giddiness	100%		74%	
Breathlessness	50%		49%	
Depressed mood (moderate or severe)	50%		49%	
Anxiety moderate or severe	50%		61%	
Confusion or disorientation	0%		26%	
Needing help with activities				
Rising and retiring	0%		23%	
Toileting	25%		13%	
Getting in and out of chair	25%		14%	
Bathing	75%		72%	
Making hot drinks	150%		32%	
Making meals	50%		74%	
ADL score[1]	2.00		1.77	
Level of informal care				
Low	25%		21%	
Moderate	25%		60%	
High	50%		19%	
Weekly social contacts[2]	17.25		19.2	

Notes
1. ADL refers to six Activities of Daily Living (Katz et al., 1963).
2. Social contacts score as used by Tunstall (1966).

seek alternative clients. She was very hostile to and dismissive of the social worker, and on the second visit would not admit her. It was decided to concentrate initially on practical assistance in the form of aids which she required, and plan the introduction of additional help through the one home help she tolerated. Helpers were introduced to gain her trust at first, and then to help with meals and check on her safety in the morning and evening. It was difficult to establish a support network as Mrs A. frequently insulted helpers. The long-suffering home help eventually withdrew and had to be replaced. Thereafter help could only be provided intermittently, Mrs A. periodically rejecting care. The social worker had to give considerable support to Mrs A.'s helpers and increased their fees for helping her. Some three years later her condition had seriously deteriorated to the point where she was virtually bedridden. She was still rejecting and hostile. At this point compulsory admission to hospital under Section 47 of the National Assistance Act was actively considered. However, the social worker was finally able to persuade her to enter hospital voluntarily after considerable effort. Mrs A.'s resistant attitude never made it possible to give her sufficient support. It was only possible to attempt to make her life more tolerable than it would otherwise have been.

The second group of cases were characterised by excessive dependence and manipulative behaviour. They were equally demanding, but required different management strategies. Goldfarb (1968) noted a pattern of neurotic behaviour in some reactions to dependency in the elderly involving an irrational search for aid from a parent or caring substitute accompanied by regression. He suggested that such a neurotic search for help often presents itself as helplessness, hypochondria, depressive and paranoid reactions, and exploitative and manipulative behaviour, compared with a 'healthy' response involving a rational search for aid.

Mrs C. suffered from leukaemia, and a heart condition restricted her mobility. She lived in a modern council flat on the ground floor. A daughter lived nearby who suffered from a chronic anxiety state and had a difficult relationship with her mother. Mrs C. tended to be very demanding and was usually dissatisfied with the help she received, tending to lapse into a 'needing care' role at frequent intervals. The first aim was to reduce her anxiety level. It was decided to enlist the help of a neighbour who already knew Mrs C. as a carer, and to extend and formalise what was already in existence. The 'letter of agreement' specified visits to check on the well-being of Mrs C., providing companionship, support and meals on a mutually-agreed basis. As the helper appeared very protective, the contract specified that the help was to be given in such a way as to maximise Mrs C.'s independence. However, the neighbour's very proximity led to increasingly unreasonable demands from Mrs C., and the social worker had to visit daily to clarify roles. Demands for additional home help were resisted because of the danger of creating further dependence. Once the initial helping relationship with the neighbour had broken down, it was necessary to structure help in great detail and short time intervals since the helpers could most easily tolerate Mrs C. in small doses and where roles were clearly defined. At length, even Mrs C.'s very supportive GP felt the need to share her care on a rota basis with other practitioners, due to the excessive demands made on him. Successful care of Mrs C. made heavy demands on the social worker in setting limits to the help provided, trying to maintain the client on an even keel and not permitting her dependence to become a destructive influence on carers. In such cases, the role of the worker was to clarify the roles of carers, avoid distorted communication in the network, and provide firm boundaries to the demands for care, whilst encouraging the client to deal with the difficulties in a more realistic fashion.

Sometimes dependent-demanding behaviour could make greater difficulties for community care than for a more structured service such as home help with specified time limits. In view of the difficulties involved in working with such cases, it is not surprising that they tended to receive less voluntary help from the scheme's helpers.

(c) Problems associated with alcohol abuse

There is a relative sparsity of literature on the problem of alcohol abuse in the elderly, although recently considerable interest has begun to develop (James, 1981). There is some evidence that use and abuse of alcohol tends to diminish with age (Mishara and Kastenbaum, 1981). This could of course reflect failure to detect drinking in the elderly, since it is more likely to be a solitary phenomenon, and less likely to be evident in behaviour such as poor work performance. Although the extent of the problem is unknown, according to one US study 6 per cent of the elderly appeared to be 'heavy drinkers' (Cahalen *et al.*, 1969).

In the community care scheme alcohol abuse was prominent in seven cases. Table 4.6 shows that these cases tended to be less expensive and less frail, but were more likely to be depressed and socially isolated. Two UK studies of alcohol abuse in the elderly (Droller, 1964; Rosin and Glatt, 1971) suggest that it is possible to distinguish two distinct groups: the long-standing excessive drink problem which has persisted into old age, and the drink problem as a recent response to stress experienced as a result of ageing, such as depression, isolation, bereavement and disability. These patterns were evident in the drink

Table 4.6 Clients with problems of alcohol abuse

	Alcohol abuse		All cases	
	Community care	**Standard provision**	**Community care**	**Standard provision**
Number of cases	7	7	92	116
Average age (years)	78		80	
Male	14%		23%	
Female	86%		77%	
Outcomes				
At home	100%	58%	67%	45%
Died	0%	14%	16%	28%
Local authority	0%	0%	4%	16%
Private residential care	0%	14%	8%	5%
Moved away	0%	0%	2%	2%
Hospital care	0%	14%	3%	4%
Resources per month				
Average cost to SSD (£)	42.42	19.67	48.55	49.23
Home help (hours)	9.40	8.67	8.20	6.71
Community care helpers (£)	14.08	-	14.92	-
Community care voluntary help (visits)	0.40	-	1.50	-
Home help as percentage of SSD cost	39	-	30	-
Community care helper as percentage of SSD cost	33	-	31	-
District nursing (visits)	0.7	-	2.5	-
Average cost to NHS (£)	59.05	83.66	80.82	81.16
Problem prevalence				
Incontinence of urine	43%		35%	
Giddiness	57%		74%	
Breathlessness	29%		49%	
Depressed mood (moderate or severe)	57%		49%	
Anxiety moderate or severe	43%		61%	
Confusion or disorientation	43%		26%	
Needing help with activities				
Rising and retiring	0%		23%	
Toileting	0%		13%	
Getting in and out of chair	0%		14%	
Bathing	100%		72%	
Making hot drinks	29%		32%	
Making meals	86%		74%	
ADL score[1]	1.57		1.77	
Level of informal care				
Low	29%		21%	
Moderate	71%		60%	
High	0%		19%	
Weekly social contacts[2]	17.7		19.2	

Notes
1. ADL refers to six Activities of Daily Living (Katz et al., 1963).
2. Social contacts score as used by Tunstall (1966).

problems of the community care group, although drink problems in the stress response group were less evident at initial assessment and only emerged through closer acquaintance with the elderly person through time. The experience of these cases was consistent with the view that alcohol abuse should be considered as a differential diagnosis in the elderly where repeated falls, confused and neglectful behaviour are evident (Wattis, 1981).

Three elderly people had a long-standing history of alcohol abuse. In these cases, the approach adopted by the team was to attempt to develop a level of acceptable or 'controlled' drinking.

Miss J. had moved into the area from London and had had a drink problem for many years; her present drinking pattern tended to be cyclical, associated with bouts of depression. She suffered from arthritis and was extremely liable to fall, particularly after drinking. She was lonely, and had no family or friends. She received home help four days per week and meals-on-wheels on two days. Her only other contacts were a monthly visit from a peripatetic warden and a weekend visit from a voluntary visitor. The social worker organised visits from two helpers to relieve her loneliness, to provide a safety check during the long periods of solitude when no other visit was due, and to provide meals if Miss J. was prepared to accept them. One helper was given a contract which specified explicitly: 'to monitor her cyclical drinking and to report back any dangers, either physical or financial'. The focus was on the realistic objective of restricting both her drinking and supply to tolerable levels.

Mr Q. was a retired labourer, living alone in a terraced house on a main road, where he had lived with his ex-publican landlady. He was very lonely, extremely unsteady on his feet, almost blind and had a long-standing drink problem. The home was neglected and his diet was poor. Support involving a home help and two helpers living nearby was established with the objectives of increasing safety, monitoring the alcohol intake, improving diet, reducing loneliness, and maintaining the home in an acceptable condition. His favourite meal, a substantial breakfast, was provided and drink was purchased for him at the local shop since otherwise he would have attempted to go out himself at great risk. With this level of support, it was possible to stabilise him for some considerable time, his morale improving through the good relationship established with the helpers to whom he would tell stories of his livelier days. It was possible to manage his alcohol intake to about one-quarter of a bottle of whisky daily, which was no mean achievement.

In both of these cases the objectives of the social worker were concerned with

Table 4.7 Clients with functional psychoses

	Functional psychoses		All cases	
	Community care	Standard provision	Community care	Standard provision
Number of cases	5	4	92	116
Average age (years)	81		80	
Male	20%		23%	
Female	80%		77%	
Outcomes				
At home	80%	25%	67%	45%
Died	0%	25%	16%	28%
Local authority	0%	25%	4%	16%
Private residential care	0%	25%	8%	5%
Moved away	20%	0%	2%	2%
Hospital care	0%	0%	3%	4%
Resources per month				
Average cost to SSD (£)	16.65	31.43	48.55	49.23
Home help (hours)	2.10	2.21	8.20	6.71
Community care helpers (£)	7.24	-	14.92	-
Community care voluntary help (visits)	3.40	-	1.50	-
Home help as percentage of SSD cost	13	-	30	-
Community care helper as percentage of SSD cost	40	-	31	-
District nursing (visits)	0	-	2.5	-
Average cost to NHS (£)	21.58	97.17	80.82	81.16
Problem prevalence				
Incontinence of urine	20%		35%	
Giddiness	80%		74%	
Breathlessness	40%		49%	
Depressed mood (moderate or severe)	100%		49%	
Anxiety moderate or severe	100%		61%	
Confusion or disorientation	20%		26%	
Needing help with activities				
Rising and retiring	20%		23%	
Toileting	0%		13%	
Getting in and out of chair	0%		14%	
Bathing	40%		72%	
Making hot drinks	0%		32%	
Making meals	60%		74%	
ADL score[1]	0.80		1.77	
Level of informal care				
Low	120%		21%	
Moderate	80%		60%	
High	0%		19%	
Weekly social contacts[2]	10.0		19.2	

Notes
1. ADL refers to six Activities of Daily Living (Katz *et al.*, 1963).
2. Social contacts score as used by Tunstall (1966).

maintenance rather than change, an approach similar to that advocated by Merry (1980). Without doubt, support was possible because both of these people had certain very appealing personality traits, to which a carer could easily relate. Nevertheless it was necessary for the social worker to monitor the care very closely and to deal with the helpers' anxieties concerning drink, especially how much should be purchased. Knowledge of the whole care network made this degree of control possible.

As far as could be ascertained, the remaining cases of alcohol abuse were all of recent onset. They were responses to stresses experienced in life subsequent to retirement, particularly loss, depression and isolation. In these cases, the social workers attempted to tackle the causes of stress, such as loneliness and isolation, and to mitigate some of the ill effects of drinking by such means as ensuring that the elderly person had an adequate diet.

(d) Problems associated with functional psychoses

There were five individuals in this category. It is evident from Table 4.7 that these cases tended to be relatively less costly, were reasonably physically active, and as might be expected were very isolated. They tended to receive relatively small amounts of other services and proportionately a great deal more support from helpers, whose costs constituted 40 per cent of social services expenditure. As can be seen, voluntary help was considerably above average. These cases posed substantial management problems, involving sizeable amounts of social worker time, not least due to the need for effective liaison with health service personnel. Activities included ensuring that diet was adequate and medication was taken, and giving reassurance to neighbours. In three cases it was necessary to initiate psychiatric treatment.

Mrs H. lived alone in a modern bungalow, and suffered great anxiety and distress both about her difficulties in coping physically, and her delusional ideas that the neighbours were planning to sacrifice her on the gallows she believed to be at her front gate. She tended to wander in the street, feeling unsafe in her own home. Her daughter lived in London, and could only visit fortnightly. Neighbours were very concerned and admission to psychiatric care on an informal basis was effected after much persuasion. She was discharged from hospital after about a month, and an attempt was made to provide home help and visits by a community care helper to give security, comfort and stimulation. This did not prove sufficient to meet her needs, and after about two months it was evident that Mrs H. had deteriorated and that her distress had increased. She was again admitted to hospital and subsequently discharged into a private residential home. Her daughter was unhappy about her mother's placement in care and felt unwilling to pay the high cost. After a few months she moved into the bungalow to live, commuting to work in London, and arranged her mother's discharge from the home. During the daughter's absence at work in the week the scheme arranged support for Mrs H., providing company, stimulation and a midday meal and made sure that medication was taken regularly. On other days she attended a day centre, a helper ensuring that she was ready, and settling her on return.

Mr S. lived on the top floor of a multi-storey block of flats. He suffered from anxiety and depression, and had paranoid ideas which tended to surface when he was under great stress. The family practitioner had provided medication for this. Although physically fit, he had clearly been very dependent on his wife, and following her death was not able to cope adequately. The focus of care was to help him come to terms with his loss, and to provide support and stimulation. A helper took him on regular visits to his wife's grave and the social worker encouraged him to take up his old hobby of winemaking. He was very competent at this, and he proudly presented the social work team with a bottle at Christmas. He was extremely demanding, at times being obviously attracted to the helper, at others responding in a very dependent fashion. One contract to her recognised this, specifying the task as visiting and 'putting up with him'.

These cases proved to be very demanding, partly because of the anxieties of neighbours and the need to reassure them both in terms of giving them some understanding of the condition of the elderly person and of assuring them that something was being done. It was especially important to be careful in the selection of (and support given to) helpers who were likely to have to deal with bizarre ideas and behaviour. Understandably, these cases required a disproportionate amount of time of the social workers. This was necessary for success in setting up packages, regular visiting, neighbour and helper support, and liaison with other agencies.

In two cases, relapse may well have been at least in part due to the difficulty of ensuring that medication was taken regularly. It is interesting to speculate whether the support of a community nurse providing phenothiazine injections might have reduced the likelihood of relapse (Post, 1966). The likelihood of relapse suggests again that closer working arrangements with relevant health service staff would be desirable in long-term care. Nonetheless, the scheme was reasonably successful in providing support for a needy group of persons who usually receive very little help.

(e) Elderly people suffering from confusional states

There were twenty-four cases who at initial assessment exhibited some degree of confusion or disorientation. This proved to be a relatively costly group, as can be seen from Table 4.8. This was both because of the intensive support they received in their own homes and because of their slightly higher rate of admission to local authority residential homes. These individuals were more likely to die within one year (Isaacs and Walkley, 1964), and were more likely to suffer from incontinence of urine. They also experienced greater difficulty in managing activities of daily living. Overall, these cases received more of their support from community care helpers and less from the home help service. It is interesting that cases in the control group were more likely to enter residential care or psychiatric hospital.

In assessment the team was careful to establish whether confusion or disorientation was of recent onset, and therefore possibly reflected temporary impairment which might be relieved by appropriate treatment of an underlying physical disorder, more appropriate use of medication, or adequate nutrition. In nearly all cases, the problem was one of long-term impairment. Such individuals are frequently difficult to help, intervention is often unsuccessful and there is little knowledge of the factors likely to determine success or failure. The only study which has identified clear predictors of outcome in the community isolated the importance of living group (Bergmann *et al.*, 1978). Elderly people living alone were least likely to remain at home over a period of one year, those living with their spouse were more likely and those with younger relatives were most likely to do so, despite the greater flow of resources to those living alone. The authors concluded that these findings suggested the need for very different care strategies for different groups, giving more domiciliary help to those not living alone.

When family support was available, work was aimed at preventing the carers from becoming overburdened and subsequently rejecting the elderly person. This involved liaison with family practitioners in an attempt to alleviate such problems as nocturnal restlessness; the provision of a wide range of practical services such as day-sitting or help with laundry; arranging periods of relief when the elderly person was particularly burdensome; or simply alleviating the constant drudgery of care; and providing opportunities for the relief of feelings of despair, anger and guilt - an approach suggested by Fuller *et al.* (1979).

However, it also seemed possible to provide effective support for some of those living alone, or for couples where both partners were mentally frail. The team appeared to learn more appropriate strategies of care, since the instances of more effective work with dementing individuals occurred in the later part of the project. In the early stages the pattern often appeared similar to that usually experienced, increasing input of resources and support being quickly defeated by pressure of circumstances associated with the elderly person's mental state.

Table 4.8 Clients suffering from confusional states

	Confusional states		All cases	
	Community care	Standard provision	Community care	Standard provision
Number of cases	24	22	92	116
Average age (years)	79		80	
Male	33%		23%	
Female	67%		77%	
Outcomes				
At home	50%	23%	67%	45%
Died	30%	50%	16%	28%
Local authority	8%	18%	4%	16%
Private residential care)	4%	0%	8%	5%
Moved away	0%	0%	2%	2%
Hospital care	8%	9%	3%	4%
Resources per month				
Average cost to SSD (£)	55.88	52.09	48.55	49.23
Home help (hours)	7.80	4.51	8.20	6.71
Community care helpers (£)	13.68	-	14.92	-
Community care voluntary help (visits)	1.60	-	1.50	-
Home help as percentage of SSD cost	26	-	30	-
Community care helper as percentage of SSD cost	33	-	31	-
District nursing (visits)	2.4	-	2.5	-
Average cost to NHS (£)	111.29	117.56	80.82	81.16
Problem prevalence				
Incontinence of urine	46%		35%	
Giddiness	75%		74%	
Breathlessness	33%		49%	
Depressed mood (moderate or severe)	29%		49%	
Anxiety moderate or severe)	38%		61%	
Confusion or disorientation	100%		26%	
Needing help with activities				
Rising and retiring	46%		23%	
Toileting	25%		13%	
Getting in and out of chair	25%		14%	
Bathing	83%		72%	
Making hot drinks	50%		32%	
Making meals	88%		74%	
ADL score[1]	2.50		1.77	
Level of informal care				
Low	8%		21%	
Moderate	71%		60%	
High	21%		19%	
Weekly social contacts[2]	21.4		19.2	

Notes
1. ADL refers to six Activities of Daily Living (Katz *et al.*, 1963).
2. Social contacts score as used by Tunstall (1966).

Later it became clear that it was with such apparently insoluble cases that a flexible response could offer some of the most exciting possibilities.

As already discussed, the scheme embodied certain principles of intervention which were particularly relevant for the management of the dementing elderly person. These were the problem-oriented assessment, a careful examination of the elderly person's current pattern of functioning with a focus on their own definition of their difficulty, and case management which could respond flexibly to the changing needs of clients and carers. The acquisition of greater confidence and experience in managing these cases can be understood in the light of four concepts - 'entrée', 'process risk', 'event risk' and 'patterning care'.

Entrée refers to the difficulty of gaining access to and acceptance by the elderly person: first for the social worker and later for the care or help which they wished to provide. This could mean at first gaining an understanding of the old person's routine, which at times required considerable persistence and 'detective work' as a means of identifying ways of establishing rapport and communication. Often it would require considerable ingenuity to relate the help that was to be provided to the elderly person's retained skills and long-term memory so as to make its acceptance more likely. This could involve strategies such as initially providing help where need was perceived by the elderly person rather than where the need was evidently greatest, to avoid rejection.

Two distinct elements of risk could be observed in the clients of the scheme. By *process risk* is meant the likelihood of increasing self-neglect, decline and reduction of coping skills, often a downward spiral which can ultimately lead to some kind of institutional care. By *event risk* is meant the loss of coping skills where normal sequential acts of daily living are not completed in their entirety, such as turning on gas taps and failing to light them, thereby causing a degree of danger for both the old person and their immediate environment. Individual cases may exhibit a mixed picture of risk, but the distinction between them is a useful one as it serves to discriminate between different types and foci of intervention.

The fourth key element which emerged can be described as *patterning care*. The objective was to build a clear regular pattern of care based initially on the positive elements retained by the old person despite their mental disability. The pattern had to be meaningful within the old person's daily routine and to relate to indicators which have meaning for them. Thus, visits on Tuesday and Thursday at 9 a.m. do not constitute such a pattern since they are not related to meaningful events within the old person's routine, Tuesday and Thursday being like any other day. Rather, the visiting and support pattern had to be built upon regular external cues such as night and morning, light and dark, and any habits which the person had retained, such as retiring to bed or rising at a certain time as a result of their previous work routine. These cues could be reinforced by carers (Berman and Rappaport, 1984). The objective was to build a pattern of care within which the old person could feel a sense of security and within which their behaviour could be reasonably predictable. Two examples of 'process risk' and one of 'event risk' may clarify these ideas:

A case exhibiting process risk was Mrs S. who had lived alone for a number of years following the death of her husband, and who had no friends in the locality. She was discharged from hospital following the detection of a heart condition and malnutrition. Home help and meals were organised but both services had difficulty gaining access either because Mrs S. was out or because she would not let them in. Neighbours were extremely concerned. On referral to the scheme she appeared disorientated, unaware of the date or time, was unable to take prescribed medication reliably, and frequently barred people from entry. She neglected her personal hygiene and the house likewise had a stale smell. She would spend much of her days in an apparently depressed state, hunched over an electric fire. After a great deal of persistence the social worker was accepted by Mrs S., probably associating her with a friendly smile and frequent contact. On occasions a uniform could assist in gaining acceptance and the part-time auxiliary nurse from the local surgery was recruited as a helper. She visited at lunch time and in the evenings, wearing her uniform on these occasions, and during the afternoon and evening involved her daughter and husband in helping Mrs S. with odd jobs. The district nursing sister from the surgery visited in the morning, and through her and the helper appropriate medication was taken. The support of the couple living next door was enlisted, made possible as they could see their part in an overall plan of care. More detailed knowledge revealed that Mrs S. was continually throwing money away in brown paper bags. The presence of soot on money identified a substantial hoard of money in the chimney. Accordingly through the Court of Protection the social worker undertook responsibility for managing her financial affairs.

The initial aims were to institute the regular provision of meals, appropriate use of medication, cleanliness and stimulation. It transpired that the only meal Mrs S. was prepared to eat was fish and chips, wrapped in newspaper. Therefore, over the Christmas period and on Sundays, frozen fish in batter was cooked for her by a helper at her own home, and wrapped in newspaper.

Once initial basic needs had been met, it was attempted to improve both Mrs

S.'s quality of experience and her immediate environment, including her choice of clothing. The offer of three dresses from a local jumble sale provoked sufficient interest for her to change her clothes. Resistance would have been more likely if only one dress had been offered. Under persuasion from people with whom she had developed a relationship of trust, she proved willing to allow her hair to be washed, an achievement which had eluded the previous best efforts of the district nurse. She also agreed to the purchase of a television set which proved a valuable distraction and enlivened her conversation. The helper switched it on at lunchtime and turned it off in the evening. The successful support of Mrs S. at home seemed dependent on the cooperation of a range of different carers. This included the family practitioner, who was an important partner in planning her care at home and even helped in arranging for the disposal and replacement of the carpet when Mrs S.'s home was being cleaned. The effectiveness of the pattern of care established was demonstrated by a degree of physical improvement, an adequate diet, the fact that wandering ceased and did not recur, and that this lady was able to remain in her own home and retain a degree of autonomy.

A second example of process risk was that of Mr and Mrs W., an elderly professional couple who had retired into the district from Scotland. Mr W. was incontinent, extremely deaf and confused. His wife exhibited loss of short-term memory, and personal distress over her difficulty in coping and consciousness of her failing mental faculties. Mrs W., who had been a very competent organised person when younger, was very ambivalent about accepting help, at times requesting help but when it was offered refusing. Home help visits were either refused or on other occasions when the home help visited the couple were out. Knowing the history the social worker took along a potential helper who had been an occupational therapist, who was thought to be likely to relate to the couple. Following this first visit, a degree of rapport was established as Mrs W. had herself worked in hospitals. The initial plan was for the helper to establish a relationship, become known, and assist wherever acceptable. Initially this help consisted of dealing with Mr W.'s hearing aid and sorting out bills. The helper was acceptable to the couple because of her willingness to provide help where they perceived a need, or simply to provide companionship, rather than to assist in home care which was clearly required but which Mrs W. found threatening. As the helper became accepted on a regular basis, it was possible also to establish visits by a home help, and this pattern of support ensured that the couple ate adequately and the home and laundry were managed, as well as giving the couple more confidence. Mrs W.'s anxiety was greatly reduced and the support continued satisfactorily until Mr W. was admitted to hospital following a stroke, and subsequently died. Following this loss, the old lady began to drink heavily. Her decline accelerated rapidly and she was admitted to long-term psychiatric care. Despite the eventual outcome of this case, the scheme had enabled the couple to remain at home together for well over a year longer than would otherwise have been possible.

An example of a case which fell predominantly into the 'event risk' category is that of Miss M. She lived alone in a three-bedroomed semi-detached house and although reasonably physically active, was quite seriously impaired, tended to wander and was prone to leave gas taps on. Gradual intellectual deterioration had been noted over the last six years following the death of a close friend with whom she had lived most of her adult life. Attempts to provide both day care and home help had been abortive as she was never in the house when home help or transport arrived and residential care had been refused. She lacked the competence to prepare meals or hot drinks for herself, and regularly purchased excessive quantities of goods at the local shop. Indeed, on the occasion of the first visit there were eight oven-ready chickens in the house - three in the kitchen, two in the lounge, two in the bedroom and one in the sitting room - all in varying states of decay. Gas taps and a gas fire were occasionally turned on and left unlit, causing a potential hazard. Nearly all the care was being provided by a neighbour who was herself unwell and finding the situation increasingly difficult, yet who felt unable to withdraw.

The initial action of the social worker was to visit her and get some idea of any pattern to her behaviour. After numerous visits she was accepted by Miss M., who responded with an expression of warmth and told the worker that she liked her. At this early stage a helper was introduced with the broad objectives of gaining her confidence, providing support and relieving the neighbour. Within a short time the neighbour was able to offer less support, due to her failing health, and a more structured programme of care was devised. It was arranged for the old lady to attend a day centre for five days per week, with a helper visiting in the morning to help her get up, provide a drink and get her ready for the transport, ensuring she did not go out before it arrived. In the late afternoon another helper collected her from the day centre where she had stayed later than other clients and had had a light tea. The second helper settled her at home in front of the television and provided her with an evening meal, often staying there for some time. Later in the evening another helper gave her a hot drink, and then assisted her to bed. The bed was moved downstairs to a warmer room because she had begun to experience difficulty in managing stairs. Over the weekends frequent visits from helpers were arranged who would take her to their own homes to provide activity and stimulation. It was also hoped that a walk might reduce the propensity to wander. At the same time attempts were made to modify the domestic environment. The gas supply was switched off except when helpers were present, and an electric convector heater was provided since it was safer than a gas fire. Her financial affairs were managed by relatives living in London who provided the social worker with money to cover the cost of meals and shopping.

After a short period the pattern appeared to be set and the tendency to wander ended, and it seemed as if the provision of order in her life had led her to feel relaxed. Once a routine was established it was possible to sustain her in her own home in comfort for a period of about two years. When breakdown finally occurred, it was due to exogenous factors rather than changes in the client. One of the helpers was leaving for a long holiday in Australia and another for a shorter holiday. It was decided that the least damaging option would be admission for short-term care to a home run by staff at the day centre whom the old lady trusted. Subsequent attempts to re-establish the pattern of care proved difficult, nocturnal wandering recurred and it was decided to admit her permanently to the same home. Two years previously she had adamantly refused, but now appeared very settled after admission. One helper noted that on moving into the home she voluntarily took off her hat which she had rarely done before, perhaps thereby indicating a degree of security.

These cases, exhibiting both 'process' and 'event' risk demonstrate how the team began to develop more useful approaches to the care of dementing elderly people as they became accustomed to greater autonomy. The initial assessment took account of not just the obvious problems at referral of the person's failure to manage adequately, but explored their pattern of coping as a whole. Not only were the negative elements of loss of faculties and skills considered, but also the positive capacities which were retained. Considerable ingenuity was shown in making help available and acceptable. Gaining 'entrée' for the helper and social worker could be unorthodox. The choice of method could depend on frequency of contact, association with pleasant past experiences or events, and an understanding of any pattern in behaviour (Snyder *et al.*, 1978). A uniform could help to gain legitimacy and persistence was often needed to convert 'letter-box dialogues' into friendly exchanges. Sometimes it was the readiness of a helper to listen, the provision of regular tasty meals, sharing a cigarette, or making a rare visit to a pub which was successful in gaining confidence and trust. A reassuring physical contact could establish communication with someone who was partially sensorily deprived. Intervention was initially focused on the elderly person's definition of a problem, emphasising such factors as loneliness, fear about declining faculties and worry about managing personal affairs. This would make help more acceptable than concentration on purely material needs. Help once accepted was used as a bridgehead for the development of a larger package of care, including provision for more instrumental needs.

'Event risk' was contained by modifications to the physical environment such as turning off the gas supply, identifying patterns of behaviour, and establishing routines in order to limit the risk of wandering, whilst the anxiety of neighbours about the risk was reduced by consultation and involvement. The downward spiral of 'process risk' was broken by organising a comprehensive network of care, which included the provision of food, medication and stimulation (Berman and Rappaport, 1984). Finally the care was structured and managed as part of a *pattern*. It required the worker to take responsibility for providing a certain level and type of care, and making it acceptable to the client (Wasser, 1971). Attempts were also made to involve helpers in other therapeutic activities as well as stimulation through social contact and recreational activity such as cooking and knitting. Most notably this involved the use of reality orientation techniques (Woods and Holden, 1981) and what Berman and Rappaport (1984) have described as 'structured cueing', to stimulate long-term memory and evoke habitual patterns of functioning. Helpers were enjoined in every interaction with the confused elderly person to convey as much information as possible, such as the day of the week, or the meal being eaten. Attempts were made to apply the principles of 24-hour reality orientation by placing certain reminder notices at strategic points in the home, such as the kitchen. This met with a limited degree of success. In one case where the elderly person had paranoid ideas, the notices were misconstrued and became part of a delusional system.

Other factors appeared to be important. First, a better preserved and more rewarding personality could predispose towards maintaining support (for example, Miss M.). Second, care required detailed coordination and was dependent on the willingness of different carers to cooperate as part of an overall plan. In all these cases the commitment of the GP was significant. Third, stability seemed significant. Once patterns of care were established, they needed to be reasonably stable. Disruption occurred less as a result of client deterioration than as a result of external events. In the case of Miss M., it was the coincidence of two central figures being away at the same time; on other occasions variations in conditions, such as a heavy fall of snow (causing a loss of reference points and also disrupting the pattern of care) threatened the continued capacity to survive at home. Perhaps the disruption of an established pattern of care may be as damaging as major social changes like moving home leading to acute decompensation (Evans, 1982).

As in the other cases suffering from mental disorder, it is worth considering whether a closer working relationship with the psychiatric services might have proved beneficial. There was no psychogeriatric service with facilities such as a specialised day hospital where early assessment could be combined with treatment and management as a joint health and social care enterprise. Nevertheless, even in the absence of such a response, it did appear that the experience of the scheme had thrust a few shafts of light into the gloomy picture of care for the mentally frail elderly by identifying some approaches worthy of further investigation.

3. Conclusions

The evidence suggests that there were clearly identifiable differences in the strategies of care provided for different types of problem, observable both in social work activity and in the variations in the mix of resources used.

The pattern of work identified is very different from that which has been described as usual in area teams (Stevenson and Parsloe, 1978; Goldberg and Warburton, 1979; Black *et al.*, 1983). These studies suggested that work with elderly people would tend to be routine and unimaginative, lacking continuity and characterised by a lack of positive aims and a reticence to deal with attitudes, behaviour and feelings. It appeared that under the community care scheme effective and varied responses were made to the needs of the mentally disordered and the physically frail. People with affective disorders were more likely to receive appropriate care than is common (Foster *et al.*, 1976) and possibly even those dementing elderly people with a poor survival chance -some of those living alone (Bergmann *et al.*, 1978) - could be supported at home with a carefully structured approach. Again, individuals who frequently pose care problems such as those at serious risk of falling and those whose difficulties are associated with alcohol abuse were more readily assisted and patients of extreme frailty could be discharged earlier from hospital care. Our observations of the work with these different cases, albeit with small numbers in each category, indicate that there is room for further testing of some of these approaches as a means of enhancing the knowledge base of social work with the elderly.

However, it was also noted that, for some groups, a more effective response could probably be achieved by a closer working relationship with the health service. This was particularly evident for those cases presenting more intractable conditions such as incontinence and functional psychoses. The lack of this health service input may well constitute a limit to the effectiveness of improved care by the social services.

CHAPTER 5

SUPPORTING THE CARERS

The elderly people helped under the community care scheme had relatively little informal social support. This was probably to be expected in a retirement resort with in-migration and lost ties of friends and family. Indeed, the saddest encounters were those where an elderly person, usually female, had moved to the area with an ailing spouse, whose wish the move had been. Caring responsibility stopped them making new ties and becoming integrated into the local community. The subsequent loss of the frail partner seemed to leave them doubly bereft. They experienced both the loss of a loved one and the loss of familiar environment, friends and family whose presence might have cushioned the effects of the initial loss. Consequently a number of people seemed to experience a sense of complete desolation.

For a significant proportion of cases - nineteen - informal contacts were few: less than four each week. Social isolation and loneliness were common for these elderly people and the focus of the workers was on constructing support networks which could, wherever possible, meet both practical and emotional needs. In one case the helper was herself elderly, and following the death of her husband felt isolated and without purpose and she gained much from participation in the scheme, which extended to boarding a client in her home at the weekend. Two years later this helper herself became a client as her health deteriorated. The opening of a new purpose-built day centre, the admissions to which were channelled through one of the scheme's social workers, helped to extend the range of provision for these very isolated individuals.

In most of the cases which had a high level of informal social support, this was due to the influence of family care (Jones *et al.*, 1983). Nevertheless, only eighteen out of the ninety-two cases had a high level of support; that is more than fourteen contacts per week. Not all of these were people living with a spouse or younger family, since families providing almost total support could be very isolated from the rest of the community. Despite serving a retirement area which reduced the availability of informal care, support of carers proved to be an important feature of the scheme's activity. This aspect of the operation of the community care schemes has been found to be more demanding where the population is less geographically mobile and a higher proportion of clients have an active support network (Challis *et al.*, 1983). Where support of carers was necessary, it was usually not due to the inadequacy of care provided but rather due to the excessive demands on the carer. In such cases, the aim was often more to redistribute the burden than to improve quality of care, providing the carer with a wider range of choice than is usually possible. It must

Table 5.1 Clients living with spouse

	Living with spouse		All cases	
	Community care	**Standard provision**	**Community care**	**Standard provision**
Number of cases	19	15	92	116
Average age (years)	78		80	
Male	58%		23%	
Female	42%		77%	
Outcomes				
At home	53%	40%	67%	45%
Died	37%	47%	16%	28%
Local authority	0%	13%	4%	16%
Private residential care	0%	0%	8%	5%
Moved away	0%	0%	2%	2%
Hospital care	10%	0%	3%	4%
Resources per month				
Average cost to SSD (£)	29.89	58.54	48.55	49.23
Home help (hours)	6.60	3.48	8.20	6.71
Community care helpers (£)	7.948	-	14.92	-
Community care voluntary help (visits)	2.70	-	1.50	-
Home help as percentage of SSD cost	37	-	30	-
Community care helper a percentage of SSD cost	26	-	31	-
District nursing (visits)	3.4	-	2.5	-
Average cost to NHS (£)	86.74	105.29	80.82	81.16
Problem prevalence				
Incontinence of urine	42%		35%	
Giddiness	90%		74%	
Breathlessness	47%		49%	
Depressed mood (moderate or severe)	52%		49%	
Anxiety moderate or severe	68%		61%	
Confusion or disorientation	42%		26%	
Needing help with activities				
Rising and retiring	42%		23%	
Toileting	21%		13%	
Getting in and out of chair	26%		14%	
Bathing	69%		72%	
Making hot drinks	68%		32%	
Making meals	84%		74%	
ADL score[1]	2.37		1.77	
Level of informal care				
Low	0%		21%	
Moderate	68%		60%	
High	32%		19%	
Weekly social contacts[2]	26.3		19.2	

Notes
1. ADL refers to six Activities of Daily Living (Katz *et al.*, 1963).
2. Social contacts score as used by Tunstall (1966).

be remembered that this description of work with carers quite properly does not cover those few cases where both elderly person and carers expressed a clear preference for residential care.

It is helpful to consider the work with informal carers in two sections: first, those where the elderly person lived with the carers, and second, those were they lived apart. As in the previous chapter, for each group of cases a summary table is given and similar caution must be exercised in making direct comparisons between experimental and control groups.

1. Elderly People Living with Carers

(a) Elderly people living with a spouse

There were eleven married couples and in all but three of these cases both partners were frail and were therefore regarded as clients of the scheme. There were therefore nineteen cases living with a spouse. It can be seen from Table 5.1 that these individuals were more likely to be male, and had a higher than average level of social contact. They were more likely to be physically frail and probably as a result more likely to enter long-term hospital care or die within a year. The level of nursing care received was relatively high although the cost was likely to be lower, due to the sharing of costs between married couples. In the absence of the scheme, some of these cases were likely to receive relatively little help and those in the comparison group were more likely to receive relatively low levels of domiciliary services.

The focus of help for a married couple was on trying to support the fragile balance which they provided for one another, while attempting to develop a more comprehensive support network. At times there were tensions in these relationships to which the worker had to be sensitive, influencing the way in which help could be given. Such tensions could arise from changes or transitions in people's lifestyle (Parkes, 1971). Changes in dependency, dominance and patterns of communication have all been found to be important aspects of family relationships in care of the elderly (Bergmann *et al.*, 1984). Necessarily the support aimed to meet both practical and emotional needs.

Mr and Mrs B. lived in a genteel but shabby ground-floor flat of a large house. Mr B. suffered from cataracts and had virtually no sight. He had a strong sense of his own dignity, having been an architect, but now he was ill-kempt and doubly incontinent, although very reticent about the problem. Mrs B. had had a replacement hip operation and suffered from a heart condition and chronic anxiety. She was only able to manoeuvre painfully with the aid of a walking frame. She was very concerned with the 'proper' maintenance of the household and tried to retain activities despite the tremendous difficulty for her, such as taking more than twenty minutes to make a cup of tea. Their relationship was a tense and difficult one, and she tended to see help as 'for Mr B.', and the social worker had to take great care in introducing help so as to avoid undermining her feeling of independence. It was important to take account of the evident friction between the couple, living in close proximity, severely restricted in their mobility and experiencing considerable frustration, in particular Mr B., who had lost the power simply to meet his basic needs. Gradually it was possible to get Mr B. to be more open about his problem of incontinence and the construction of a network of care involved careful consultation with the hospital, district nursing and home help services. In order to provide for both rehabilitation and relief of tension, it was arranged for Mrs B. to attend the local day hospital. Eventually, the pattern of care provided a degree of cover throughout the day:

Morning: District nurse visited, assisted with washing and changed urine bag.
Mid-morning: Home help. On certain days Mrs B. attended day hospital.
Lunch-time: Meals-on-wheels or community care helper.
Tea-time: Community care helper with private help on some days. Volunteer assisted with shopping.
Evening: District nurse visited, assisted with washing and changed urine bag.

Sometimes a spouse would be unwilling to relinquish care tasks despite experiencing great difficulty due to failing health and being very isolated. In such cases a helper would provide companionship and reassurance and gradually would undertake more as the carer developed confidence.

In seven of the eleven married couples, one partner had died within a year. In three cases where the scheme had initially taken on only one partner - the husband, who was being cared for by a more active wife - the bereavement led to considerable support being given to the wife, who became a client in her own right. These were cases who would be unlikely to receive a great deal of support from the social services department in ordinary circumstances.

Mrs C. was caring for her bedridden husband, a full-time activity leaving them very isolated. She had difficulty taking advantage of home help, since she perceived their needs less in terms of home care, which she had managed all her life, than problems of her own isolation, the need for additional company for her husband and relief sitting. Following the bereavement she became extremely distressed and felt unable to go out of the home and became very dependent on the scheme for support. The social worker adopted a behavioural approach to reduce her anxiety gradually, by arranging for her to go out further by stages with the support of a helper, the contract specifying a programme of increasing independence.

Table 5.2 Clients living with informal carers other than spouse

	Living with carer		All cases	
	Community care	Standard provision	Community care	Standard provision
Number of cases	9	10	92	116
Average age (years)	81		80	
Male	13%		23%	
Female	87%		77%	
Outcomes				
At home	33%	20%	67%	45%
Died	22%	20%	16%	28%
Local authority	11%	40%	4%	16%
Private residential care	33%	20%	8%	5%
Moved away	0%	0%	2%	2%
Hospital care	0%	0%	3%	4%
Resources per month				
Average cost to SSD (£)	50.66	89.87	48.55	49.23
Home help (hours)	2.00	0.38	8.20	6.71
Community care helpers (£)	13.88	-	14.92	-
Community care voluntary help (visits)	0.30	-	1.50	-
Home help as percentage of SSD cost	8	-	30	-
Community care helper a percentage of SSD cost	46	-	31	-
District nursing (visits)	4.5	-	2.5	-
Average cost to NHS (£)	135.44	58.50	80.82	81.16
Problem prevalence				
Incontinence of urine	22%		35%	
Giddiness	67%		74%	
Breathlessness	44%		49%	
Depressed mood (moderate or severe)	33%		49%	
Anxiety moderate or severe	44%		61%	
Confusion or disorientation	22%		26%	
Needing help with activities				
Rising and retiring	44%		23%	
Toileting	33%		13%	
Getting in and out of chair	33%		14%	
Bathing	89%		72%	
Making hot drinks	67%		32%	
Making meals	89%		74%	
ADL score[1]	2.56		1.77	
Level of informal care				
Low	-		21%	
Moderate	78%		60%	
High	22%		19%	
Weekly social contacts[2]	24.0		19.2	

Notes
1. ADL refers to six Activities of Daily Living (Katz *et al.*, 1963).
2. Social contacts score as used by Tunstall (1966).

The work of assisting bereaved elderly people was undertaken both directly by the social worker and by certain selected helpers. In one case the helper, an ex-nurse, showed great sensitivity in her support of a bereaved spouse. She enabled the old lady to perceive the relationship as reciprocal, where they shared their troubles, which greatly increased the old lady's sense of self-respect. Mrs L. commented on their relationship: 'I'm able to talk to her about my worries and she tells me about her family and that relieves her a bit too. Even if she stopped doing it (helping in the project) she'd probably still come and see me. It's become a friendship ... sometimes it's like having a daughter; she'll ring me in the evening to see if I'm alright but sometimes I try to beat her to it'.

(b) Elderly people living with other informal carers

Nine elderly people lived with other informal carers. Four were two elderly sisters and two friends living together, one of each pair being extremely frail and therefore dependent on the other. Four elderly people were living with a younger relative, in each case a daughter. In one of these cases, both the mother (aged 90 and blind) and her daughter (in her 60s and crippled by arthritis) were recipients of the scheme in their own right. Table 5.2 shows that these cases had relatively high levels of social contact, experienced more difficulty in activities of daily living and were more likely to receive district nursing than the usual run of cases. Support from helpers constituted a much higher than average proportion of social services support, since other services tended to be less readily available to those living with others. For those people in the comparison group, receipt of home help was very unlikely (Levin, 1982). Differences in NHS costs were entirely due to the greater use of acute facilities by community care cases.

Those most likely to experience breakdown in this group were those living with another elderly partner, where a fragile equilibrium was being maintained, such as two sisters and two elderly friends. The main focus of care where elderly clients were living with others was to provide relief to the carer or less frail partners.

On one occasion the involvement of the scheme occurred at the time when a crucial decision had to be made. Miss B. was a woman in her early 40s, caring for a frail elderly mother whose condition had deteriorated to the point where she was bedridden and required frequent attention. Miss B. was at the time undertaking a full-time job which, combined with the care of her mother, became overwhelming. Initially considerable time was spent helping Miss B. with her decision whether or not to continue working, and when this decision was made, working with her in identifying realistic limits to her commitment in a routine of care so that she would not be overburdened with the task.

In another case the long-standing effects of care were wearing down a stepdaughter to the point where she was actively considering whether she could continue. Mr H., aged 72, was paralysed down one side and had lost the power of speech, having suffered a stroke some years ago. The carer was initially very tense and anxious, at times insisting on managing alone and at others stating that the hospital would have to cope. The social worker had to avoid making hasty decisions, work through these conflicting feelings expressed by the step daughter, and subsequently plan the level of care with her. It was noticeable how positively she responded given the opportunity to discuss the problems of care and the effects on her. She experienced considerable difficulty helping her father upstairs and safely to bed since he was a heavy man, whereas she was very slight and had a weakness in one arm. A helper was organised to help the stepdaughter assist her father upstairs each evening, while on two occasions each week a helper sat with Mr H. for the evening while his relative went out. At a later stage, a helper with a nursing background helped the carer to bath Mr H. as the district nurse was unable to fit into the stepdaughter's routine. She, provided with greater support and relief, and knowing where she could turn, became visibly more relaxed and tended to adopt a protective attitude to the helpers, insisting she could manage over the Christmas period in order to give them relief.

In those cases where clients were living with family, the relatives' attitude to help proved as crucial as that of the client. Understandably, many relatives felt guilty in articulating their difficulties in caring for a loved one, and providing the opportunity to express these feelings could be an essential first step (Allen *et al.*, 1983). Usually the elderly people were willing to cooperate with plans developed to relieve their relatives, since they were often aware of and wished to reduce the burden of care. Even where clients felt a degree of reluctance or resentment at these arrangements, careful handling of the situation caused such feelings to be short-lived, and they often came to appreciate the stimulation of a new person in their lives. Indeed, one danger was that the client might be less cooperative with a member of the family than with a helper where the relationship began with a 'clean slate'. In order to avoid the destructive elements of competition or jealousy, the social worker needed to be aware of these possibilities and prepare both family and helper. The most successful arrangements appeared to be those where family and helper understood each other's roles clearly and the risk of misunderstanding was reduced.

2. Elderly People Living Apart from Carers

As can be seen from Table 5.3 there were sixteen cases in this group who received a high level of informal support or who had an identifiable principal

Table 5.3 Clients with considerable informal help but not living with carer

	Not living with carer		All cases	
	Community care	**Standard provision**	**Community care**	**Standard provision**
Number of cases	16	12	92	116
Average age (years)	81		80	
Male	19%		23%	
Female	81%		77%	
Outcomes				
At home	69%	16%	67%	45%
Died	6%	50%	16%	28%
Local authority	13%	17%	4%	16%
Private residential care	6%	8%	8%	5%
Moved away	6%	0%	2%	2%
Hospital care	0%	9%	3%	4%
Resources per month				
Average cost to SSD (£)	65.29	32.64	48.55	49.23
Home help (hours)	8.90	3.34	8.20	6.71
Community care helpers (£)	21.04	-	14.92	-
Community care voluntary help (visits)	0.60	-	1.50	-
Home help as percentage of SSD cost	28	-	30	-
Community care helper as percentage of SSD cost	27	-	31	-
District nursing (visits)	1.6	-	2.5	-
Average cost to NHS (£)	70.24	51.65	80.82	81.16
Problem prevalence				
Incontinence of urine	31%		35%	
Giddiness	75%		74%	
Breathlessness	50%		49%	
Depressed mood (moderate or severe)	32%		49%	
Anxiety moderate or severe	50%		61%	
Confusion or disorientation	25%		26%	
Needing help with activities				
Rising and retiring	19%		23%	
Toileting	13%		13%	
Getting in and out of chair	13%		14%	
Bathing	94%		72%	
Making hot drinks	31%		32%	
Making meals	94%		74%	
ADL score[1]	1.81		1.77	
Level of informal care				
Low	0%		21%	
Moderate	69%		60%	
High	31%		19%	
Weekly social contacts[2]	21.8		19.2	

Notes
1. ADL refers to six Activities of Daily Living (Katz *et al.*, 1963).
2. Social contacts score as used by Tunstall (1966).

carer. These clients were particularly likely to experience difficulties with the preparation of meals and were likely to receive quite high levels of expenditure from the community care scheme, aimed at providing relief to carers. It is helpful to consider separately those whose support came from family members and those who were dependent on friends and neighbours. Again, those not receiving community care were unlikely to receive substantial levels of domiciliary support and made less use of acute health facilities.

(a) Elderly people supported by family members

Sixteen elderly people had family members living in the area. Ten of these families were regularly involved at least on a weekly basis. In these cases, the focus of intervention was on the relief of stress, avoiding unreasonable or excessive demands on the carer, or reducing their anxieties and fears for the safety of the old person.

In the case of Mrs N., who lived alone and was extremely prone to falling and whose daughter lived in the neighbourhood, helpers provided regular 'check-ups' at times when the old lady would be alone for long periods. A helper's task was specified as 'to visit Mrs N. to check up on her well-being, so as to alleviate her own and her daughter's fear that she might fall and be unattended for a long time'.

Sometimes, family members were trying to cope with an excessive range of personal and caring commitments.

Mr P., a man in his 50s, was married with two children. The marriage was an unhappy one and his wife had a poor relationship with his elderly mother, living two miles away, who was practically bedridden. His mother was very demanding and the bulk of the care fell to him, visiting on the way to and from work each day, at lunchtimes and sometimes returning again in the evening. The only other relative in the vicinity was a sister who herself suffered from a very serious illness. It was possible to devise a less demanding care schedule with Mr P., involving home help on certain days and community care helpers on others, establishing an explicit rota of shared care. The presence of other visitors made Mr P.'s mother less demanding, and although these arrangements did not resolve an unhappy domestic situation, it enabled Mr P. to cope with it more comfortably.

Difficult relationships were also evident between an old person and her familycarer.

Mrs C. lived about a mile from her daughter. Their relationship had always been a troubled one, with Mrs C. tending to manipulate her daughter in order to achieve her ends by means of hypochondria and apparent illness. The daughter found it difficult to cope, and was treated with psychotropic medication for her anxiety state. It proved possible to reduce the demands made on Mrs C.'s daughter by structuring and defining her role in caring in relation to the home help and additional visits by helpers. At the same time, it was essential for the social worker to ensure the helpers were not placed in a similar situation as the daughter by the old lady, and therefore to be firm in resisting demands.

Involvement with clients' families usually took place at a time of anxiety, stress and tension, when people were demanding speedy solutions to the problems of caring for an elderly relative. In such cases, the involvement of the family was sought in care planning and evaluating alternative courses of action, and sometimes it was necessary to help them come to terms with a degree of risk which the old person had chosen in order to remain in their own home. The social worker had to act as mediator between family and client in situations which, unless handled with care, would cause an already disenchanted relative to withdraw completely, or result in serious tensions between helper and relative. Beneath apparent lack of care could lie more long-standing difficulties and resentment.

Mrs J., aged 84, was almost blind and suffered from a heart condition and arthritis. She had lived alone since the death of her husband some three years earlier, and was extremely lonely and miserable. At the time of her husband's death they had both been living in an old people's home, an arrangement which he had hoped to make permanent, but subsequently she had returned to live in their home. The old lady was extremely defensive about her ability to manage and had refused home help at the time of referral to the scheme. Yet she frequently fell and had no means of summoning help. Her daughter lived nearby but felt unable to tolerate the old lady's occasional incontinence, was unhappy about her decision to leave residential care and tended to blame her mother for her father's death. It proved difficult to gain Mrs J.'s confidence and make help acceptable, but a helper was introduced to visit and provide some companionship. This soon extended to making light meals. Mrs J.'s tendency to fall increased notably within a short space of time, and it became necessary to provide regular, reliable support throughout the week. This involved day care, home help, assistance with meals and visits for companionship. Most weeks, her daughter had either visited or taken the old lady to spend the day with her on Sundays and this was made part of the care plan. However, the daughter often failed in this and Mrs J. for her part was unable to admit that the arrangement was not satisfactory, and accept additional help on Sundays, probably fearing that this would lead to her daughter not visiting. The obvious potential gap in care caused frustration to the social worker, who was placed in an impasse, and to the helpers, who were concerned about risk on Sundays. The problem was further compounded when Mrs J. attempted to make her daughter feel guilty for not visiting as conscientiously as the helpers, and then passed her daughter's comments back to the helpers. Inevitably the relationship between daughter and helpers became strained, and the social worker had to take great care to keep the network in balance.

Comprehending the nature of long-standing family relations problems was important, not necessarily in an attempt to resolve deep-seated difficulties, which might in any case be results of aspects of personality unamenable to change, but rather to maintain equilibrium in a package of care and where possible avoid unnecessary conflicts. Furthermore, the team had no remit from families to become involved with such difficulties except to the extent that they affected the care of the elderly person. Nevertheless, supporting an elderly person with these limited objectives could still prove very demanding, since these broader problems of family relationships would frequently influence the care of the elderly person and were likely to be important determinants of outcomes (Bergmann *et al.*, 1984).

In addition to situations where family care was under stress, there were six cases where it was unreliable or relatively infrequent (less than weekly) although there were relatives living nearby. In two cases, there was a very poor relationship between the old person and their family; in one case the family member suffered from serious mental illness, and in the other had extensive work commitments. This left only two cases where an apparent lack of interest could not be explained. In these cases, attempts to involve family members were not conspicuously successful because of long-standing difficulties and the attitudes of both parent and child. The evidence, albeit in an area where family support was generally less available than in other areas, appeared to bear out the argument of Isaacs *et al.* (1972) that neglect by families is rare.

It appeared that where substantial support was provided and risk considerably reduced, relatives tended to feel more at ease. Where a final decision was taken to enter residential care it was after careful consideration, and less likely to evoke the feelings of guilt and remorse in families than where a hasty decision had been made (Allen *et al.*, 1983).

(b) Elderly people supported by other informal carers

Only a few of the old people without family support had substantial levels of informal care, usually because they had lived in a stable neighbourhood for a long time. They were unlikely to be in-migrants. Such elderly people with a good social network were sometimes reluctant to admit that there was any deficit in their pattern of care, and considerable sensitivity was required to overcome their fears that additional care would detract from what friends and neighbours would offer. Often the cooperation of friends and neighbours was enlisted in clarifying for the client the role of the scheme. By supporting a friend or neighbour in their involvement with the old person, it was hoped to reduce the risk that their sense of commitment would be undermined, and of their reducing their contact once a statutory agency became involved (Abrams, 1977). Broadly, the scheme had three functions: the first was that of gap-filling and oversight; the second consisted of providing support and back-up for carers; and the third involved devising realistic boundaries and limits to commitment to avoid carers being overwhelmed. These are illustrated below.

The gap-filling role and general oversight of a fairly sound support network can be observed in the case of Miss G. She was confined to bed or a wheelchair and was closely involved with the local church and had a great deal of visitors. During the week the informal carers, district nursing and home help service covered her needs adequately, except on weekends and at bedtimes. The social worker had to ensure that these gaps were filled and check that the network functioned smoothly.

A second type of activity was the provision of support and back-up to carers. On one occasion an elderly person was very dependent on a neighbour, herself elderly, and here part of the efforts of a community care helper were focused on maintaining the elderly neighbour because she was central to the support network. On another occasion, a neighbour who had been about to withdraw her involvement with an elderly person felt able to continue in her role as principal carer when given relief and support in helping, saying that she was able to continue in the knowledge that she could turn to the community care social worker when she needed to. For this carer, the very existence of the scheme, and the ready availability of someone with whom she could discuss the difficulties and obtain practical relief, made much other help unnecessary. A similar phenomenon was noted by Fuller *et al.* (1979) in providing support to relatives caring for dementing elderly people.

On some occasions the amount of care neighbours were providing placed them under a great deal of strain, and in these situations realistic boundaries to their involvement had to be worked out. The very existence of the social worker acting as 'case manager' relieved carers of sole and inescapable responsibility, which could be a major penalty of involvement in informal care and might ultimately lead to withdrawal. In the case of an extremely sick man, the neighbour had become so deeply involved and her tolerance so stretched that she and her family were actively considering moving house to escape his demands. A temporary admission to hospital for the old man became her 'breaking point' at which she decided to do no more. However, when the scheme became involved, and clear limits were defined for her responsibilities, she was happy to remain involved free of the sole responsibility of care.

3. Conclusion

It was noticeable that, under normal circumstances in the comparison group, those with informal carers were less likely to receive domiciliary services. The level of provision of home help for cases with carers was much closer to the average for all cases under community care than under standard provision. This goes some way towards rectifying the balance which is tilted against informal carers in the allocation of resources (Charlesworth *et al.*, 1984). Through the community care scheme more resources were therefore made available to support informal care. In addition, other forms of support were devised to assist carers, such as a sitting-in arrangement, and the continuity of care provided by a responsible case manager ensured that carers knew where to turn for help and receive support and guidance. These are important needs which have been identified as unmet in other studies (Sainsbury and Grad, 1971; Wheatley, 1980). Allen *et al.* (1983) argue that for services to meet carers' needs more effectively requires sensitive professional assessment, greater appropriateness of services to individual needs and greater influence of carers in the decision about the nature and type of care. The evidence of this chapter suggests that the community care approach moved closer in this direction than is commonly the case.

CHAPTER 6

DEVELOPING COMMUNITY SUPPORT

It was recognised before the scheme entered the field that the needs of frail elderly people required not merely the more effective use of existing resources, but also the provision of additional support. During the original planning phase of the scheme, one important theme had been the possibility of treating the local community and clients' existing networks as potential resources for providing care (Collins and Pancoast, 1977). Elderly clients, who often had little informal support, required the creation of new care networks which made the development of substitute care crucial. The practical expression of this approach, to meet multiple needs - physical, social and emotional - was the recruitment of members of the local community as helpers. The term 'helpers', which emerged quite early in the life of the scheme, captures quite effectively the social workers' deliberate focus on people with a predominantly caring motivation, but for whom payment can be important, and who will occupy a position on a continuum between pure voluntarism and employment status.

This chapter considers the relationship between helpers and the team social workers and the nature of their caring activities for elderly people.

1. Social Work and Helpers

In this section we consider some of the activities undertaken by and demands made on social workers as a consequence of working with members of the community as resources in the care of elderly people. Of particular importance are the processes of recruitment of helpers, matching of client and helper, support and turnover.

(a) Recruitment of helpers

There were three potential sources of helpers for the scheme: first, strangers from outside a client's social environment; second, neighbours either centrally or peripherally part of the elderly person's network; and third, members of the family. The latter two groups were dependent on known clients and, therefore, in order to provide an initial pool of potential helpers suitable for matching with individual clients, recruitment of people in the first category was decided on at the commencement of the scheme. However, this posed a real dilemma in balancing the need for a pool of available helpers with, in the first instance, very few clients to provide for. This is not of course uncommon in the early phase of projects (Goldberg and Connelly, 1982) and despite attempts to sustain interest, out of the first twenty-one helpers who appeared suitable, only six actually reached the point of direct involvement with clients.

Initially notices were displayed in libraries, newsagents' windows, post offices and the local newspapers. The response from most of these was relatively small and the use of a local free advertising paper proved to be the most effective medium. After about a year therefore, advertising was concentrated in this free newspaper. Advertisements stressed 'caring' attitudes, local loyalty and the possibility of payment, pointing out the needs of the town's old people. The appeal tended to be at the general level such as 'to help the old people of Town A to remain in their own homes'. Other sources of recruitment such as word of mouth continued to play a part once the scheme was under way, and a number of 'client-specific' helpers were recruited from elderly people's networks.

The main source of recruitment for the 104 helpers involved in the first year's care of ninety-two cases is shown in Table 6.1. It is likely that these figures understate the importance of the local free advertising press, reflecting as they do the experience of the early phase of the scheme. Nevertheless, the importance of informal networks is noticeable as the second largest source of recruitment. This included family and neighbours of clients as well as helpers who were introduced by existing helpers. Three helpers were family members of clients: one niece and two daughters. The niece had not been involved in any caring activity prior to the intervention of the scheme and was unemployed after leaving school. The two daughters were both under considerable strain in caring for their elderly parents and their position as helpers made it possible to structure their caring activity and avoid excessive involvement. One daughter, caring for a sick husband and frail mother, had to work part-time to augment the family budget. The result of excessive commitment was that she was under

Table 6.1
Main source of recruitment of helpers

Source	N
Advertisements in local advertising press	57
Contacts with informal networks	16
Advertisements in other local press	15
Social services department (social worker)	5
General publicity (media)	5
Other (library, Citizens Advice Bureaux, jobcentre)	6
Number of helpers	104

great stress and coping only because of regular psychotropic medication from her GP. The scheme provided her with equivalent income to her existing job, enabled her to care for her mother and to help several other clients in addition. The other daughter, similarly, helped other clients as well as her own mother. In addition a few helpers were suggested by social workers, and others had heard of the scheme through the local radio or press.

On occasions, as has been attempted with foster care for children, specific advertisements were placed to deal with unusually difficult needs. These included one for companionship for a man who had lost the power of speech after a severe stroke, in order to provide relief for his stepdaughter. Such forms of recruitment were, however, rare. Although other methods such as posters and door-to-door leaflets were considered, these were not used because of the effectiveness of newspaper advertisements. However, elsewhere in subsequent projects a leaflet appealing for helpers distributed in public places such as shops and libraries has met with some degree of success, and some helpers have been recruited through voluntary agencies and job centres.

(b) Selection of helpers

Telephone discussion was often sufficient to eliminate certain enquiries, and interviews were arranged with potential helpers who seemed both interested and suitable. Wherever possible interviews took place in the person's home, partly because a visit to the home can yield another dimension to the worker's understanding of the person and partly because this was more informal, comfortable and convenient for the potential helper. This approach was reinforced by the scarcity of interviewing facilities at the office.

At the beginning of the interview a brief outline was given of the scheme, its objectives and the practical implications of participation for the helper. It was emphasised that helping in the scheme could not be considered as a job in the usual sense and that the scheme could not guarantee a regular income, since changes might occur in the life of the elderly person being helped. In those cases where the individual's need and desire for a regular wage clearly outweighed their interest in work with the elderly, it was usually mutually agreed to proceed no further.

In the rest of the interview, a simple form was used to ensure that the information collected by each worker was similar. The form covered basic details such as whether the person had transport and times of availability, as well as more general information such as the person's previous employment experience, involvement in caring activities, family circumstances, possible areas of difficulty, their reasons for applying and expectations from the scheme. These were all factors expected to influence the ways in which a person could contribute and to help determine with whom the person could be matched.

The previous caring experience of the potential helper, whether on a formal employed basis or informal basis, was considered particularly important. Caring for a frail elderly person, whether in a nursing home or in their own home, was likely to mean that the person had developed a realistic appreciation of the difficulties which potential clients can experience and the problems which can arise from individual reactions to dependency. In certain cases, discussion of previous caring activities identified possible areas of difficulty or activities with which the person felt uncomfortable. These could include helping a person who was incontinent or suffering from mental disorder. Similarly a helper unduly preoccupied with hygiene was liable to experience considerable difficulty in tolerating standards lower than their own. Some people appeared to experience difficulty at the thought of leaving an old person alone at night in the knowledge that, however carefully planned, there was a degree of risk. The individual's motivation to help was also relevant since it appeared that for some an overriding need to help and nurture could prevent them from effectively helping an old person to preserve as much independence as possible.

Potential external constraints which could impinge on the ability and willingness to help were also explored during the initial interview. It was possible that family relationships, especially the attitude of a husband, could be strained by the wife engaging in new activities of her own, whilst for younger people it was important to assess the extent to which parents were supportive and understood what was entailed. These constraints should not be underestimated. Indeed, in some cases, it was only the payment offered by the scheme that made helping legitimate in the eyes of husbands, although this was not a prime reason for the wife's involvement. Constraints of a more practical kind also were significant for some helpers. These included dependence on public transport in an area where this was often unavailable in the evenings, and distance from potential clients.

The team had few initial preconceptions about the attributes of a suitable helper, save a caring attitude and sound commonsense. However, qualities which influenced the selection process included a liking and enthusiasm for work with the elderly, an approach and manner which communicated care and concern without being patronising, a belief in the right to dignity and choice in old age, a sense of commitment to the activity, and the capacity to respond to possible difficulties, such as illness or a fall, in a calm and reasonably competent fashion. It was noticeable that the commitment to and belief in the elderly person's right to choice and independence was particularly evident in a number of people who had worked in nursing homes or as nursing auxiliaries. It seemed as if, for some of these people, the scheme offered a means of redressing the balance of the negative experiences of institutional care.

The question of references was debated at some length. On the one hand, the lengthy processes which are involved in the selection of foster parents, such as checking police records, were seen as too detailed for a scheme which sought to involve members of the local community more closely in caring for elderly people and where the relationship between project and helper was to be as informal as possible. Equally, however, the need for great care in selection was recognised, since strangers were being introduced into the homes of vulnerable people. In practice the team asked for two references, ideally one from an ex-employer and one of a more personal nature. The idea of seeking references was never questioned or thought intrusive by the helpers; it was understood as reasonable that, given the degree of close and even intimate contact that could occur between helper and client, such precautions were necessary. Of course, obtaining references could be difficult for people who had not been in employment for a long time, and on occasions where nothing untoward was evident in the interview, it was decided to accept one reference, perhaps from a local shopkeeper or even a neighbour. An additional check was usually made of social services department records, in order to ascertain whether there was any information to which particular attention should be paid in the interview or, in the extreme, more serious factors such as a record of unreliability or uncontrolled behaviour. Achieving the balance between informality and partnership with helpers on the one hand and the responsibility to protect elderly people on the other was a difficult one, and procedures were regularly reviewed.

Following receipt of satisfactory references a letter of acceptance was sent to new helpers, welcoming them to the scheme. In certain cases this would be obviated by immediate telephone contact to arrange to introduce them to a client. Where interview or references were unsatisfactory and this had not been discussed in the interview, a letter was sent to applicants thanking them for their enquiry, stating that the scheme could not use their offer of help, and where it was felt helpers might be better involved with other agencies an attempt was made to redirect them.

A wide range of helpers was recruited, ranging from people with relevant employment experience as nurses or home helps to young mothers with time to spare. A few young people were recruited, but unsurprisingly the most successful of these proved to be those with a strong interest in a career in nursing. Some helpers were already involved with individual clients, such as relatives who were incorporated in a more structured pattern of care or neighbours who were already part of an elderly person's network. The age, sex and previous experience of the helpers are shown in Tables 6.2 and 6.3. Nearly all helpers were female, although more men became involved on an informal basis as a result of their wives' involvement. The age of the helpers was also revealing, 39 per cent being of an age where they were highly unlikely to re-enter the labour market. Sixty people (58 per cent) had previous relevant work experience. Nearly one-half of these had worked either in residential homes or hospitals for the elderly as unqualified carers. Nearly one-quarter more were qualified nurses. In addition to these sixty people, a substantial proportion of others had relevant life-experience in caring for elderly relatives.

Table 6.2
Age and sex of helpers

Characteristics of helpers	**%**
Age	
Less than 21	6
21-29	13
30-39	24
40-49	18
50-59	26
60 and over	13
Sex	
Male	6
Female	94
Number of helpers	104

Table 6.3
Previous relevant work experience of helpers

Work background	**%**
Qualified nurse (SRN, SEN)	23
Nursing auxiliary or care attendant	48
Home help	10
Hospital domestic	10
Other (e.g. community worker, sheltered housing)	9
Number of helpers	60

(c) Matching carer and care-giver

It was attempted to 'match' individual helpers and clients using the kind of detail that is more usually associated with foster care placements for children.

The matching process was greatly facilitated by the prior recruitment of a pool of potential helpers. In considering who would best relate to a particular elderly person, attention was paid to factors such as personality, attitudes and coping strengths in addition to obvious features such as availability and geographical proximity.

Previous experience might equip helpers particularly well for some clients. An elderly person who was extremely sick and receiving much nursing care could be reassured by a person with nursing experience. Such a person was able to feed back relevant information to the social worker so that appropriate action could be taken. Attitudes and beliefs also influenced matching decisions, since some helpers found dirty conditions or incontinence difficult to tolerate. Some people who had worked in care settings where there were always staff on duty, experienced difficulty in leaving elderly people alone at night. Since help was more likely to be effectively provided by those who could tolerate certain hazards, attitude to risk was considered a necessary component in matching.

Personality also played a part in the matching of client and helper, as some helpers appeared more able to tolerate dependency and cope with manipulative behaviour than others. Where an elderly person apparently tended to manipulate their care network it was useful to involve a helper who could recognise what was going on, avoid being drawn into the process, and yet respond to appropriate demands. Again, helpers with a tendency towards 'cosseting' or 'overprotectiveness' were thought very unsuitable for an elderly person where the care objectives were to increase independence. Conversely, a person with a rather businesslike manner was likely to be suited to an elderly person whose needs were predominantly practical. Matching had to be concerned not only with the helper and elderly person, but also the congruence between helper and the existing care network, both formal and informal. This was obviously the case with significant informal carers, but also where formal carers, such as a home help, had a long-established relationship with the elderly person and where carers were likely to meet one another regularly.

Undoubtedly, there were a number of helpers whose personal characteristics made them acceptable to a wide range of elderly people, and in rural districts the opportunities for matching were greatly reduced. Nevertheless, the idea of matching - devising a 'fit' between the needs of the elderly person, the care network and the helper - appeared crucial for the effective interweaving of care.

(d) Introducing helpers

Introduction of a helper to an elderly person usually followed a briefing discussion with the helper about the elderly person and their needs, the objectives of help, general guidance about possible approaches and consideration of difficulties which might arise. During a joint visit at which the social worker would introduce the helper and client, precise responsibilities and tasks were discussed. Arrangements about fees were usually made with helpers after this first joint visit, since discussions were then more realistic. Fees were a matter for social workers and helpers, clients not being involved. These arrangements were formalised by a letter of agreement or 'contract' which specified the care objectives, the particular tasks expected of the helper and the fee to be paid. This made explicit the degree of commitment and the expectations of the social services department.

Soon after the introduction of a helper to an elderly person, consideration was given to providing some 'back-up' to the helper who was most closely involved. From the beginning, most cases had more than one helper, and they proved more than willing to substitute for one another at times of domestic crisis, illness or holiday. At times they arranged this informally. Where only one helper was involved, it was usually considered desirable to introduce another, albeit with only a small commitment, to alleviate the possible anxiety of the elderly person that their helper might be ill and unable to come. The introduction of new helpers into an existing care network was a more complex process than initial introduction, since it was necessary to take into account not only the match between helper and elderly person but also the new helper's fit with the existing network and their relationship with other helpers.

From an early stage, clarification of roles and commitments was essential in those cases where several helpers were involved in care. Naturally, helpers tended to provide care in very individual ways, and the elderly people would respond differently to each of them. In order to avoid any element of competition among helpers for the attention of the client, each helper was introduced to the others involved. Where necessary, group meetings were arranged by the social worker to share ideas about care and identify any difficulties experienced. Contact often led to friendships and a willingness to back one another up should the need arise. Such arrangements were reported to the social worker, as coordinator of care, to avoid misunderstandings and the risk of one helper's goodwill being exploited by another. Regular communication reduced the danger that some helpers might go far beyond the terms of the agreement, thereby creating expectations on the part of the elderly person of a level of care which would not be met by other helpers who might need to substitute for them on either a temporary or permanent basis.

(e) Payment of helpers

Following introduction of helper to client, any necessary adjustment to the proposed fee could be madc and thc contract re specified. However, although the fee paid was in theory subject to negotiation between helper and social worker, in practice helpers tended to be unwilling to negotiate and would

Table 6.4
Rate paid per helper visit, £ at 1977 prices

Group	Rate £
All cases	1.75
Dependency Group 1*	1.11
Dependency Group 2*	2.27
Dependency Group 3*	1.37
Dependency Group 4*	1.49

*Dependency levels are defined in Chapter 2. The least dependent are in Group 1 and the most dependent in Group 4.

accept the fee offered. Indeed, some helpers said that they found the idea of bargaining unacceptable, since to appear to be 'in it only for the money' would be to offend their sense of self-esteem. Since helpers were unwilling to broach the issue of extra tasks they had undertaken or the appropriateness of payment received, it appeared clear that the social workers had to take the lead in reviewing activities and recompense.

Contracts, or letters of agreement, specified a level of payment for tasks rather than the amount of time spent in their performance. This combined a precise statement of what was required with the principle of flexibility which was central to the scheme. The wording of the letter of agreement read 'the contract is for the performance of the duties rather than the amount of time spent on the duties'. Initially weekly sets of tasks and rates of payment were specified, but experience of the first six months of operation led to the standardisation of arrangements based on a fee per visit. This proved to be both more precise and flexible, allowing for extra visits to be made in response to ill-health or other deterioration, with the minimum of extra administration.

The level of payment for any particular set of tasks would vary according to the nature of the tasks, whether the helper was asked to undertake the activity at short notice or at inconvenient times such as evenings or weekends, or had to travel a long distance, or if the elderly person had personality or other characteristics making helping more unpleasant or difficult. Factors such as earnings limits and other circumstances of the helper also influenced the amounts paid, as did the team's awareness of local rates for similar activity. The team did not specify any fees for particular activities, having to take into account a wide range of factors for each case. Nevertheless it was regarded as important that each worker should keep within similar boundaries for similar tasks, so as to avoid a sense of injustice or unfairness between helpers. Careful discussion amongst team members of payment levels, particularly for any new tasks, served to standardise the amounts paid by allowing norms to emerge. The average payment per visit (which usually lasted between one and two hours) specified for the 427 contracts which covered the year's care of ninety-two clients was £1.75 at 1977 prices, ranging from £1-£3. This rate varied substantially with client dependency, as can be seen in Table 6.4.

At first it may appear surprising that there is not a clear relationship between cost and dependency, but there are several explanations for this. First, those in Dependency Group 2 were most likely to be living alone, and therefore the cost per visit would not be shared as in higher dependency cases. Secondly, within this group were some of the more difficult cases with psychiatric disorders, drink problems and unrewarding personality characteristics. These were factors likely to be taken into account by the social workers in the fees paid.

In the interests of equity, as the scheme developed across the local authority the social workers formalised the norms of payment which had developed earlier into more precise and explicit criteria for payment. Rigidity was avoided, allowing response to individual circumstances by specified 'bands' or ranges of payment. Within a given range, an individual worker could vary the fee as circumstances dictated. There were five bands. The lowest was concerned with the least demanding visits, and the second band with more demanding visits to more dependent clients, unpleasant tasks or awkward hours. The third band was concerned with whole day support either in the elderly person's home or the helper's home, and the fourth with night-sitting. The fifth band, the most expensive, related to short-term family placement.

Payment for the tasks specified in a contract was arranged following the completion of a claim form by the helper. This would be countersigned by the social worker and forwarded to the treasurer's department of the local authority. A cheque was then sent to the helper when the claim had been processed. Such a centralised system was inevitably cumbersome, involving stretched lines of communication giving increased opportunities for information loss and delay. To minimise administrative upheaval, helpers' fees were processed on the weekly payroll despite their not being formally classified as employees. This system was not designed for the scheme and was made to work principally by goodwill and cooperation on all sides. Only in the case of small and incidental travelling expenses was it possible for helpers to be paid directly from the local office account. The payment system represented a clear example of one of the many constraints facing innovation, namely the powerful pressure to conform to the requirements of existing structures. It required a great deal of liaison and negotiation with other departments of the local authority and an acquisition by the team members of detailed knowledge of National Insurance, taxation and benefit thresholds which could influence helpers' payments.

(f) Support of helpers

As we have seen, the basis of support to helpers was a readiness to respond to their needs. It began with the careful planning of the initial approach to and early phases of the relationship with the elderly person and their family, identifying possible difficulties and considering ways of handling them. Contact between social worker and helper was most frequent in the early stages of the helping relationship when any uncertainty or difficulties would be likely to emerge. It subsequently varied according to the needs and demands of the elderly person and the expectations of the helper.

A number of principles underlay the approach to helper support.

(i) Maintaining boundaries

Through time the contact between client and helper would take on a life of its own beyond that prescribed at the beginning. The social worker had however to protect helpers from the risk of overinvolvement, which could otherwise lead to their feeling excessively responsible and anxious for the elderly person. This required the worker to provide a framework and the boundaries within which a caring relationship could safely develop.

A second aspect of boundary maintenance which became apparent was in situations where helpers experienced role conflict as a result of their previous employment; for instance when a GP recognised a former community nurse when visiting a patient and requested her to administer an enema.

The maintenance of appropriate boundaries raised the important issue of achieving the right balance between control and direction on the one hand and informality and helper initiative on the other, as the team was anxious to avoid the experience of lack of direction complained of by participants in some voluntary schemes (Davies, 1977b).

(ii) Balancing needs and demands

Crucial to helper support was the objective that helping should be a satisfactory experience for both helper and helped. There was always a danger, recognised by team members in their desire to maximise the skills and abilities of individual helpers, that those who were competent in dealing with a particular kind of problem such as incontinence or mental frailty might be used excessively with difficult cases. In order to provide satisfaction it was seen as important that helpers involved with several clients had a suitable 'mix' of cases. Indeed, one helper commented that one visit to a pleasant old lady made up for all the other demanding individuals.

Similarly, it was important to make sure that the tasks were within the level of competence of any given helper. One helper, unsure whether she could cope with toileting an elderly woman, found the experience too much for her, which became evident to the old lady. The social worker had to respond quickly by giving this helper a less intimate activity with another client to restore her confidence and providing the elderly lady with another helper, since following this episode of apparent rejection there was little possibility of a relationship developing.

The need for support of individual helpers varied in relation to their original expressed motivations for participation in the scheme. Thus, for example, those hoping for employment in the social services at some later date were more likely to wish to participate in care planning and monitoring progress. In a few cases these helpers were asked to keep notes of their visits and observations as an additional task. Other helpers whose motivations were associated with a desire for increased social contact particularly valued group meetings. It also appeared that in general working-class helpers seemed to desire more direction and supervision than the more middle-class helpers (Qureshi *et al.*, 1983).

(iii) Ensuring financial payments remain appropriate

As tasks and difficulties in care increased with dependency, the team was conscious of the need to review payments and whether they adequately reflected current circumstances, such as changes in the elderly person's circumstances, additional tasks undertaken or the effects of inflation.

(iv) Recognition of helpers' own needs and difficulties

On occasions helpers with very extensive family responsibilities, for example caring for an elderly parent or handicapped child, appeared to have chosen involvement with the scheme as an escape from these demands or even to provide them with a legitimate activity outside the confines of their own homes. Others experienced problems such as marital or child management difficulties. Such individuals on occasions indicated a need for support or advice in coping with their domestic difficulties. In such situations the scheme social worker would offer support through a particular crisis or suggest facilities or agencies which could offer help, but would avoid giving professional help. This could be a difficult decision to take since a helper with personal problems might experience the response as rejection and a failure to meet their needs.

(v) Group support and informal helper networks

While helper support was usually undertaken on an individual basis, there were occasions when a group basis was more appropriate. General group support took the form of a regular coffee morning, organised once a month by the team. It gave the helpers an opportunity to meet socially, discuss common problems and pass on important general items of news. On a few occasions the coffee mornings were used to provide an element of training, discussing such issues as health problems and financial benefits for the elderly. Consideration was given to more systematic training which has developed in the scheme elsewhere, involving issues such as lifting, welfare rights and understanding the effects of illness (Challis *et al.*, 1983). However, at the time this was decided against for fear of losing certain helpers for whom training would be too formal, and of creating an 'elite' of trained helpers. At a more task-related level, some elderly people would have a number of different helpers working with them and as we have noted small group meetings of these helpers would be arranged. These groups, concerned with one elderly person, tended to develop a clear sense of identity and purpose, and some helpers would refer to such gatherings as 'their section'. The groups meant that back-up to individual helpers was usually readily available and that relief could be given without substituting a stranger into the elderly person's home. On occasions when a difficulty arose at the last minute, helpers would contact one another to ensure that particular needs were met. The social work team, while encouraging this growth of informal contacts, saw it as their role to monitor any informal back-up arrangements to ensure that no helper was exploited by others.

(vi) Acceptance of ultimate responsibility for client welfare

Two features of the scheme valued by helpers were the clarity of their functions and the overall responsibility of an accountable agency. In day-to-day practice this meant that the social work team had to be receptive to helpers' suggestions about extra needs, to accept the responsibility for managing crises and liaising with other agencies, and to assist helpers to withdraw from a case when the difficulties and demands proved too great for them. Finally they had to make the ultimate decision when the scheme should no longer continue and to help the elderly person come to terms with the need for institutional care.

However, the lack of a departmental out-of-hours service, so that only police or the health service were available at night, posed a real problem for helpers. In the event of any serious difficulty occuring at night without access to advice or someone to take the crucial decision, perhaps an excessive responsibility was placed by the social services separtment on individual helpers. To some extent this problem was resolved informally by helpers spending the night in a client's home and social workers being contacted at home in the evenings and weekends. However, such arrangements cannot be entirely adequate and the absence of more formal support was an unresolved problem.

(g) Turnover among helpers

Of the 104 helpers, one-third remained in the scheme for more than a year, but one-half were involved for less than six months (Table 6.5). Nearly all the turnover was due to 'natural causes', that is to say a change in personal circumstances such as a new job, the helpers' or their families' health, moving house or pregnancy. However, in ten cases helpers had left because of unsatisfying experiences with the scheme. The reasons given are shown in Table 6.6.

Table 6.5
Turnover of helpers

Length of time in scheme	%
Less than six months	49
More than six but less than twelve months	32
Twelve months or more	19
Number of helpers	104

Table 6.6
Helpers leaving project for reasons other than 'natural wastage'

Reason	N
'Client too demanding'	3
'Client felt to require institutional care'	2
Tax and national insurance difficulty	2
'Client unpleasant/unrewarding'	1
'Task/activity too boring'	1
'Wanted social work support'	1
Number of helpers	10

Three helpers felt that the client had been too demanding. One of these was a neighbour whose help and payment by the scheme made the old lady more unreasonable. It was as if she felt that the relationship between her and her neighbour had been changed by the formalisation of her involvement. When the helper decided to cease helping through the scheme, she continued to help informally. In the case of two clients the helpers felt that they needed institutional care but the elderly person adamantly refused. The helpers felt that to continue to support them at home went against their own better judgement. Two helpers experienced difficulty with reconciling the payments from community care with their other income and supplements such as housing benefit. This became so complicated that they ceased helping on a paid basis although both continued to visit the elderly clients on a voluntary basis. One helper had to deal with a difficult elderly woman who was aggressive and unpleasant to her; one felt that her tasks were not demanding enough; and one woman, a single parent with multiple problems, had wanted personal help from the community care team.

A detailed study of helpers (Qureshi *et al.*, 1983) also examined a second topic related to helper turnover. This was to identify the factors associated with sustained involvment in caring. Of particular importance were gaining a sense of usefulness and purpose, commitment to the scheme itself and receiving payment. However, the factor which most successfully identified sustained involvement proved to be previous employment experience with elderly people (Qureshi *et al.*, 1983). Dealing with people who were extremely frail and who could be difficult or confused was no easy task. Clearly, people who had worked in relevant occupations had realistic expectations and were likely to feel confident enough to sustain their involvement.

(h) The status of helpers

The official status of helpers was that they were not employees of the local authority but 'agents' for which they received a fee. A parallel to this is the way in which some local authorities used to 'contract out' certain services for the visually handicapped and the hard of hearing to the relevant national voluntary organisation. When helpers were visiting client's homes they were insured for injury and third-party liability through the local authority's general insurance cover. However, the issue of helper status was an area of continuing negotiation between the local authority and other agencies. Three factors were pertinent to this.

(i) Both the Inland Revenue and the National Insurance section of the Department of Health and Social Security saw the relationship between the helper and the social services department as akin to employment for their purposes. This was the case even for helpers receiving clients into their own homes, which was unlike the ruling made for foster parents (National Foster Care Association, 1981). It was therefore agreed that where helpers received sufficient payment from the scheme to be liable for tax or National Insurance contributions these should be deducted at source. Similarly, where helpers were eligible to receive statutory sick pay then this would be paid by the social services department on the basis of an employer/employee relationship. However, in practice these arrangements were relevant to very few helpers. Less than one in ten was in a position where deduction of tax or National Insurance was required.

(ii) A small number of helpers, because of their ability and energy, undertook a very considerable amount of care and it is likely that their interests would have been better served had they been subject to conditions of service with a suitable job description. This would have entitled them to paid holidays and similar benefits.

(iii) However, the use of helpers from a wide range of backgrounds and experience was essential to the effectiveness of the scheme. The majority of helpers were not, and did not wish to be, used intensively for several clients as were the few helpers referred to above. Classifying all helpers as employees would have excluded people over retirement age and others not eligible for employment. It would not necessarily have conferred additional benefits on most helpers since they would have only been eligible for 'casual' terms and conditions. Furthermore, other helpers said that they would be unwilling to accept the conditions of formal local authority employment for a relatively small amount of activity, since it could involve form-filling and medical examinations. A longer-term danger of using an employment-based approach might be an increasing pressure to deploy an existing workforce according to the demands of guaranteed weeks rather than according to the needs of elderly people. Currently, helpers have been administratively classified as employees, but usually without age and other restrictions being imposed.

In retrospect, the resolution of this apparent dilemma (between the risks of exploitation of helpers on the one hand and inflexible and inappropriate responses to elderly people on the other) requires two complementary approaches. A scheme for long-term care of the elderly at home needs to be able to employ a small group of permanent home care staff who can undertake the full extent of personal care, domestic and social tasks and also to be able in addition to pay a wide range of other people as and when required to undertake some care tasks on a flexible basis.

2. Helpers and Clients

The tasks specified on the contracts provided a basis for assessing the inputs made by helpers, and the contracts over one year were collated for each case. However, it must be remembered that, as in any caring relationship, helpers assisted clients in a variety of other ways which were not recorded on the contracts.

(a) Tasks undertaken by helpers

The contracts issued covered a wide range of activities from practical help with daily living to more therapeutic objectives such as accompanying a phobic old lady on short walks of increasing length, or reactivating old interests and skills.

There were 427 contracts specifying 1,096 tasks for 104 helpers issued in the care of the ninety-two clients over one year. The number of contracts per case over one year ranged from none to nineteen. Those clients on whose behalf a large number of contracts were issued were the most dependent. Each contract therefore specified on average between two and three tasks which could be divided into eight categories: 'help at night and morning', 'help with personal care', 'help with daily household activities', 'help with weekly household activities', 'social and therapeutic activities', 'family support activities', 'assessment and enabling' and 'back-up/support'. Table 6.7 shows the breakdown of tasks in these different categories.

Table 6.7
Tasks specified in contracts with helpers

Task type	%
Help at night and morning	9
Help with personal care	16
Help with daily household care	28
Help with weekly household care	19
Therapeutic activities	21
Carer support	4
Assessment and enabling	2
Back-up or support of helpers	1
Number of tasks	1,096

It can be seen that personal care activities, both night and morning and otherwise, constituted one-quarter of the help provided; nearly one-half involved household activities; and one-fifth of the help provided was concerned to raise morale and reactivate social skills. The tasks undertaken within each of these broad categories can be examined further. The range and extent of activities undertaken are wider both in type and time of response than those which would be typically expected of a domiciliary care service. Helpers themselves, particularly those who had worked in caring occupations such as former home helps and nurses, were anxious to stress the difference between the 'task' approach with its flexibility and the more rigid 'hours' approach usual when dealing with clients in an employed capacity. This difference was valued greatly by them.

(i) Night and morning tasks

These constituted slightly less than one-tenth of the help provided for the most frail. Table 6.8 shows that most of these activities were concerned with retiring to bed rather than getting up. An example is Miss G., who spent the day in her wheelchair but was unable to transfer from chair to bed without help, and had to retire to bed at 6 p.m. which was the latest time when the nursing service was available. The scheme made it possible for her to retire to bed considerably later and to enjoy evening television programmes.

Table 6.8. Helpers' activities at night and morning

Getting up	8
Dressing	17
Retiring to bed	5
Number of tasks undertaken night and morning	100

(ii) Personal care activities

The range of personal care activities was very wide (Table 6.9). The most important were check-up visits (41 per cent), which helped to minimise the length of solitude of an elderly person otherwise at risk. A significant amount of help involved helping people with toileting (21 per cent) and bathing and washing (12 per cent). For many cases there was no one else to do this and as a result valuable cooperation developed with the district nursing service. For some confused and disorientated clients, helpers supervised their medication. This could avoid the development of a toxic confusional state superimposed on their level of dementia. In some instances day care, particularly for elderly demented people, was made possible only because helpers prepared and settled the client at the beginning and end of the day. A small proportion of tasks, 7 per cent, were more comprehensive. These were activities such as boarding out, or day care of the elderly person in a helper's home.

Table 6.9. Helpers' tasks in personal care

Task	%
Check-up visits	41
Toileting and commode	21
Bathing and washing; hair care	12
Prepare and settle before and after day care	9
Supervision of medication	7
Boarding-out; day care at helpers' home; night-sitting	7
Helping in emergencies	2
Improve hygiene/cleanliness	1
Number of tasks	177

(iii) Daily household tasks

Help provided during the day was often ancillary to more basic tasks such as check-up visits, or providing stimulation and support. One of the most common forms of help given was with meals and snacks, which comprised over one-half of this group of activities. There are a number of reasons for this. First, the meals-on-wheels service was insufficiently frequent, being unavailable at weekends, the food arrived too early to be eaten whilst hot and could not be readily reheated, and sometimes people did not find it appetising and as a result did without a main meal. Second, the provision of food, however appetising, was insufficient for many people since they required stimulation and encouragement to eat it. Third, helpers often provided meals in the evenings and at weekends. Fourth, in certain cases meals of an unusual kind had to be provided.

A second item was daily housework. This consisted of routine activities, such as washing up, particularly at weekends or in the evening when the home help service was not available. Providing an elderly person with hot drinks consisted of more than one-tenth of these activities, often part of a late evening visit. The provision of fuel and regular checking of coal fires was part of these activities, as was the care of pets, involving tasks such as exercising dogs and feeding cats, who might have been crucial to an old person's desire to continue at home. The tasks are shown in Table 6.10.

Table 6.10. Helpers' tasks in daily household care

Task	%
Meals and snacks/encourage to eat	63
Daily household jobs	20
Provision of drinks	12
Help with domestic pets	3
Assist with coal fire	2
Number of tasks	312

(iv) Weekly or less frequent household care tasks

Most of the basic household tasks were carried out by the home help service, but there were certain infrequent activities such as shopping for less routine items, for example clothes, or the collection of prescriptions. In certain cases the helper would take the elderly person out shopping so that they could again choose their own purchases. This was inevitably time-consuming. The second largest group of activities were 'one-off' activities such as odd jobs, errands and accompanying elderly people to appointments with opticians or to outpatient departments. Often the support of a helper was sufficient for the old person to undertake the effort of keeping an appointment to which there was in any case no other means of transport.

Laundry and washing of soiled linen formed 19 per cent of activities, the latter reflecting the lack of an incontinence laundry service. As was described earlier, on occasions the handling of substantial amounts of soiled laundry posed a real obstacle to continued home care. Transporting and escorting clients to day hospital enabled some people to receive treatment which they would otherwise not have received. For a number of people, particularly those with difficulty in maintaining continence, a lengthy ambulance journey was a serious disincentive to continuing valuable treatment. However, a direct and comfortable car journey could make it worthwhile for them to attend. In a small number of cases, usually where there was a problem of mental frailty, helpers, under the direction of the social worker, assisted elderly people to manage their finances. Routine housework hardly featured at all in the tasks specified. Where ordinary housework was undertaken it was as part of an attempt to re-involve the old person in the care of their own home, or on a few occasions helping to clean out a home which had become particularly foul.

The range and frequency of weekly household tasks are shown in Table 6.11.

Table 6.11. Helpers' tasks in weekly household care

Task	%
Shopping, prescriptions, etc.	31
Odd jobs, errands, appointments	23
Washing soiled linen	13
Transporting/escorting	12
Laundry	7
Managing finances	6
Housework activities	5
Cleaning neglected and foul home	3
Number of tasks	203

(v) Social and therapeutic tasks

These activities constituted one-fifth of the tasks specified, although this is probably an underestimate since some activities of this type, such as encouraging an apathetic person to eat or re-engage them in home care, have been recorded as instrumental activities. The most important aspect was to deal with loneliness and isolation. Activities to improve the quality of life were the second highest group. These ranged from playing games with an elderly person to taking them on outings. On occasions an outing was of importance for other reasons than stimulation. One contract arranged for a helper to take a chronically anxious man, who had been unable to come to terms with his wife's death, to place flowers regularly on her grave, and to assist him come to terms with the loss. Therapeutic activities were the next most important of this group, accounting for 16 per cent of these tasks. They ranged from helping clients to deal with their anxieties both specific and general, and supporting the recently bereaved by giving them an opportunity to talk about their loss, through to activities of a rehabilitative nature, such as helping a person to regain their confidence and to recover lost skills. One example of this was the behavioural approach to the agoraphobic elderly lady described earlier. Related to these activities was the stimulation or reactivitation of old interests, as with the man who was encouraged to take up his old hobby of wine-making. In a few cases rehabilitation was attempted by a helper who was a retired physiotherapist. Helpers were also involved in relation to institutional care. For example, helpers visited their clients in hospital to prepare them for their discharge, or in one case to help prepare an old person for entry to residential care.

The therapeutic and morale-raising tasks are shown in Table 6.12.

Table 6.12
Social and therapeutic tasks undertaken by helpers

Task type	**%**
Companionship or relieve loneliness	45
Specific activity, e.g. games, outing	19
Therapeutic activities	17
Stimulate old interest	15
Rehabilitation - exercises	2
Visit or support in institutional care	1
Number of tasks	235

(vi) Tasks related to support of informal carers

Indirectly a number of instrumental tasks already discussed will have been designed to provide relief to informal carers. Nevertheless, on occasions it was clearly specified in contracts that tasks were designed for the relief of carers. There were three kinds of task. The most common of these was where helpers were asked to relieve a carer of a specific activity. One example was of a stepdaughter who wanted someone to sit with her father at certain times so that she could attend evening classes. The next most frequent form of help was to assist a carer with a task she could no longer manage single-handed: for example dressing or bathing an old person. The third group of tasks involved direct support for the carers themselves, for instance providing an isolated wife with companionship and giving them an opportunity to share their anxieties. These activities are shown in Table 6.13.

Table 6.13
Support to informal carer provided by helpers

Task type	%
Relief or assistance; fit into carer's routine	37
Assist carer jointly with practical task	33
General support for carer	30
Number of tasks	46

(vii) Other tasks

There were two other areas of activity listed in Table 6.7 which accounted for only 3 per cent of the tasks undertaken by helpers. These were 'assessment and enabling' and 'back-up or support of other helpers'.

Involvement of helpers in assessment and enabling was necessary in certain cases. Where mental frailty was a significant factor it was difficult to discern the extent of difficulty or the ability to cope. Over a period of time the helper could glean valuable information so that care could more effectively be planned. For example, a contract with a suspicious elderly woman read: 'Visit Mrs. S with the hope of establishing a relationship with her that might allow provision of a meal and assistance into bed'.

The 'back-up' contracts were sometimes arranged by the social workers to cover periods of sickness over public holidays. Sometimes helpers had arranged cover with other helpers in a personal crisis, such as a child's sickness. On such occasions the social worker might issue a retrospective contract to cover the activity undertaken.

(b) Helper tasks and client dependency

Table 6.14 shows the tasks undertaken for cases in each of the four categories of dependency, except the very small number of back-up/support contracts. As might be expected, the Table shows that the nature of the tasks was associated with the level of dependency.

Table 6.14 Helper activity by dependency level

Task type	Dependency Group			
	1 %	2 %	3 %	4 %
Help at night and morning	3	4	5	20
Help with personal care	8	18	15	18
Help with daily home care	13	27	35	31
Help with weekly home care	23	23	24	7
Therapeutic activities	45	23	15	17
Carer support	6	2	4	6
Assessment or enabling	2	2	2	1
Number of tasks	111	416	238	326

It can be seen that the proportion of tasks directed towards therapeutic activities, such as raising morale or developing interests, tended to decrease with dependency. This is not surprising since it would be in Dependency Groups 1 and 2 where problems of depression and anxiety were predominant. In the more dependent cases aspects of basic care were more pressing. The distribution of personal care activities seems less clearly associated with dependency than might have been expected. However, whereas for Dependency Groups 1 and 2 (the less physically frail) 'check-up' visits constituted more than half of these activities, virtually none were 'check-up' visits in Dependency Group 4, where tasks were more concerned with actual physical care. If both rising and retiring and personal care tasks are considered together, then there is a clearer difference between low and high dependency.

Help with daily home care proved to be important in all cases. The most important task in this domain proved to be help with meals. This ranged from encouragement and assistance in preparation and consumption for the more depressed and apathetic individuals, to actual provision and supervision in cases suffering from dementia.

Dependency also influenced the number of tasks which were undertaken for clients. Over one year the number of tasks undertaken increased with dependency, from 7.4 per case in Dependency Group 1 to 17.4 per case in Dependency Group 4. This was also reflected in the average number of contracts issued over the year which ranged from 2.9 for Dependency Group 1 to 6.2 for Dependency Group 4.

(c) Client-helper relationships: the shift towards informal care

The social workers saw helpers as having a separate and distinct contribution to make to the care of the elderly. It was not simply care to meet basic instrumental needs of daily living, however important this was, but care with an affective basis which in many respects resembled that of informal care. Nonetheless, initially the relationship between client and helper was a formal one; carer and cared for were in many cases strangers introduced by a third party, and the activities and objectives of the helper were spelled out in a formal letter of agreement. However, interviews with helpers who had been involved with a client for a considerable time indicated that the importance of the contract had diminished (Qureshi *et al.*, 1983). For these people, a relationship had developed with the elderly person whom they helped and the tasks and activities undertaken had broadened out, albeit within the original planned approach.

The development of this relationship, where the original formal approach grew into a personal exchange between helper and helped - in short the move towards informal care - could be observed in four ways (Qureshi *et al.*, 1983). First, helpers undertook tasks which were not required in the original contract. They tended to do more and different tasks for their clients. Second, helpers developed strong attachments to individual clients and were unwilling to change, even when for other reasons this might have been convenient for them. People would retain contact with clients even after leaving the scheme. Third, in many cases a feeling of personal responsibility emerged, a feeling which some helpers likened to their responsibility for dependent members of their families such as children. Fourth, helpers with families tended to involve them in looking after the elderly person. Husbands would do odd jobs in people's homes, young children visited and elderly people were taken for meals to helpers' homes.

These developments for some helpers flowed almost imperceptibly from their helping the elderly person, so that identification of needs, meeting them and sharing their family life appeared to them a natural development of which they were almost unaware. For others, the non-instrumental quasi-informal care was an important reward for participating in the scheme. This appeared to be particularly true for people who had worked in relevant occupations, but wished the scheme to provide more than the job had done. In short, they perceived the caring exchange as something more than one between two strangers, providing the opportunity for informal care relationships to develop. Thus, for example, one helper stressed the importance of doing things with the old person rather than for them. Of course, as we have discussed earlier, the development of informal caring relationships within the scheme could have disadvantages too. Helpers could be exposed to manipulation by clients, and it was important that the social worker knew the extent of helpers' commitment. At times the contract would be used by both social worker and helper to limit overinvolvement, avoid exploitation and prevent one helper creating unrealistic expectations that could not be met by others.

Clients also frequently perceived the relationship as like informal care. In a number of cases the helper was perceived as if they were a substitute family member. This was particularly noticeable where a client had little contact with their family. It has already been noted how one elderly woman described how she and the helper would keep in touch in the evening by telephone, just as she would with a daughter. One man, feeling somewhat rejected by his own daughter, described with relish the meals provided by a helper and noted the fact that she undertook sewing and clothes-mending for him just like a daughter might do. Other clients perceived their helpers more as friends. One lady recounted a story of how the helper had taken her and an elderly friend to her own home for tea. Reciprocity was also made possible. One client who had not been out of her home for a long while took her helper to a pub, where the old lady was able to enjoy a glass of stout for the first time in many years. At Christmas time it was noticeable the extent to which helpers took clients into their own homes for the day. One helper described this as akin to having a lonely aunt, and therefore a moral obligation at Christmas. Of course, the sharing of a helper's home was more difficult in cases where the elderly person suffered from incontinence. On the three occasions when helpers were family members and actual informal carers, the scheme appeared to improve the informal caring relationship by relieving the stress which the carer experienced. For example, one daughter after receiving help from the scheme over some nine months moved to another county to be nearer relatives. In a letter to the social work team she said: 'Who would have thought that mother at 88 years old would have been able to start a new life with us in Suffolk. I am sure that without the extra time and attention I was able to give her and the help we had from the social services department it would not have been possible ... Community care has done so much for my mother - she is almost a new woman'.

However, whilst clients clearly appreciated the relationships which they developed with helpers, they also seemed to welcome the formal arrangement, for regularity, reliability and quality. For example, one elderly woman, finding that her helper was paid, said: 'That's good. So often these voluntary people come, then wave goodbye and that's the last you see of them'. This lady perceived the involvement of the social services and the fact that the helper was paid as likely to produce more regular and reliable support. An elderly gentleman who was very satisfied with the help he received from the scheme, clearly had lower expectations of voluntary help. Commenting on his low opinion of the food provided by the meals-on-wheels service he said: 'What can you expect, they're only voluntary'. For this man, a service whose providers were paid by the social services department was expected to be of higher quality. There is an apparent contradiction in this valuation by clients of formal aspects of the community care scheme and their satisfaction with the informal relationships which it generated. This contradiction can perhaps be most readily understood in the light of exchange theory. Exchange theory (Dowd, 1975) would suggest that elderly people, unable to reciprocate in a caring exchange by giving, are able to relax in the knowledge that provision by a third party, in this case the social services department, can equalise the exchange. Such an equalised exchange is compatible with the maintenance of the elderly person's self-respect and dignity.

5. Conclusions

A recent review of research in social care of the elderly concluded that social workers' 'roles as mobilisers of resources, coordinators of services and resource persons to a variety of other carers or caring schemes may have to expand considerably' (Goldberg and Connelly, 1982, p.114). The analysis of approaches to work with helpers provides one example of how this role expansion might occur, by decentralising control of resources to individual fieldworkers.

However, it would be mistaken to see the mobilisation of community resources as a sufficient end in itself. This would be to neglect the personal context of individual need and in the social care of the elderly would maintain the false dichotomy so often posed between practical and other forms of help. As Stevenson argues 'if social work is *only* about promoting, stimulating and supporting community networks, then some other occupational group will have to move in or be invented to offer service to those with specific and complex psychological difficulties' (Stevenson, 1981c, p.19). Thus case management is required, as well as enhanced care from community and other resources. The evidence of the community care scheme suggests the interdependence of the organisation of social care, the handling of specific and complex social and psychological difficulties, and the mobilisation of community resources.

CHAPTER 7

THE OUTCOME OF CARE

Our analysis of the outcome of the scheme is based on comparison of the effects of the experimental scheme with those of the standard range of provision received by the control group. The principles which influenced our choice of outcome and effectiveness indicators were discussed in Chapter 2. A range of different outcomes were examined. First, the destinational outcomes of elderly people over four years were considered, comparing the likelihood of remaining at home or entering institutional care. The remaining outcomes were concerned with measured differences between the groups rather than events. These factors were changes in the quality of life and health status of the elderly person, changes in the effects on family and informal carers and changes in the extensiveness of informal caring networks.

1. Patterns of Institutionalisation and Survival

(a) Location of elderly people after one year

Location was defined as the elderly person's permanent place of residence twelve months from the first assessment and again in subsequent years. So if an elderly person was in hospital for treatment after twelve months, but was to be discharged home in the future, their location would be defined as at home. In the case of elderly people for whom plans were indeterminate at the time, such as those in hospital where it was not clear whether their stay was permanent or temporary, location was determined with the advantage of hindsight.

Table 7.1 shows the location of seventy-four matched cases over a four-year period. There are very clear differences between the two groups after one year. Those receiving community care were far more likely to remain in their own homes (68 per cent compared with 34 per cent), were less likely to enter residential care (12 per cent compared with 27 per cent), and there appeared to be a marked difference in the death rate (14 per cent compared with 33 per cent). These differences between the outcomes of the two groups were statistically significant ($chi^2 = 24.54$; $p < .001$); that is to say the differences are unlikely to have occurred by chance and may be attributed to effects of alternative forms of care.

A similar pattern was evident for the full unmatched samples of cases, ninety-two in the community care scheme and 116 in the comparison group, as can be seen in Table 7.2. Whilst 66 per cent (sixty-one) of the community care scheme cases remained in their own homes, only 45 per cent (fifty-two) of the comparison group did so. Similarly, whereas 4 per cent (four) of the community care scheme clients had entered local authority homes, 16 per cent

Table 7.1 Location of matched pairs of cases over four years

	Year 1				Year 2				Year 3				Year 4			
	CCS		Std. Prov.		CCS		Std. Prov		CCS		Std. Prov.		CCS		Std. Prov	
	N	%	N	%	N	%	N	%	N	%	N	%	N	%	N	%
Own home	51	69	25	34	37	50	15	20	26	35	9	12	17	23	8	11
Local authority care	3	4	16	22	4	5	17	23	6	8	15	20	4	5	9	12
Private residential care	6	8	4	5	11	15	8	11	10	14	8	11	7	10	6	8
Hospital care	3	4	4	5	2	3	2	3	6	8	1	1	4	5	2	3
Died	10	14	24	33	19	26	30	40	24	32	39	53	39	53	47	63
Moved away	1	1	1	1	1	1	2	3	2	3	2	3	3	4	2	3
Total	74		74		74		74		74		74		74		74	

(eighteen) of the comparison group had done so. Significant differences in the death rate also remained evident, 16 per cent (fifteen) in the community care scheme and 28 per cent (thirty-two) in the comparison group. These differences in outcome were also significant ($chi^2 = 20.1$; $p < .01$).

Table 7.2.
Location of the community care and comparison groups after twelve months

Outcome	Community care group N	%	Comparison group N	%
Own home	61	66	52	45
Local authority care	4	4	18	16
Private residential care	7	7	6	5
Hospital care	3	3	5	4
Died	15	16	32	28
Moved away	2	2	3	2
Totals	92	100	116	100

(b) Location of elderly people over four years

One year is, of course, an insufficient period over which to judge these outcomes. It can be seen from Table 7.1 that the advantage of community care continues beyond the first year. In the first year the death rate, that is the proportion of cases who died, was 14 per cent for community care and 33 per cent for standard services. Although a few more people died proportionately in the experimental group during the second year, there was still a substantial difference in favour of the community care group, 26 per cent compared with 40 per cent. By the end of four years this advantage still remained, 53 per cent compared with 63 per cent. Examining admissions to residential care, it appeared that in the second year it was entry to private residential homes which increased in both groups. However, the relative advantage of community care remained, in that a lower proportion of this group were in residential homes overall.

Over the third year it appeared that there had been a slight increase in admission of community care cases to long-term hospital care, although it was less evident in year four. This trend was to be expected, since a number of cases had remained in their own homes until their physical condition made long-term hospital care the only feasible option. Clearly there are implications in this for closer collaboration between the social services and the National

Health Service in the care of the very frail. By the end of the fourth year, the proportions of cases in institutional care were similar, and twice as many who had received the community care scheme remained in their own homes.

(c) Reasons for admission to residential homes

Detailed information was only available for the first year of each elderly person's period of care. Since the main objective of the scheme was to reduce the need for admission to institutional care, it is helpful to examine the reasons for entry to long-term care. There were fifteen such cases, fourteen of whom survived the one year follow-up period, one having died in hospital. Four were admitted to long-term hospital care and the rest entered residential homes. The prime reasons for entry to institutional care are summarised in Table 7.3 and appeared to be factors beyond the control of the social work team. For twelve of the clients, the reasons for admission were either health-related, or concerned with exogenous events such as a fall, or the death of a carer. Two people made a positive decision to go into a home, leaving only one case whose entry would be described as for 'negative' reasons. In this case there was a dispute about the client between two daughters who could not agree how to share the care for their mother, despite the efforts of the social worker. It was probably more satisfactory for the old lady to be in a residential home than to be the centre of a family conflict.

Table 7.3
Reasons for entry to long-term institutional care among community care clients

Reasons	N
Serious decline in physical health	7
Following a fall	2
Dementia and associated behaviour patterns	2
Family discord	1
Death of carer	1
Personal choice	2
Number of clients	15

The differences between the groups were largely due to the experimental group having a lower probability of entry to local authority residential care. There was little difference between the numbers entering private residential care and hospital care in the two groups. An examination of the process of entry to private and local authority residential care provides some explanation for this. Over the whole of the two samples of cases, of the thirteen elderly people who entered private homes for long-term care, eight came direct from hospital, whereas of the twenty-two cases entering local authority residential homes twenty-one came directly from their own homes. It appeared that a significant proportion of people entering private residential homes were placed there following involvement of hospital social work staff. One reason might be that transfer to a private home would release hospital beds in circumstances where the local authority waiting list was long. A second might be that it had been decided that community support was no longer a reasonable alternative. Conversely, the entrants to local authority homes came directly from their own homes, and there was therefore more opportunity to prevent these admissions by the provision of additional community support. This interpretation is consistent with the history of the seven elderly people in the community care group who entered private homes. Of these, four were admitted to private residential homes from hospital when it had been decided by all parties that continued community support was no longer a realistic alternative. There were diverse reasons for entry among the remaining three. One elderly person had the arrangements made by their relatives during a period of turmoil in the family; one entered by choice having experienced the home during a period of short-term care; and a third entered a home following a relationship which was made as a result of a boarding-out arrangement.

(d) Possible explanations of differences in the probability of death

Differences in survival rates were less expected than differences in institutional admission. Nevertheless, this has been observed in other studies (Ratna, 1982; Hendriksen *et al.*, 1984; Vetter *et al.*, 1984). Here we consider some of the factors which may have influenced this finding.

Three possible explanations are considered. First, whether there were important dissimilarities between experimental and control group cases. Second, we examine the possible effect on survival of differences in admission to institutional care, and third we consider whether the nature of the service itself could have been influential.

(i) Group similarities and differences

Before any conclusions of experimental effect may be drawn, it is essential to assess whether members of the comparison group were more frail or vulnerable than their counterparts in the experimental group. A number of studies have identified a range of characteristics consistently associated with non-survival in elderly populations. The influence of poor memory, physical disability, organic brain syndrome and other psychiatric disorders is frequently noted (Kay *et al.*, 1962, 1966; Palmore, 1969; Gilmore, 1975). Social factors may influence survival as well as physical and psychiatric disorders. Lieberman (1971) has suggested that the influence of poor cognitive functioning is particularly potent for those elderly people undergoing stressful experiences. Berkmann and Syme (1979) found an association between the extent of social support and mortality that was independent of factors such as physical symptomatology, health care provision and physical inactivity. The most significant components of the social network influencing survival were found to be intimate ties of marriage and contacts with friends or relatives. In another study, Blazer (1981) found that as well as physical and cognitive impairments, lack of perceived social support and impaired roles and attachments were significant predictors of mortality. Kastenbaum and Kastenbaum (1971) have suggested that the elderly person's survival can be influenced by the psychological mechanism of hope, and for some 'learned hopelessness' can be crucial. Tobin and Lieberman (1976), examining admissions to residential homes, found that many of the negative effects usually associated with institutional care, including high mortality, could be traced to a process of 'giving up' prior to admission to residential care.

In matching cases, particular attention had been paid to achieving similarity with respect to physical frailty, confusion, incontinence, social support, age and sex, which should therefore have reduced the likelihood of significant differences in vulnerability between the groups. However, it was naturally impossible to match by all the factors which might conceivably influence the probabilities of death or admission to institutions for long-term care. Therefore, the matched groups were compared on a wide range of criteria so as to reveal any differences which might partly account for the effects observed. No significant differences could be found between the community care scheme cases and comparison group in functional status, poor memory, or other correlates of organic brain disease (Bergmann *et al.*, 1975). In order to test for the possible effect of physical frailty, a fourth category of dependency was developed of the extremely frail consisting of those who were bedridden, chairbound or suffering from faecal incontinence, by further dividing into two the highest dependency group of cases. However, more of the matched cases in the community care group (fourteen) fell into this high dependency category than in the comparison group (nine). Therefore, there was no evidence that greater frailty in the comparison group could explain the differences in survival rates. Although there was no significant difference between the groups in terms of overall social support, the community care scheme cases did have more contact with neighbours, but this element of social support is unlikely to be an adequate explanation of the variations in survival. Also, cases were only matched for the *extensiveness* of their social support rather than for its *quality*. However, changes both in quality and extensiveness could have occurred as a result of enhanced care. Finally, the reduced death rate was evident in the unmatched cases as well as the matched ones (Table 7.2).

(ii) Relocation effects

An alternative explanation for the difference in death rates could be the changes occurring in care. These could be a single permanent relocation from a client's own home to institutional care, or a series of temporary relocations from one hospital to another or to residential homes. In their review of research on relocation of the elderly, Yawney and Slover (1973) note that adverse effects are most frequently observed at the 'impact stage', the period immediately following the move. It is at this time that increased mortality is most likely, some studies suggesting a doubling of the death rate over this first year, with the first three months being a critical period.

An examination of the possible impact of relocation on the elderly people was undertaken by first examining whether relocation from home to institution had an effect. Of the fifteen community care cases who died, twelve (80 per cent) were living at home and had not made a permanent move to institutional care, compared with nineteen of the thirty-two control group cases (59 per cent). This does not either confirm or refute the relocation hypothesis, although the difference in proportions is consistent with an explanation that the higher death rate can be partly accounted for by relocation. A second element of relocation which might be expected to have a negative impact was the number of moves which a frail elderly person experienced as they moved from treatment to convalescence to their own homes. However, there is no evidence that the comparison group cases experienced more 'disturbance' than the community care cases. The average number of 'moves' experienced by elderly people in the community care scheme was 1.27, compared with 1.28 for their counterparts. The average number of 'moves' for elderly people who died was 1.47 for the recipients of community care and 1.53 for recipients of standard provision. This provides little evidence to suggest that disturbance played a significant part in the observed variation in death rates. A third aspect could be the person's willingness to move. Schulz and Brenner (1977) suggest that controllability and predictability can reduce the negative impact of stressful experiences such as relocation and it is probable that the recipients of community care enjoyed greater choice and control over their destination. Indeed, interviews suggested that, for those who entered a residential home, it was a positive decision for a higher proportion of the recipients of community care than of standard provision. The existence of the community care scheme made it possible for elderly people to die in their own homes, or at least spend fewer of their last weeks in institutional care. Of the fifteen community care cases who died, nine (60 per cent) either died in their own homes or had been in hospital for less than one week before their death. Only eight (25 per cent) of the thirty-two cases receiving standard provision who died did so in their own homes or within a week of admission to an institution.

(iii) The effects of service provision

The nature, type and extent of services may also affect survival. Garraway *et al.* (1980) found that the acute outcome of stroke appeared to be influenced by whether treatment was provided in a specialist unit or in a general medical ward, only 19 per cent of the specialist unit cases dying, compared with 28 per cent of the general medical ward cases.

A community-oriented psychogeriatric service which used a predominantly social approach has demonstrated a lower death rate than other services (Ratna, 1982). In part this could be due to the prevention of admission to institutional care. Regular surveillance of elderly people in the community can also be significant. Vetter *et al.* (1984) examined the effects of a health visitor screening and monitoring elderly people. They noted in an urban area that there was a greater use of domiciliary social services and a decline in mortality. Screening of elderly people at three-monthly intervals over a three-year period in Denmark reduced both institutionalisation and mortality rates (Hendriksen *et al.*, 1984).

A number of studies have suggested that social support can influence mortality (Berkmann and Syme, 1979; Blazer, 1981). A significant increase in the number and quality of contacts was observed for the elderly persons receiving community care. Frequently these contacts developed into important relationships which were experienced by elderly people as similar to informal care (Qureshi *et al.*, 1983). It was certainly the objective of the community care social workers to provide social support which wherever possible would meet both practical and emotional needs. Thus, aware of the need to improve the low morale of many elderly people, they tended for instance to involve the elderly person more closely wherever possible in the planning of care. At follow-up, survivors in the community were asked whether they had anyone in whom they could confide, studies having suggested that this may be an important buffer mediating the effects of social stress (Brown and Harris, 1978; Miller and Ingham, 1976; Murphy, 1982). Whereas 58 per cent of the comparison group felt that they had no confidant, only 15 per cent of the community care scheme felt this, as can be seen in Table 7.4. Of the recipients of community care, 43 per cent answered that they would either confide in the community care scheme social workers or one of their helpers. Only 8 per cent of the recipients of standard provision felt that they could confide in the social worker or the home help organiser.

Table 7.4
Confiding relationships of clients

	Community care %	Standard provision %
None	15	58
Family	16	11
Other informal carer	23	19
Social services personnel (including community care helpers)	43	8
Other	3	4

In the absence of evidence to the contrary, one interpretation is that at least some of the difference in the death rate between the two groups was due to the different experiences of the process of care itself. There was a highly significant positive change in a measure of 'felt capacity to cope' for the community care scheme cases. This would indicate that clients would be less prone to 'giving up', a cause to which Tobin and Lieberman (1976) traced many of the negative effects usually associated with institutional care. Furthermore, there was evidence that the scheme workers liaised closely with GPs and arranged for geriatric assessment and review in a significant number of cases. Access to medical care was thus made easier for community care clients. The presence of one person coordinating care regularly was probably also important. Hendriksen *et al.* (1984) noted that this imparted a sense of confidence and security in elderly people, and led to a decline in both institutionalisation and mortality rates.

The Appendix to Chapter 9 of *Matching Resources to Needs* (Davies and Challis, 1986) further explores variations in mortality.

2. Changes in Quality of Life of the Elderly Person

Changes in quality of life were seen as changes evident between the two interviews undertaken with the elderly person. The domains or dimensions of quality of life which the indicators of outcome represent were discussed in Challis (1981). There were seven dimensions identified, the first five of which relate to aspects of the elderly person and the others to their broader social network. They were defined as:

(i) 'Nurturance', or basic physical care covering the usual activities of daily living (Katz *et al.*, 1963), such as toileting and bathing. It also included factors such as the security of those at risk of falling or self-neglect.

(ii) 'Compensation for disability', covering 'instrumental self-maintenance behaviours' including activities involved in home care such as meal preparation and shopping.

(iii) 'Independence', referring not just to the residential independence of the elderly person, but also to their felt independence and self-respect in retaining a degree of control over their own life.

(iv) 'Morale', ranging from conceptions of personal growth and life satisfaction to overt psychopathology in the form of depression and anxiety.

(v) 'Social integration' referring to aspects of boredom and loneliness, the presence or absence of a confidant and the extensiveness of social networks.

(vi) 'Family effects': the problems of stress and difficulties experienced by family and informal carers.

(vii) 'Community effects': the effect of a new caring scheme on the extensiveness of the network of existing and potential carers and their willingness to undertake care.

The indicators of outcome within these domains are described in more detail in Appendix A.

The outcome variables concerning client state were analysed in order to test whether differences observed between community care and standard provision were due to clients having received the experiment ('group effects'), or due to their degree of disability ('disability effects') or to a combination of both of these ('interaction effects'). The method used to answer this was analysis of variance.

(a) Cases included in the analysis and the allowance for missing information

In order to avoid loss of information, all cases who were fully interviewed at follow-up from the original total of 208 community care and comparison group cases were used in these analyses. This gave 135 cases in all, since the higher death rate in the comparison group meant that the matched cases who were re-interviewed were only a portion of the original group of 148. To ensure that the changes observed were not due to the effect of initial differences between the two groups, the analyses were re-run with each of the variables listed in Table 2.2 which had differentiated the two samples as a covariate. This effectively removed initial differences between the groups before comparing the outcomes. These checks did not influence the results.

Full interviews could not be conducted with all those elderly people who entered residential care because of their personal circumstances or condition. Complete interview data were not available for thirteen of the thirty-five cases in residential care although partial interviews were conducted with all but three of them. Those in hospital were not interviewed at follow-up.

For elderly people in residential care, both those interviewed and those seen but not fully interviewed, there were very different subjective responses. These ranged from feeling contented and settled, to feeling unhappy and distressed. On the other hand, there was a much greater degree of uniformity about the quality of care. This was at least adequate and usually a marked improvement on their previous circumstances as a result of entry to a residential home. In order to examine whether the lack of interview data for certain of the residential care cases could influence the analyses of outcomes, a double-check was made for the quality of care variables. For the analysis of those in residential care, cases with missing information were allotted the mean value for each of the quality of care variables in residential homes and for the other those cases were excluded. This, however, made no substantive differences to the findings, and the results shown are those for cases fully interviewed. For the more general outcomes indicating subjective well-being, it did not seem realistic to follow the same procedure, since feelings and attitudes were so varied. Therefore only those cases with full interview data were included.

Save for two variables, analyses were based on persons both resident in their own homes and in residential care. For those two - 'Increase in Social Contacts' and 'Need for Services' - the analyses were conducted only for persons living in their own homes at the time of the post-test interviews since the information related to shortfalls in home care only.

(b) Effects on Subjective Well-being and Quality of Care

The results of the analyses are shown in Tables 7.5 and 7.6 respectively. The tables show the mean change for the community care cases and the comparison group on each outcome indicator and the results of the analyses to show whether differences could be attributed to the effect of receipt of community care ('group'), the elderly person's frailty ('disability') or to a combination of both ('interaction'). Where a statistically significant difference is noted against any of these effects, it indicates that the difference between the two groups is

Table 7.5 Subjective well-being outcomes

Variable	Descriptive statistics			Analysis of variance		
		Community care	Standard provision	Effect	F	Significance
1. Felt capacity to cope	Mean	5.03	.66	Group	55.38	.001
	Variance	10.89	11.31	Disability	.15	NS
	Standard error	.41	.42	Interaction	.49	NS
2. Depressed mood	Mean	-.68	-.17	Group	7.61	.007
	Variance	1.57	.75	Disability	.68	NS
	Standard error	.15	.16	Interaction	.78	NS
3. Anxiety	Mean	-.39	-.2	Group	2.3	NS
	Variance	.74	.39	Disability	.49	NS
	Standard error	.12	.08	Interaction	1.27	NS
4. Boredom	Mean	-.36	1.06	Group	29.68	.001
	Variance	2.14	2.06	Disability	.87	NS
	Standard error	.18	.18	Interaction	.06	NS
5. Felt degree of control over own life	Mean	2.41	.92	Group	3.07	.08
	Variance	18.83	22.33	Disability	.83	NS
	Standard error	.53	.59	Interaction	.07	NS
6. Reduction in loneliness	Mean	1.46	-.36	Group	34.78	.001
	Variance	2.41	3.59	Disability	.16	NS
	Standard error	.19	.24	Interaction	.05	NS
7. Reduction in general dissatisfaction	Mean	.99	-.59	Group	28.43	.001
	Variance	3.71	1.8	Disability	.01	NS
	Standard error	.24	.17	Interaction	.08	NS
8. Reduction in dissatisfaction with life development	Mean	.38	-.23	Group	9.97	.002
	Variance	1.5	.82	Disability	.18	NS
	Standard error	.15	.11	Interaction	.27	NS
9. Morale	Mean	2.99	-1.00	Group	36.97	.001
	Variance	14.69	12.54	Disability	.01	NS
	Standard error	.47	.44	Interaction	.16	NS

highly unlikely to have occured by chance.

It can be seen that for all variables with the exception of three - Felt Degree of Control Over Own Life, Anxiety and Improvement in Diet - there were significant positive changes in favour of the community care scheme ('group effects', Tables 7.5 and 7.6). Subjective Well-being had improved and practical needs had been met. There was a greater reduction in need for additional care among community care cases as perceived by both interviewer and elderly person. The improvements for those people receiving community care in help with getting up and going to bed and with daily household needs were particularly great for those who were very frail ('Interaction effects'; see Table 7.6). This was to be expected since the most frail would be those with the greatest difficulty in rising and retiring, and meal preparation. In addition, the very disabled tended to benefit more than other cases, although the improvement was greater for community care in daily household needs, personal care and weekly home care ('Group effects' and 'Disability effects', see Table 7.6).

Except for two variables it appeared that there were no differences of substance between analyses comparing cases in their own homes and analyses comparing those in residential care also. However, with the residential care cases included, a higher proportion of whom were in the comparison group, the advantage to community care was slightly reduced, as might be expected. For those remaining in their own homes, community care made significant improvements in Quality of Diet ($F = 13.8, p < .001$) and anxiety ($F = 3.83, p < .05$). Since this difference was not apparent when considering those in residential homes as well as those in their own homes, it appeared that residential care was particularly effective in meeting these needs for the comparison group.

Overall it is clear that for most of these aspects of quality of life, there was a significant gain for the elderly people in the community care group. The morale effects which were observed are not dissimilar to those of an earlier study in the care of the elderly where the more intensive work of qualified social workers, and the additional resources which they tapped, appeared to cause a higher proportion of cases to improve in morale, and a lower proportion to deteriorate (Goldberg *et al.*, 1970). These improvements might have influenced survival in the present study through such intermediate factors as improving the old person's confidence in coping. The justification for such an inference is strengthened by the greater number of those receiving community care who said that they had a person in whom they could confide (Table 7.4).

3. Changes in Health Status of Elderly People

It was not expected that community care, a scheme for social not health care,

Table 7.6 Quality of care outcomes

Variable	Descriptive statistics			Analysis of variance		
		Community care	Standard provision	Effect	F	Significance
1. Need for additional help night and morning[1]	Mean	-.58	.13	Group	5.13	.025
	Variance	3.14	3.29	Disability	1.27	NS
	Standard error	.21	.21	Interaction	5.34	.02
2. Need for additional help with personal care/security needs[1]	Mean	-9.47	-1.29	Group	22.62	.001
	Variance	72.55	124.81	Disability	1.85	NS
	Standard error	1.00	1.28	Interaction	2.00	NS
3. Need for additional help with daily household needs[1]	Mean	-6.68	-1.71	Group	14.52	.001
	Variance	56.48	50.76	Disability	8.25	.005
	Standard error	.89	.82	Interaction	5.94	.016
4. Need for additional help with weekly household needs[1]	Mean	-4.77	-1.94	Group	15.47	.001
	Variance	19.54	15.53	Disability	.58	NS
	Standard error	.52	.45	Interaction	.12	NS
5. Adequacy of help night and morning[2]	Mean	3.18	2.54	Group	.15	NS
	Variance	43.00	41.17	Disability	1.74	NS
	Standard error	.77	.74	Interaction	7.06	.009
6. Adequacy of help with personal care/security needs[2]	Mean	5.33	1.46	Group	35.68	.001
	Variance	13.23	20.64	Disability	3.78	.05
	Standard error	.43	.52	Interaction	.26	NS
7. Adequacy of help with daily household needs[2]	Mean	6.20	1.83	Group	15.74	.001
	Variance	43.37	50.73	Disability	1.02	NS
	Standard error	.78	.82	Interaction	.009	NS

8. Adequacy of help with weekly household needs[2]	Mean	3.19	.85	Group	20.79	.001
	Variance	14.47	12.01	Disability	12.29	.001
	Standard error	.45	.39	Interaction	.41	NS
9. Improvement in quality of diet	Mean	1.92	1.86	Group	1.53	NS
	Variance	42.69	44.63	Disability	.18	NS
	Standard error	.80	.84	Interaction	.34	NS
10.Increase in social contacts[3]	Mean	5.66	-.77	Group	20.18	.001
	Variance	76.16	22.65	Disability	1.88	NS
	Standard error	1.12	.66	Interaction	.08	NS
11.Reduction in need for extra services[3]	Mean	2.44	-.69	Group	70.66	.001
	Variance	4.72	2.87	Disability	.02	NS
	Standard error	.28	.15	Interaction	.72	NS

Notes
1. 'Need for additional care' is an interviewer assessment of the shortfall of available care with each particular activity.
2. 'Adequacy of care' refers to the elderly person's perception of the reliability, effectiveness and sufficiency of the care provided.
3. Only tested for those elderly people remaining in their own homes for whom it was relevant.

was likely to effect changes in functional state or health. However, one aspect of more intensive social work might be to alert other agencies to unmet needs, such as treatable ailments in an elderly person.

Two health-related outcomes were examined. The first was a measure of functional health, a count of the six basic Activities of Daily Living (ADL), such as bathing, with which the elderly person required assistance, an indicator commonly used in the USA (Katz *et al.*, 1963). The second measure was a composite variable, General Health, consisting of the sum of a series of three-point ratings of problems with eyesight, hearing, breathlessness, giddiness, risk of falling, incontinence, and a self-assessment. Outcome was defined as the change between the first and second assessment, and since a positive score on either variable would constitute a decline in health, the lower the value, the greater the benefit to the elderly person. The analyses of these two outcomes are shown in Table 7.7. As before, analysis of variance was used.

It can be seen that there is a tendency to increasing ill-health in both groups, as in other studies (Goldberg *et al.*, 1970), although this was significantly less for the experimental than for the comparison group on the functional status indicator. The General Health change was not significantly different. It is unlikely that this finding of less impaired functional health for the community care group can be explained by the different rates of attrition within the two groups. Since the death rate was higher in the comparison group, it is likely that those whose health was declining most died, whereas in the community care scheme a smaller proportion of similar cases died. It is therefore likely that any attrition effect would tend to have caused the average state of health of survivors in the comparison group to be better than that of the community care group.

A more likely explanation can be found in the activities of the community care scheme social workers, who, by establishing close contact with a local geriatrician and liaising with GPs, ensured that a number of elderly people attended the day hospital with the objective of assessment and improving mobility. There is evidence that even the very frail can show improved mobility and capacity for activities of daily living if treatment is initiated (Bergmann and Jacoby, 1983). In particular, through encouragement and by provision of transport where a roundabout ambulance journey was too tiring for the elderly person, people were enabled to receive treatment who otherwise would not have done so. In addition, helpers were encouraged to take elderly people out wherever possible to stimulate their independence when previously they had been effectively housebound. Similar support, help, encouragement and contact with medical services was not available to elderly people in the comparison area, which may account for the differences between the groups. It is noteworthy that lower rates of decline have also been observed elsewhere

Table 7.7 Health care outcomes

Variable	Descriptive statistics	Community care	Standard provision	Analysis of variance: Effect	F	Significance
1. Change in functional state (ADL)	Mean	.14	.67	Group	6.71	.01
	Variance	.98	2.00	Disability	.82	NS
	Standard error	.12	.17	Interaction	.07	NS
2. Change in general health	Mean	.38	.98	Group	2.39	NS
	Variance	3.50	7.29	Disability	.25	NS
	Standard error	.23	.34	Interaction	2.59	NS

where elderly people's health and social status are more closely monitored (Tulloch and Moore, 1979; Luker, 1981).

4. Outcomes for Family and Informal Carers

There were relatively few elderly people in the area with family living nearby and providing care, or carers such as neighbours providing a substantial amount of care which would clearly identify them as a principal carer. This is characteristic of a retirement area, to which people will often have moved from over fifty miles away (Karn, 1977). Consequently, in only between one-quarter and one-fifth of the cases, forty-two in all, was information from a principal carer available. Only twenty-nine of these overall could be followed up, because the elderly person had died or moved away.

Outcomes for principal carers were defined as changes in the effects of their care role on their daily life. Nine variables were considered in the assessment of effects on families and carers. These were three-point ratings of the severity of difficulty experienced in different spheres of life such as mental health or social life. One variable - Subjective Burden - represented the carers' overall perception of the extent of burden, again on a three-point scale. The interviews were analysed to examine whether or not changes in these outcomes could be attributed to the effect of receiving the community care scheme (Group effect) using analysis of variance. The results are shown in Table 7.8.

It can be seen that it is in only in three variables - Subjective Burden, Extent of Strain and Mental Health Difficulties - where differences between the community care scheme and the comparison group approach a satisfactory level of significance. In these three variables, those carers who received help from the community care scheme appear to have fared more satisfactorily than their counterparts in the comparison group. However, the scale of significance of these differences is not surprising in view of the very small numbers of cases for whom information was available.

Stress and subjective burden appeared to be reduced to a greater extent in the community care scheme than in the comparison group. Practical difficulties such as disruption of household routine, employment and social life appeared to be reduced in both groups. There was no significant difference between them. It is interesting to consider why subjective stress may have been more effectively reduced by community care. For a number of cases in the comparison group, the only means of achieving relief was admission to a residential home of the elderly person in circumstances in which this might be desired by neither the family nor the elderly person. Such a solution may itself provoke guilt and distress (Allen *et al.*, 1983). One family, having arranged for their mother to enter an elderly persons' home in response to their difficulties, felt it necessary for her to move back to live in their home again, because of her

Table 7.8 Outcomes for principal carers

Variable	Descriptive statistics			Analysis of variance		
		Community care	Standard provision	Effect	F	Significance
1. Level of subjective burden	Mean	-1.12	-.33	Group	5.21	.03
	Variance	.61	1.15			
	Standard error	.19	.31			
2. Extent of strain	Mean	-1.24	-.50	Group	3.01	.09
	Variance	.94	1.73			
	Standard error	.24	.38			
3. Mental health difficulties	Mean	-.82	-.25	Group	3.02	.09
	Variance	.65	.93			
	Standard error	.19	.28			
4. Difficulties in social life	Mean	-.71	-.67	Group	.48	NS
	Variance	.72	.97			
	Standard error	.21	.28			
5. Difficulties in household routine	Mean	-.76	-.42	Group	.96	NS
	Variance	1.07	.63			
	Standard error	.25	.23			
6. Difficulties in employment	Mean	-.18	-.01	Group	1.32	NS
	Variance	.28	.02			
	Standard error	.13	.01			
7. Financial difficulties	Mean	-.12	-.25	Group	.83	NS
	Variance	.11	.20			
	Standard error	.08	.13			
8. Difficulties with children	Mean	.06	-.17	Group	.48	NS
	Variance	.06	.33			
	Standard error	.06	.17			
9. Physical health difficulties	Mean	-.41	-.33	Group	.09	NS
	Variance	.38	.61			
	Standard error	.15	.23			

distress, despite the difficulties it entailed. On the other hand, a neighbour of an elderly woman, experiencing difficulties in coping with care, felt happy at continuing with support from the community care scheme in the knowledge that further back-up was readily available if she should require it, and no longer feeling that she alone was responsible. The more practical difficulties were reduced for carers either by admission to residential care or by more adequate care at home.

These findings are compatible with other studies of family care of the frail elderly. Often people would cope (albeit with difficulty) with the physical demands of care, but the mental effort involved was daunting. A major problem was the forced assumption of total responsibility, with services only available when the carer reached breaking point (Isaacs *et al.*, 1972; Levin, 1982). One study noted: 'What many families and particularly the principal carers within the family wanted was understanding and an opportunity to talk out a situation' (Nissel and Bonnerjea, 1982, p.64). This was more readily available from community care, where case-management responsibility made it possible to relieve the total responsibility of the family, and provide emotional and practical support more closely tailored to the needs of carers.

5. The Impact of Community Care on Caring Networks

One fear which was expressed about the development of the community care scheme was that it could lead to a decline in the provision of informal care, causing 'a negative relationship between formal and informal care' (Abrams, 1977), perhaps by introducing what Hirsch (1977) has described as a commercialisation effect. In order to assess the apparent effects on networks, at the follow-up elderly people living at home were asked about the extent of change in help given. The results from these questions are shown in Table 7.9 separately for family and other informal carers. It can be seen that there is little difference between the groups. If anything there was less decline in the supportive activities of informal carers among those receiving community

Table 7.9 Effects on informal care over one year

	Family carers		Other informal carers	
	Community care %	Standard provision %	Community care %	Standard provision %
Increased care	12	8	22	24
Same level of care	83	84	59	48
Reduced care	5	8	19	28

care, particularly among carers who were not related to the client. From this evidence, anxiety that the introduction of the scheme might have a destructive effect on informal care appears unfounded.

6. Summary and Conclusion

The available evidence suggests that the community care scheme was able to achieve considerable improvements both for the elderly people and their families. In particular:

(i) Significantly fewer people were admitted to institutional care and significantly fewer died, effects most noticeable over the first year. This latter finding was initially unexpected, although other studies which have systematically monitored care and health status suggest not dissimilar findings (Hendriksen *et al.*, 1984; Vetter *et al.*, 1984).

(ii) The reduction in admission to institutional care was not achieved at the price of a poorer quality of life for elderly people, since the community care scheme was able to achieve greater benefits in terms of Subjective Well-being and Quality of Care than the standard provision of domiciliary and residential care.

(iii) The community care group appeared to show less decline in their physical abilities. This has also been demonstrated in other work where elderly people are more closely monitored and gain access to appropriate treatment (Tulloch and Moore, 1979; Luker, 1981; Bergmann and Jacoby, 1983).

(iv) Informal carers of clients receiving community care seemed to feel less burdened as a result of the help given and possibly suffered less mental stress and strain.

(v) Close confiding relationships were developed between the elderly people receiving the scheme and community care helpers and social workers. Those receiving community care were considerably more likely to have a person in whom they could confide than those receiving standard provision.

(vi) The community care scheme did not appear to have any negative effects on the availability of informal care networks; indeed it appeared that carers were if anything less likely to reduce their support when the scheme was involved.

CHAPTER 8

THE COSTS OF CARE

The last chapter was concerned with the effectiveness of care. Here we consider the costs of care for those receiving community care and standard provision. First, we outline the principles which guide our approach to costing. (They are discussed in more detail in Davies and Challis, 1986, Chapter 10.) In the subsequent sections of this chapter we describe the costing process for different agencies and interest groups before considering the different costs incurred by them as a result of community care and standard provision.

1. Principles of Costing

Three factors were particularly important: our concern to deal with the 'opportunity costs' of different forms of care; the need to discount future costs to render them comparable with present levels, and the divergence between private and social costs. Let us consider each in turn.

(a) Opportunity costs

The costing of care is a complex process not only due to the multiplicity of costs involved but also because the conventions of financial accounting used by public agencies do not always adequately reflect the consumption of real resources (Sugden and Williams, 1978). This information may therefore be an insufficient guide for making decisions. Costing analyses are usually concerned with decisions about whether to provide a little more or a little less of a service. These decisions require knowledge about the cost of an additional unit of service (or output): the marginal cost. Costing information held in the accounting system of agencies usually refers, however, to average costs. Our approach to costing used the economist's concept of 'opportunity cost', which means that the cost of using a resource in one particular way is not the money cost or the price of the resource but is the benefit foregone by losing its best alternative use.

There is, of course, no uniquely correct opportunity cost; rather it will depend on the validity of different assumptions and expectations about the context within which decisions have to be made. This study took place in the context of an ageing population with a rising need and demand for care services. Therefore, the most that could reasonably be expected of a successful scheme to maintain elderly people at home would be a slower rate of growth required in the development of services such as residential care, and not a reduction of that provision. Hence, the opportunity cost would reflect increasing provision of a range of services, involving both capital and current expenditure, based on 'long-run' marginal cost, not on the 'short-run' cost which would exclude any allowance for capital.

(b) Discounting future costs

In comparing the costs and benefits of different courses of action, we have to take account of the differential timing of those costs and benefits. For example, a decision to develop a specialised fostering service will involve a substantial investment now in staff, recruitment and training followed only later by a stream of benefits as the foster-parents receive children. Costs incurred now need to be compared with benefits enjoyed tomorrow. In making an assessment of the present cost of, say, a new residential home, we have to 'discount' part of its cost since this will give benefit to future residents. A discount can be seen as akin to an interest rate, and different assumptions as to the correct discount rate and the period over which discounting has taken place will obviously affect our cost judgements. For example, in the case of investment in a building, the usual discounting period is sixty years (see Knapp, 1984, Chap. 7). Consequently, in our analyses we have used three different discount rates - 5, 7 and 10 per cent - to compare the effect of these different assumptions.

(c) The divergence between private and social costs

As we discussed in Chapter 2, costs, like benefits, affect a number of different parties and will appear different according to the standpoint of each. For example, the private costs to the social services department ignores costs or savings which might affect the National Health Service. By taking account of the cost of alternative courses of action to society as a whole ('social cost') we are able to take the possible range of factors into account.

Nine different interest groups could be identified, each of whom would have a different opportunity cost as a result of the introduction of a new care scheme for the elderly (Davies and Challis, 1981). These groups were:

1. The social services department
2. The National Health Service
3. Local authority housing department
4. The Department of Health and Social Security
5. Private and voluntary welfare agencies
6. Elderly people receiving care
7. Informal carers of elderly people
8. The controllers of public expenditure
9. Society as a whole

Information on unit costs and service use was collected to permit estimates of income and expenditure to be made for each of these different 'accounts'. In the following sections we discuss the unit costs of the various services and then consider the costs incurred by the relevant parties.

2. Costs to the Social Services Department

It is helpful to discuss the costing of social services in four sections: residential care, day care, social worker time and domiciliary services. The unit costs used, derived from the local authority accounts, were those in force when the scheme commenced in 1977. These 1977 costs were expressed in terms of a November 1976 price base.

(a) Residential care

There are two components in the cost of residential care: recurrent costs and capital costs. Recurrent costs include staffing costs and hotel costs such as heating, lighting and maintaining the fabric of the building, less credits consisting principally of residents' contributions. In view of the expectation of rising demand, the costs of a new home which had opened the year before the scheme was launched provided the basis for cost estimates, since with a home operating at full capacity, the marginal cost of residential care could be deemed equivalent to the average cost of a place in a new home. As information on individual financial contributions was not available, the average financial contribution of elderly people throughout the authority was used to make judgements of net cost.

Capital costs consist of capital and loan charges to the local authority or the discounted replacement cost. Local information was available about the building cost of new homes which is relevant for the estimation of long-run marginal cost. During 1977, the year of the scheme's commencement, two new homes were constructed. At the prevailing price level the cost of these two homes were £362,000 and £365,000, an average of £363,500. These figures did not include an allowance for the cost of the land required for building. Following Wager (1972) and Wright *et al.* (1981) it was assumed that an acre of land would be required for the construction of a new old people's home. For the outer south-east region, the weighted average price for one acre of private housing land was £18,892 (Department of the Environment, 1978). The estimated capital cost of a home was thus increased to £383,392. The cost per week per place for a home with forty beds discounted over a period of sixty years - the expected life of the building - could therefore be calculated by adding the running costs to this estimate of capital costs. Table 8.1 shows the costs of revenue account net expenditure and opportunity cost at three different discount rates for residential care. It appeared that, depending on the discount rate, residential care would cost between £65 and £75 per week.

Table 8.1
Social services department costs, £ at 1977 prices

	Revenue account £	Discount rates 5% £	7% £	10% £
1. Residential care per resident week				
Revenue account				
Running costs	56.21			
Debt charges	23.14			
Maintenance costs	0.40			
Less average resident contribution	-16.00			
Total	63.75			
Opportunity costs				
Running costs		56.21	56.21	56.21
Capital costs		9.71	13.09	18.44
Total		65.92	69.30	74.65
2. Day care in purpose-built centre				
Revenue account				
Running costs	7.59			
Capital and loan charges	1.41			
Total	9.00			
Opportunity costs				
Running costs		7.59	7.59	7.59
Capital costs		0.85	1.15	1.62
Total		8.44	8.74	9.21
3. Domiciliary services				
Opportunity costs				
Day care in residential home (per session)			2.69	
Home help (per hour)			1.66	
Meals on wheels (per meal)			0.40	
Telephones (per month)			2.54	
Sheltered housing special grant (per week)			2.25	
Social work (per hour)				
Community care			2.64	
Area team			2.28	

(b) Day care

Day care was provided both in residential homes and also in a purpose-built day centre. The cost of these two different forms of provision varied considerably. The cost of day care in a residential home was considered to be relatively low, consisting of transport, the midday meal and a snack, a chair in a lounge, some attention from staff and a small share of activity costs. This daily cost was estimated to be £2.69. No capital allowance was made since the admission of elderly people for day care was acceptable only in such small numbers that they were catered for by the existing facilities of the home.

A purpose-built day centre was a substantial capital investment. A new day centre which opened in the year the scheme commenced provided the basis for estimation of the capital component. The building costs were £78,000, to which must be added, as in the case of a residential home, the cost of one acre of land, at £18,892. This was discounted over sixty years at three different rates. The running costs, based on an 85 per cent occupancy rate for five days per week over a forty-seven week year were £7.59 per day including transport, as shown in Table 8.1.

(c) Fieldwork

Perhaps the most complicated estimation of cost to the social services department was for social work. The community care staff were of more senior status than those working with the elderly in the comparison group, which may slightly exaggerate the costs of social work compared with subsequent developments of the scheme. The unit cost of fieldworker time included departmental overheads such as transport, clerical support, office accommodation and a central administration cost. At 1977 prices this was £2.64 per hour for community care and £2.28 for the area teams.

The costing of social work time was handled by dividing the activity into three component parts: research, development and running costs. Development activity (which would not be undertaken by workers in the comparison group to a similar degree) included liaison with other agencies, developing new systems of working and negotiating their acceptance with a range of personnel, such as departmental management and the treasurer's and personnel departments. The costs of such developmental activities were treated as an investment, only a discounted capital allowance being charged to the period in which they occurred. The return from this investment would be enjoyed not only over the duration of the original scheme but also in other parts of the department and indeed in other authorities. The running costs were divided into general (or overhead) activities such as recruiting and supporting helpers, and costs associated with individual clients. Research activities were not included as part of the costs of care, and the proportion allocated to development and overhead time was raised accordingly. The basis for the allocation of social worker time into each of these categories - research, development and running costs - was the entries of workers in their diaries and casenotes described in Chapter 3.

The costs of social worker time which could readily be attributed to clients varied throughout the life of the scheme, but during the period most representative of a fully operating service never fell below 30 per cent. Development activities ranged from 18 per cent to 60 per cent of time during different phases of the scheme. Much of the development cost was unique to the establishment of this first scheme. In order to compare the costs with running a scheme elsewhere, the development costs should reflect those when the scheme was running with a reasonable caseload. This represented up to 30 per cent of time. Subsequent experience suggests that much less is required to operate an established service. Discounting these costs over a relatively conservative three to five-year period at different rates indicates a development cost of between £1 and £1.50 per client/month. Overhead running costs tended to amount to about 20 per cent of fieldworker time during the most representative period. However, part of this cost might also be considered an investment since helpers once recruited would often stay for a considerable period of time. Taking a range of discount rates over a three-year period and discounting from one-half to no part of the overhead costs provides a range of overhead costs from £1.50 to £3 per client month.

Therefore, using several different assumptions about discounting, the fixed cost of social worker time, which should be added to the variable cost in Table 8.7 ranges from £2.50 to £4.50 per client month.

However, information on social worker activities in the comparison group was much less readily available. Certainly there were a number of cases which received little or no social worker contact, but others received quite substantial inputs of time and effort, some outside normal office hours. This was less frequently recorded in detail and there was no reliable method of recording fixed costs for the comparison group. Accordingly there was some underestimation of social worker costs in the comparison area.

(d) Domiciliary services

The unit costs of these services are summarised in Table 8.1. The gross cost of the home help service, consisting of wages plus overheads, was £1.66 per hour. The meals service was provided on an agency basis by the Women's Royal Voluntary Service (WRVS), which received a grant for the purpose. From the extent of the grant and number of meals served, it was possible to estimate a unit cost of 40 pence per meal. The rental charge for telephones provided to elderly people was £2.54 per month. The capital cost of aids was discounted over their expected life, which was in many cases relatively brief. Neither in community care nor in the comparison group were there people whose homes had been specially adapted by the local authority, and minor adaptations such as handrails or ramps were discounted as if they were aids.

The social services department made a grant to the housing authority at a level estimated to meet the social care element of sheltered housing. The unit cost to the authority was calculated as the average grant per unit, at £9 per client per month.

For the community care group, direct payments were also made to helpers for caring tasks. These reflected their cash value at the time of payment. To render them comparable with other costs they were deflated to the same price base by means of the Retail Price Index. This was felt to be the most realistic basis since what helpers were prepared to accept should most closely approximate to their experience of daily expenditure as represented by this index. Since contracts were short-term and open to renegotiation, it was assumed that payments reflected helpers' valuation of their leisure and their perception of the balance of advantages and disadvantages of helping. Although a contractual relationship could result in exploitation, the team was concerned to avoid this danger and these contracts were regularly reviewed.

However, helpers themselves might possibly have borne costs. Their payments were arranged within the framework of regulations governing eligibility for social security benefits and liability for tax. There was some evidence that these factors affected both the decision to offer help and the amount proffered. It appeared that any opportunity costs to the helper and the wider society were imposed by fiscal regulations or by the exclusion of these people from the labour market by personal circumstance such as retirement age or caring for young children, and not by the existence of the new scheme.

3. Costs to the National Health Service

The rising demand for health care services from an ageing population requires us to consider health service costs in the context of increasing levels of provision, both of hospital and community health services. Although it is possible that enhanced community care from the social services department might relieve some demands on community nursing services, it would not be sufficient to affect the price of those services. We consider hospital and primary health care services separately.

(a) Hospital services

Information about direct treatment services, medical and paramedical supporting services and general services were extracted from records for the relevant local hospitals. Comparable data for broader geographical areas were extracted from the *Health Service Costing Returns* for 1977 (Department of Health and Social Security, 1979). Hospitals into which the elderly people were admitted were classified into three groups: those providing acute hospital care, long-stay geriatric hospital care and psychiatric care.

The capital cost of hospital buildings is not included in the Costing Returns. However, the capital costs estimated by Wright *et al.* (1981) based on DHSS building cost estimates at March 1977 prices provided an appropriate costing basis for three situations: the construction of a new building (at a capital cost of £20,000 per bed), the upgrading of an existing building (at a capital cost of £12,000 per bed) and the improvement of an existing building without

Table 8.2
Total hospital resource costs per inpatient day by discount rate and capital expenditure scenario, £ at 1977 prices

Capital scenario and hospital type	Revenue Account	Discount Rate		
		5%	7%	10%
	£	£	£	£
New building costing (£20,000 per bed)				
Acute care	28.20	31.10	32.06	33.70
Long stay care	16.97	19.87	20.83	22.47
Psychiatric care	13.21	16.11	17.06	18.76
Day hospital (1)	9.56	12.46	13.42	15.06
Upgrading buildings costing (£12,000 per bed)				
Acute care		29.94	30.05	31.51
Long stay care		18.71	19.27	20.28
Psychiatric care		14.95	15.51	16.52
Day hospital (1)		11.30	11.86	12.87
Improved buildings costing (£1,000 per bed)				
Acute care		28.34	28.40	28.47
Long stay care		17.11	17.17	17.24
Psychiatric care		13.35	13.41	13.48
Day hospital (1)		9.70	9.76	9.83

Notes
1. Revenue account expenditure is invariable with different capital assumptions.
2. Figures are for geriatric care.
3. The local day hospital was part of a unit with inpatient facilities. In the absence of separate data, the capital costs for inpatient beds were applied to these facilities.

structural alteration (at a capital cost of £1,000 per bed). Each of these represent possible NHS levels of investment to meet rising demand for health care.

Table 8.2 shows estimates for total costs for patients in each type of hospital, for revenue expenditure and three rates of discount over a sixty-year period, with different possible levels of capital expenditure. It is clear that differences in the discount rates for capital expenditure substantially affect the total costs of long-term care. Outpatient costs were not compiled since in total they were too small to make a material difference to the results of the analysis.

(b) Community health services

The costs of community nursing consist predominantly of salary costs, travelling expenses and administrative overheads. The estimates of home nursing costs by Wright *et al.* (1981) for an urban area took account of the overheads of central administration, drugs, dressings and telephones, and are shown in Table 8.3. It was assumed that an average visit to an elderly person would take half an hour. The nursing service provided evidence of the number of formal visits made to each elderly person in the sample during the study period; however, this information did not document whether each visit was made by a state registered nurse (SRN), a state enrolled nurse (SEN), or a nursing auxiliary. It was, however, not unreasonable to assume that on the whole the pattern of visiting to elderly people would reflect the distribution of the different grades in the district. In the area there were thirty-one SRNs, ten SENs and fifteen nursing auxiliaries. Computing a weighted average cost per visit of half an hour on the basis of this distribution, the cost per visit for community nursing was calculated to be £1.52. Health visiting was very rare for these elderly people, and like community psychiatric nursing was given a similar unit cost.

Table 8.3
Estimated costs of home nursing, £ at 1977 prices

Nurse grade	Cost element	
	Patient care (£ per hour)	Visiting (£ per visit)
District nurse (SRN and RMN)	3.10	0.50
'Practical' nurse (SEN)	1.96	0.36
Nursing auxiliary	1.40	0.34

Source: Wright *et al.* (1982).

It was not possible to assess the cost of visits and services to individual elderly people by general practitioners. The failure to account for this community health care resource is unlikely to influence the comparison between care at home and residential care significantly, since the general practitioner services were provided to elderly people in both settings and their cost was small in relation to other components of costs to the National Health Service. Furthermore, any difference between hospital and community costs to the National Health Service - though not to social opportunity cost - would also have to take account of the continued receipt by GPs of capitation fees for patients in hospital.

The length of a visit by a chiropodist was assumed to be half an hour. Wright *et al.* (1981) estimated the cost of chiropody to be £2.14 per hour. Aids were discounted over their expected life. The unit costs of community health services are listed in Table 8.4.

Table 8.4.
Unit cost of community health services, £ at 1977 prices

Service type	£
Community nursing (per visit)	1.52
Domiciliary chiropody (per visit)	1.07
Aids - discounted over expected life	variable

4. Costs to the Local Authority Housing Department

The housing department was particularly likely to be affected by the adoption of community care through the costs of increased demand for units of special housing, and a greater likelihood of elderly people remaining in their own homes. However, this effect was less likely to be evident in a twelve-month follow-up period than it would be over a longer time scale. This is because people entering long-term care would often retain their homes for an overlapping period.

Subsidies from the housing revenue account, rent and rate rebates (now housing benefit) are also important. Data on the receipt of these subsidies were obtained from the interviews. Where the interview data were unreliable because some people were unsure whether they received benefits or of the precise amount, financial assessments made by the social services department were used. Where these was not available, but it was evident that these housing subsidies were being received, an estimate was made taking into acount the relationship between the average rebate and the value of an elderly person's home.

5. Costs to the Social Security Agency

As with housing benefits, income data were gathered by interview from the elderly persons themselves and checked with a financial assessment undertaken by the social services department if available.

Flows of benefits through time were checked against individual changes in circumstances and appropriate adjustments made. Thus, for example, an elderly person in hospital would receive their full pension plus the payment of a home rent allowance. After eight weeks the pension was subject to reduction by the amount of the prevailing pocket money rate. Similarly, for elderly people entering residential care, their home rent allowance was usually paid for three months, after which time a discretionary judgement was made according to individual circumstances.

Payment towards the cost of residential care in a private home varied with the circumstances of the individual old person and the charging policy of the home, but was around £31 per week with additional contributions made from the pension and benefits such as attendance allowance. Although some homes exceeded this figure, adhering to it in our analyses was expected, if anything, to bias costs against community care.

The levels of benefit prevailing at the time of the scheme's commencement and used in costing are shown in Table 8.5 (DHSS, 1978).

6. Costs to Private and Voluntary Welfare Agencies

In practice the only substantial private or voluntary provision used by the elderly people in the study proved to be residential care, although one or two elderly people paid for private domestic help. Allowance was made for this in the costs to elderly people and in their receipt of benefits.

7. Costs to Clients

Elderly people incurred different resource costs according to whether they were living at home or in institutional care. Living at home involves expenditure on food, heating and light. Interviews with individual elderly people provided details about their actual income, which, wherever possible, were checked with a local authority financial assessment. However, no attempt was made to collect data on general items of personal consumption from them. In order to obtain estimates of consumption by elderly people with different levels of income, the interview information was used to provide sufficient information to place each elderly person into the appropriate personal consumption bracket of the Family Expenditure Survey (Department of Employment, 1978). For elderly people in institutional care, the level of personal consumption was deemed to be the equivalent 'pocket money' allowances for that setting. This provided the pattern for living expenses in

Table 8.5
Weekly rates of benefit paid by the Department of Health and Social Security, 1977

Benefit	£
Pension	
Single person	15.30*
Married woman	9.20*
Attendance allowance	
Higher rate	12.20
Lower rate	8.15
Exceptional circumstances additions	
Laundry	0.33
Diet	
Higher rate	1.75
Lower rate	0.75
Heating	
Higher rate	2.10
Middle rate	1.40
Lower	.70
Average addition	1.24
Average rent allowance	
Local authority tenants	6.38
Private tenants	4.25
Owner occupiers	2.93
Institutional 'pocket money' rate	
Hospital	3.00
Local authority home	3.00
Private residential home	5.25
Private residential care	
Maximum fees allowance	31.00

Notes: * Plus 25p if aged 80 or over.

Table 8.6, with the housing element excluded. In addition, actual rent and rate payments, net of rebates, were calculated and if the elderly person was an owner-occupier, the potential value of an annuity purchaseable from the capital value of the house was calculated as if a rent payment.

Table 8.6
Personal consumption by weekly income level, £ at 1977 prices

Weekly per capita income	Personal consumption	
	Single £	Couple £
£15 and less than £20	14.50	(
£20 and less than £25	16.03	(26.07
£25 and less than £30	18.68	(
£30 and less than £35	(21.51	29.13
£35 and less than £40	(	30.70
£40 and less than £50	(26.92	37.72
£50 and less than £60	(	44.32
£60.00 or more[1]	43.01	45.76
£80.00 or more	-	69.42
Hospital care	3.00	6.00
Local authority home	3.00	6.00
Private residential home	5.50	10.00

Note
1. The Family Expenditure Survey tabulation for single persons does not state a mean for persons in receipt of a weekly per capita income of £60 and less than £80.

Source: Family Expenditure Survey (1977).

8. Costs to Families and Informal Carers

Most informal carers did not seem to bear substantial financial caring costs which could be ascertained from interviews. The major 'costs' appeared to take the form of stress, strain and social limitation. Although these 'psychic' costs seemed more important than material costs, no attempt was made to attach a financial value to them since feelings of stress, tension and burden were seen as indicators of effectiveness of care. Only in a few cases was there evidence of costs which were readily quantifiable; for example, the earnings foregone by a single daughter who had given up work to care for a bedridden mother or by a son and daughter-in-law, both retired and in poor health, who daily travelled forty miles to provide care for their mother. In these cases, the age and circumstances of the carer were such as to permit a reasonable judgement of the costs incurred. In other cases, minor costs were incurred, such as as gifts, or visiting for mainly social reasons, but it appeared that these costs were likely to be similar whether or not the elderly person were in residential care.

9. Public Expenditure Costs

The public expenditure costs consisted of the revenue account expenditure, including debt charges, of the social services department, revenue account expenditure of the National Health Service, housing subsidies received by elderly people, and the cost of state benefits, including pension, supplementary benefit and attendance allowance.

10. Social Opportunity Costs

This was the most overarching cost concept of all. It consisted of service costs to the social services department and the National Health Service, capital elements being discounted at different rates. Social security payments and housing subsidies which were transfer payments did not correspond to flows of real resources and were therefore ignored. However, the personal consumption of the elderly person on food, fuel and other living expenses was included, as were the costs incurred by family and informal carers. The opportunity cost of housing occupied by an elderly person was included as the final element of social opportunity cost.

In order to make an assessment of the opportunity cost of the housing foregone, a market assessment of the value of the elderly person's housing, whether public or private sector, was made at May 1980 prices by an experienced valuer. These were deflated to a November 1976 price base by means of the housing component of the Retail Price Index. The estimated value was discounted over a period of sixty years to obtain a weekly cost for each unit of housing. This approach made it possible to reflect both the size and quality of accommodation foregone more exactly than an assessment of replacement value.

The cost to the rest of society of housing an elderly person will differ depending up whether the old person lives alone or with others, and whether or not if they left home they would release space that could be put to alternative use. The detailed knowledge of each case made it possible to take individual account of these differences. In the case of a frail elderly couple who were mutually supportive, for whom the entry of one into care would mean the entry of the other, then the discounted cost of housing was shared between the two. In the case of an elderly person sharing a home with one or more others who would remain in the home should the old person enter institutional care then their accommodation costs were deemed to be nil. In a case where the accommodation released would be filled by another person, then the estimated value of that proportion of the dwelling was treated as the housing cost of the elderly person.

11. The Costs of Community Care and Standard Services

It can be seen that for each group of interests identified there is an 'opportunity' cost of community care. As we have seen, decisions about what is the most realistic estimate of 'opportunity costs' ultimately depend on a judgement about what is the likely alternative to any course of action. In our case, this is whether the adoption of community care is likely to affect the costs of any of the 'parties' discussed. Although in many cases the private costs of the individual agency are likely to be equivalent to the opportunity cost, at times this may disguise the real resource consequences. For example the cost to the social services department of a new home could reasonably be seen as the opportunity cost of residential care for that agency. However, the revenue cost to the National Health Service of hospital beds takes no account of capital costs and will therefore be an underestimate.

The cost elements for the seventy-four matched pairs of cases are shown, both annually and per month of survival for each of the nine cost accounts in Table 8.7. Where it is useful to do so, both revenue account expenditure and opportunity costs at different rates of discount are provided. The costs for matched pairs broken down into the four Dependency Groups for the three major costs 'accounts' - the social services department, the National Health Service and society as a whole - are shown in Tables 8.8 to 8.10. The latter two accounts include an allowance for capital facilities discounted at 7 per cent, on the assumption that health service investment would be directed at the upgrading of facilities. Although Table 8.7 is highly detailed, a number of points can clearly be seen.

Table 8.7 Costs of matched pairs annually and per month of survival, £ at 1977 prices

Cost account	Annual cost		Cost per month	
	Community care £	Standard provision £	Community care £	Standard provision £
1. Cost to the social services department[1]				
Total SSD cost (revenue account)	638.95	701.74	51.54	58.80
Total SSD opportunity cost (5%)	634.19	746.23	51.24	62.79
Total SSD opportunity cost (7%)	640.36	776.09	51.72	65.26
Total SSD opportunity cost (10%)	650.11	823.35	52.48	69.18
Residential care (revenue account)	116.18	555.78	9.05	46.06
Residential care opportunity cost (5%)	120.13	574.70	9.36	47.63
Residential care opportunity cost (7%)	126.29	604.17	9.84	50.08
Residential care opportunity cost (10%)	136.04	650.81	10.60	53.94
Day care centre (revenue account)	0.00	14.11	0.00	1.09
Day care centre opportunity cost (5%)	0.00	14.31	0.00	1.10
Day care centre opportunity cost (7%)	0.00	14.70	0.00	1.13
Day care centre opportunity cost (10%)	0.00	15.33	0.00	1.18
Day care in a residential home	16.58	6.36	1.28	0.52
Home help	179.15	110.14	14.44	9.62
Area team social work	20.36	30.49	1.59	2.81
Community care social work	97.28	0.00	8.36	0.00
Community care helper costs	201.14	0.00	16.20	0.00
Meals on wheels	9.54	9.68	0.74	0.96
Telephone for disabled person	3.33	3.57	0.29	0.29
2. Cost to the National Health Service				
Total NHS cost (revenue account)	778.00	707.81	68.98	74.92
Total NHS opportunity cost (5%)	830.26	761.46	73.51	80.16
Total NHS opportunity cost (7%)	857.23	784.45	75.89	82.66
Total NHS opportunity cost (10%)	892.02	818.11	78.92	86.06

General hospital cost (revenue account)	400.89	226.36	36.05	32.29
General hospital opportunity cost (5%)	425.64	240.32	38.28	34.29
General hospital opportunity cost (7%)	433.59	244.82	38.99	34.93
General hospital opportunity cost (10%)	447.95	252.93	40.29	36.09
Geriatric hospital cost (revenue account)	176.81	283.22	16.12	22.19
Geriatric hospital opportunity cost (5%)	194.94	312.26	17.77	24.47
Geriatric hospital opportunity cost (7%)	200.77	321.60	18.30	25.19
Geriatric hospital opportunity cost (10%)	211.29	338.46	19.26	26.52
Psychiatric hospital cost (revenue account)	19.64	54.63	1.51	4.86
Psychiatric hospital opportunity cost (5%)	22.22	61.82	1.71	5.49
Psychiatric hospital opportunity cost (7%)	23.06	64.14	1.77	5.70
Psychiatric hospital opportunity cost (10%)	24.56	68.31	1.89	6.07
Geriatric day hospital (revenue account)	64.85	42.76	5.15	5.24
Geriatric day hospital opportunity cost (5%)	76.66	50.55	6.09	6.19
Geriatric day hospital opportunity cost (7%)	80.46	53.05	6.39	6.49
Geriatric day hospital opportunity cost (10%)	87.31	57.57	6.94	7.05
Psychiatric day hospital cost (revenue account)	14.73	0.00	1.13	0.00
Psychiatric day hospital opportunity cost (5%)	17.41	0.00	1.34	0.00
Psychiatric day hospital opportunity cost (7%)	18.27	0.00	1.41	0.00
Psychiatric day hospital opportunity cost (10%)	19.82	0.00	1.53	0.00
Community nursing cost	50.77	50.88	4.53	5.24
Chiropody cost	1.69	1.37	0.14	0.13
3. Private residential care	31.29	79.82	2.41	7.95
4. Department of Health and Social Security				
Supplementary benefit and pensions	979.88	809.52	80.74	78.87
5. Elderly person				
Personal consumption costs (excluding housing)	660.53	470.84	54.20	45.82
Total opportunity cost (including housing)	1,112.29	1,064.65	90.85	101.60
6. Informal carers[2]	74.32	43.51	5.72	10.88

Cost account	Annual cost		Cost per month	
	Community care £	Standard provision £	Community care £	Standard provision £
7. Local authority departments				
Housing rents	86.07	40.13	7.06	4.19
Housing subsidies	11.06	11.99	0.90	1.14
Local authority housing opportunity costs (5%)[3]	119.43	56.31	10.12	6.00
Local authority housing opportunity costs (7%)[3]	161.03	75.93	13.56	8.10
Local authority housing opportunity costs (10%)[3]	226.76	106.95	19.10	11.40
8. Public expenditure total cost	2,407.89	2,231.03	202.17	213.98
9. Social opportunity cost				
Housing opportunity cost (5%)[3]	422.53	389.41	34.54	38.61
Housing opportunity cost (7%)[3]	569.71	525.05	46.57	52.05
Housing opportunity cost (10%)[3]	802.46	739.56	65.59	73.32
Social opportunity cost (5%)	2,669.72	2,497.64	222.89	246.72
Social opportunity cost (7%)	2,850.02	2,686.13	237.77	265.15
Social opportunity cost (10%)	3,127.31	2,981.57	260.59	293.73

Notes
1. Only the major components of cost are included. Small items such as aids, holidays and sheltered housing contribution are not shown.
2. Cases not matched by economic circumstances of informal carers.
3. Cases were not matched by housing values. Differences are thus due both to variation in housing usage and in part to variations in housing value.

Table 8.8.
Cost per case to the social services department for matched cases by Dependency Group (revenue account),£ at1977 prices

Dependency Group	Annual cost		Per month of survival	
	Community care	Standard services	Experimental	Control
1	341	314	28	25
2	537	904	43	73
3	784	678	63	58
4	881	410	71	42

Table 8.9.
Cost per case to the National Health Service for matched cases by Dependency Group (assuming 7% discount rate) £ at 1977 prices

Dependency Group	Annual cost		Per month of survival	
	Community care	Standard services	Experimental	Control
1	-	403	-	42
2	927	663	74	69
3	1043	1192	85	121
4	1001	713	115	86

Table 8.10
Social opportunity cost per case for matched cases by Dependency Group (assuming 7% discount rate),£ at 1977 prices

Dependency Group	Annual cost		Per month of survival	
	Community care	Standard services	Experimental	Control
1	1576	2119	130	198
2	2869	2795	228	252
3	3009	3106	243	326
4	3404	1934	313	237

(a) Costs to the social services department

The community care scheme appeared less costly overall to the social services department than the provision of standard services and also less costly per month of survival. It is clear that this was due largely to the lower level of expenditure on residential care for community care recipients. There is also evidence in the scheme of substantially greater expenditure on social work and some additional home help provision. The higher social work cost was indicative of the more intensive level of activity expected in view of smaller caseloads. Helper costs, naturally, were not incurred by standard services. The structure of the costs of community care clearly reflects the policy of greater investment in home care. An examination of the costs of the four Dependency Groups suggested that the main cost advantage to the social services department of the new scheme was for those in Dependency Group 2. The most frail elderly people, those in Dependency Group 4, appeared to receive significantly fewer resources from standard provision. They were likely to be receiving a substantial amount of informal support and the relatively low level of help under standard provision is consistent with the argument that services have tended to discriminate against carers (Charlesworth *et al.*, 1984). The higher costs of the community care group indicate that the scheme went some way towards redressing this balance. Conversely, under community care there appeared to be a clear cost by dependency gradient, the more dependent receiving more resources.

(b) Costs to the National Health Service

The longer survival of the community care group, on average six weeks longer, tended to make costs to the health service greater. Adjusting these figures by length of survival suggests that the community care scheme was less expensive. The components of National Health Service costs indicate why this was so. Community care cases were more likely to enter acute facilities, which are relatively expensive. This more than offset their lower use of geriatric and psychiatric inpatient facilities. It is interesting to speculate whether additional community services of sufficient scale could release resources from long-term hospital care for short episodes of acute inpatient care. However, there might in the event be little saving due to the greater cost of acute facilities. There is again a closer relationship between cost and dependency for community care. The slightly lower cost of district nursing in the community care scheme could possibly reflect a degree of substitution at the margin of helper support for 'non-nursing duties' which was indicated in interviews with nursing managers.

(c) Costs to elderly people and informal carers
Monthly costs to informal carers appeared less for community care, reflecting the longer survival rate. However, caution must be exercised since cases were not matched by carers' financial circumstances. The higher consumption costs of elderly people in community care in part reflect a longer survival period, but also a reduced rate of entry to institutional care. Personal consumption in institutional settings tends to be low, reflected in the 'pocket money' allowance. Private residential care costs were lower under community care, reflecting a reduced rate of admission.

(d) Costs to other local authority departments
Local authority housing department costs were higher for community care. This was to be expected and reflected the greater and longer use of housing as a result of not entering institutional care. However, again some caution should be exercised since cases were not matched by housing circumstances.

(e) Costs to the public purse and society as a whole
The community care group appeared to have lower public expenditure and social opportunity costs per month of survival. However, it seemed that the greater length of survival of these cases made their costs higher over one year. The social opportunity cost for the four dependency groups suggested a clear relationship between dependency and cost for community care: as a result more resources were received by the most frail. This was not evident for standard provision.

However, this analysis of costs is only over a one-year period. In a longer period there could be a crossover between the apparently lower scheme costs and those of standard services. This might occur due to the relatively greater influence of housing costs in subsequent years for those remaining in their own homes. However, over four years this does not appear to be the case (Chesterman *et al.*, 1986). Indeed, the picture appears to remain surprisingly stable. The community care group had, by the end of four years, survived on average thirty weeks longer than the comparison group. For the social services department the community care scheme appeared to be cheaper overall and per month of survival over the four-year period. The cumulative cost (the sum of the four years) of the scheme remained at about 90 per cent of that of standard provision. The cumulative cost of community care to the National Health Service appeared higher over four years. It rose from being 10 per cent higher at the end of one year to 26 per cent higher than standard provision at the end of four years. However, when comparison is made of the cost per month of survival, even at the end of four years there was no difference between the costs of community care and standard provision. Social costs similarly remained higher on a cumulative basis for community care than standard provision. The costs rose from about 7 per cent more in the first to about 20 per cent more at the end of four years. Again, however, as in the first year, community care had lower social costs per month of survival at the end of four years.

Analysis of costs alone does not, of course, tackle the crucial issue of identifying those cases for whom community care was most appropriate. This requires simultaneous consideration of both costs and effectiveness and is the subject of the next chapter.

CHAPTER 9

COSTS AND OUTCOMES: THE ISSUE OF COST-EFFECTIVENESS

We have so far considered the different outcomes and comparative costs for those receiving community care and standard provision. This is not, of course, sufficient. The main concern for policy and practice is to identify those clients for whom the new approach to care is more (or less) cost-effective. In this chapter we tackle this question by comparing the cost of achieving improvements in well-being for elderly clients in different circumstances, using two different modes of care: community care and standard provision. We examine this from the standpoint of three different 'cost accounts': the social services department, the National Health Service and society as a whole. In the first section we explain the method used to analyse the relationship between costs and outcomes. The following three sections consider the results of the cost-effectiveness question for each of the three 'accounts' in turn.

1. The Approach to the Analysis

As we explained in Chapter 2, our approach to the cost-effectiveness question was guided by the 'production of welfare' framework (Davies and Challis, 1981; Davies and Knapp, 1981; Knapp, 1984; Davies, 1986). Made specific to our context of care of the elderly, the central proposition of the production of welfare theory is that:

> *The outcome of care ('output') for elderly clients is determined by the level and type of care services received ('resource inputs'), the elderly person's individual characteristics and circumstances ('quasi-inputs') and the way in which services combine with client circumstances and characteristics.*

Our concern was thus to explain how the costs of care ('resource inputs') varied as a result of the characteristics and circumstances of clients ('quasi-inputs') and changes in client well-being ('outputs'). This involved estimating the overall effects of outcomes and client circumstances on costs using the statistical technique of multiple regression analysis. In this way we were able to derive a series of equations which explained the extent to which a combination of circumstances such as the health and dependency of old people, and changes in their morale and quality of care caused the costs of care to vary. This approach reflected the reality of service provision where decisions about what level of resources to give to a client are influenced by the multiple needs and problems of each case.

(a) Variables used in the analysis

(i) Costs

Costs were the dependent variables of the analyses. In each case they were the total costs over the one-year period of monitoring. The costs to the social services department consisted of the revenue account expenditure per case including an allowance for capital elements. The costs to the National Health Service consisted of the cost of services provided plus an allowance for a capital element at a 7 per cent discount rate based on the assumption of upgrading of facilities. The measure of social opportunity cost consisted of: the costs of health and social services (including a capital element based on a discount rate of 7 per cent), the costs of private residential homes, the opportunity costs of the elderly person's housing (using a 7 per cent discount rate), the costs incurred by informal carers (such as employment foregone) and the costs of resources consumed in daily living by the elderly person.

(ii) Outputs

One outcome was length of survival which appeared to be influenced by the form of care which people received. The other outputs were defined as changes in an elderly person's state or circumstances between the first and second assessments. Social care outputs were classified into one of two broad types, namely life satisfaction/psychological well-being and adequacy or quality of care. It was possible to reduce the number of variables in this way because of the degree of correlation between individual variables. Hence our analysis could be simplified at a very low cost in loss of information.

'Morale' was used as a proxy variable for the range of elements of subjective well-being and was measured by responses to the Philadephia Geriatric Centre Morale Scale (Lawton, 1975). Quality of care was assessed by constructing a composite variable made up of ratings of the amount of shortfall of the elderly person's care in the areas of rising and retiring, personal care, daily household care and weekly household care.

Two health care outputs were considered: the change in functional capacity, and the change in the degree of severity of health-related conditions. The first was derived from the Index of Activities of Daily Living (Katz *et al.*, 1963). The second measure - General Health - was the sum of severity ratings for eight symptom-related items. These were self-rated health and ratings based on information concerning eyesight, hearing, breathlessness, giddiness, risk of falling, and incontinence of urine and faeces. It might seem that the health care indicators, being functional and physical symptom-related, tend to neglect psychiatric disorders in the elderly. However, to avoid complication, it was assumed that changes in mood state would be captured by the morale indicator (Lohmann, 1977).

In order to make the variables of comparable magnitude and to make change scores meaningful, each variable was transformed into a measure of percentage improvement. They are described in more detail in Appendix A. Because these output indicators were expressed as percentage improvements, initial levels of well-being were included in the analyses to provide a baseline measure.

It was inevitable that for some of the cases it was not possible to ascertain the actual outcomes for those output variables which were derived from interview assessment, such as Quality of Care. This was so because some people did not survive the year and others could not be interviewed for various reasons. However, although for some cases outcomes were unobserved, the production of care process was just as real for these individuals as for others. To estimate costs for survivors alone would be distorting since the needs and circumstances of non-survivors in practice influence expenditure decisions, and therefore the operation of the scheme, just as much they would for those for whom outcomes were observed. In these cases of unobserved outcomes, the mean value of the group was assigned to the unobserved variable to avoid bias in the estimate of the cost effect of these variables. In view of the greater death rate and decline in states of welfare in the group receiving standard services, this tends toward bias against finding an advantage to community care since missing cases were attributed levels of output higher than would really have been the case. Alternative assumptions which were tested produced not dissimilar results (Davies and Challis, 1986).

(iii) Quasi-inputs

These are factors which mediate and influence the relationship between costs and outcomes. These were of five types: Social Support, Dependency and Health, Personality and Attitude to Help, Aspects of the Physical Environment, and Other Factors. They are listed with the output indicators in Table 9.1, and are described in Appendix A.

The variables Age and Sex were not used in the initial estimation since it was expected that both would be closely associated with dependency. Since the need for the provision of long-term care is substantially determined by dependency, it was thought that age and sex could mask this important relationship. Age is likely to be highly correlated with dependency. Sex may reflect different propensities to suffer certain health conditions (Mayer-Gross *et al.*, 1977; Yarnell and St Leger, 1979) and capacity to cope. These variables were therefore examined by considering their effect on costs only after the other characteristics had been taken into account.

(b) The estimation procedure and interpretation of tables

The seventy-four matched pairs of cases were used in these analyses since these

Table 9.1
Predictor variables used in the cost estimation

Domain	Variable	Variable form
Outputs		
	Quality of Care	Per cent improvement or decline
	Subjective Well-being	Per cent improvement or decline
	Survival	Months survived
	General Health	Per cent improvement or decline
Quasi-inputs		
Health and dependency		
	Eyesight difficulties	None, moderate,severe
	Hearing difficulties	None, moderate,severe
	Giddiness	None, moderate,severe
	Breathlessness	None, moderate,severe
	Risk of falling	None, moderate,severe
	Incontinence of urine	None, occasional,frequent
	Incontinence of faeces	None, occasional, frequent
	Dependency states	Dependency Groups 1, 2, 3 and 4
	Confusion/disorientation	Sum of responses to items concerning behaviour, appearance, memory; range 0-9
	Depressed mood	None, mild, moderate, severe
	Felt capacity to cope	Sum of responses to four questions concerning capacity to cope with different areas of daily living; range 4-16
	Loneliness	Sum of responses to two questions concerning felt loneliness and dissatisfaction; range 0-6
	Anxiety	None, mild, moderate, severe
Social support		
	All informal care	Total weekly social contacts
	Support of spouse	Present or absent
	Support from children	Weekly social contacts
	Support from relatives	Weekly social contacts
	Support from neighbours and friends	Weekly social contacts
Personality and attitudes to help		
	Hostile-rejecting attitude to help	Characteristic present or absent
	Passive-dependent attitude to help	Characteristic present or absent
	Dependent-demanding attitude to help	Characteristic present or absent
Physical environment and other factors		
	Shortcomings in housing	Number of identified problems
	Overall suitability of housing	Suitable, unsuitable, detrimental
	Elderly persons's dissatisfaction with housing	Number of reasons
	Age	
	Sex	
	Whether retired to area	
	Recent bereavement	

were the two groups between whom there was the least degree of variation due to the characteristics of the elderly person. Separate estimates were made for the experimental and control groups. Our concern was to find a combination of variables that would explain the most of the variation in costs (the 'best fit'). Independent variables were only included if their coefficients had a 't' statistic with a value greater than 1, which would therefore improve the 'goodness of fit'. Further details are given in *Matching Resources to Needs* (Chaps 11 and 12). These equations provided the basis both to predict the cost of certain levels of outcome for clients in different circumstances and to further examine the process of care.

In the sections which follow we describe how costs varied according to the circumstances of the clients, and then examine the expected costs of care for different groups of elderly people receiving community care and standard provision. However, before progressing further in the discussion of the findings, it would be helpful to pause and provide an explanation of the tables which show our cost equations. In the absence of this explanation they could appear unnecessarily complicated and daunting. Tables 9.2, 9.3, 9.6, 9.7, 9.9 and 9.10. show the variables which proved to significantly influence the cost of care. The effect on cost, either positive or negative, of each variable is shown and the statistical significance of this effect. The variables are of two kinds, outcomes or outputs (effects on client well-being) and quasi-inputs (circumstances and characteristics of clients). Let us consider each in turn.

The outcome variables inevitably appear the more complex for several reasons. First, there are quadratic or squared terms in the equations. These are there because the relationship between cost and outcome is not linear; that is to say, for example, that increasing the quality of care by a given amount from an already high level is more costly than from a lower level. Thus, to increase to 24-hour cover the care of an elderly person already receiving cover twelve hours a day is probably more expensive than to provide 12-hour cover for someone currently receiving none. Second, there are interaction terms or joint effects between the outputs, for instance between Subjective Well-being and Quality of Care. Sometimes two outputs may be produced together in a less costly fashion than one alone, for example when a home help who visits to provide household care also raises an elderly person's morale. Third, there are interaction terms or joint effects between outcome and dependency, reflecting the fact that achieving well-being for the highly dependent might be more costly than for the less dependent. We shall not discuss the outcome indicators further here since they have mainly been used in the comparison of the cost of outcomes between community care and standard provision later in the chapter.

The 'quasi-input' or client characteristics variables are more readily understood. Those which appear in the equations with highly significant cost effects can be used to further understand the care process and the particular circumstances that influenced fieldworkers' decisions. Thus, for example, a positive cost effect for confusion and disorientation indicates that clients with these characteristics were more costly than others to support, whilst a negative cost effect for support by a spouse would indicate that such cases tended to be less costly than others due to the influence of family support. Linking these statistical findings with our observations about care processes in Chapters 3, 4 and 5 helps to clarify further the factors which were influential in decision-making.

2. Costs and Outcomes for the Social Services Department

The cost which we sought to explain was the total cost to the social services department as described earlier in this chapter. A number of possible forms of the relationship between costs and outcomes were considered, from the simplest where each element is additive in its effect on cost to more complex formulations (see *Matching Resources to Needs*, Chap. 11). These latter versions contained interaction terms which postulated, for example, that outputs would be more or less costly for elderly people with different levels of dependency or social support. However, the small number of cases would not permit all the possible forms of the relationship between costs and outcomes to be examined.

The final forms were chosen by criteria of goodness of fit and relative simplicity. As noted earlier, this permitted interactions between outcomes and dependency - possible differences in cost for improvements in Subjective Well-being and Quality of Care for people with different levels of frailty. These effects were represented in the equations by terms relating Subjective Well-being to Dependency Group (e.g. MDG4) and Quality of Care to Dependency Group (e.g. QDG4). Quadratic terms (e.g. Quality of Life^2, Q^2) were tested to see whether the cost of, say, improving Quality of Care increases the higher the level of care. The effect of services producing two outputs at the same time (joint supply), for example a service designed to meet practical needs also raising morale, was also examined by interaction terms between Subjective Well-being and Quality of Care (e.g. MQ).

The final equations were reasonably effective in explaining variations in cost; explaining 50 per cent and 70 per cent for community care and standard services respectively. Tables 9.2 and 9.3 show these equations for both modes of care and indicate the effect of each variable on cost and its statistical significance.

Table 9.2
Costs of outputs to the social services department in community care, 'outcome by dependency' relationship, £ at 1977 prices

Variable type	Variable	Cost effect £	p
Outputs			
	MDG2 (Subjective Well-being x Dependency Group 2)	7.74	.083
	MDG4 (Subjective Well-being x Dependency Group 4)	-11.37	.218
	QDG1 (Quality of Care x Dependency Group 1)	5.35	.120
	MQDG3 (Subjective Well-being x Quality of Care x Dependency Group 3 interaction)	0.062	.014
	MQDG4 (Subjective Well-being x Quality of Care x Dependency Group 3 interaction)	0.121	.029
	M^2 (Subjective Well-being)^2	-0.093	.010
	Q^2 (Quality of Care)^2	-0.039	.005
	$(MQ)^2$ (Subjective Well-being x Quality of Care)^2	0.03*	.004
	Survival (months)	85.83	.002
Quasi-inputs			
Health and dependency			
	Incontinence of urine	211.80	.079
	Mental clarity (lack of dementia)	-41.36	.182
	Loneliness	117.79	.034
Social support			
	Support from spouse	-23.87	.269
	Support from relatives	-54.36	.040
Personality/attitude			
	Refusing-rejecting attitude to help	-256.00	.069
Physical environment			
	Unsuitable housing	-77.40	.320
Initial level of well-being			
	Subjective well-being	-22.95	.184
	Quality of care	55.98	.692
	(Constant)	668.23	.295
	Equation	$R^2 = .52$ Adj $F = 3.19$	$R^2 = .35$ $p < .001$

* coefficient multiplied by 10,000

Table 9.3
Costs of outputs to the social services department in standard provision, 'outcome by dependency' relationship, £ at 1977 prices

Variable type	Variable	Cost effect £	p
Outputs			
	QDG2 (Quality of Care x Dependency Group 2)	-1.76	.237
	QDG3 (Quality of Care x Dependency Group 3)	5.79	.158
	M^2(Subjective Well-being)^2	-0.121	.139
	Q^2(Quality of Care)^2	-0.074	.148
	$(MQ)^2$(Subjective Well-being x Quality of Care interaction)^2	0.01*	.017
	Survival	47.28	.017
Quasi-inputs			
Health and dependency			
	Giddiness	218.57	.410
	Hearing difficulty	297.48	.056
	Dependency Group 3	-952.61	.087
	Depressed mood	-180.65	.180
	Felt capacity to cope	71.92	.030
Personality and attitudes			
	Passive-dependent attitude to help	546.10	.020
Initial level of well-being			
	Subjective Well-being	-11.39	.680
	Quality of Care	95.25	.527
	(Constant)	251.39	.832
Equation		$R^2 = .70$ Adj $R^2 = .62$ F=9.45	$p < 001$

* coefficient multiplied by 10,000

(a) Factors influencing the relationship between costs and outcomes: The process of care

The equations, their significant variables and the signs of individual coefficients provide important clues to the different care processes occurring in community care and standard provision.

(i) Health and dependency

Several health and dependency characteristics influenced the cost of care. The negative effect of incontinence of urine in the community care group is perhaps best explained by the fact that the scheme made it more possible for those with this condition to remain at home, although it presented a particular problem in the absence of specific services for incontinence. The positive cost effect of a confusional state in the community care scheme was to be expected despite the low level of significance in view of the difficulty of caring for the demented elderly. It was clear that these individuals tended to be on average more expensive than individuals with predominantly physical disorders, whether because of a higher rate of admission to residential homes in the early phase of the scheme or more intensive support at home in the later stages. Giddiness had a positive effect on costs for the group of elderly people receiving standard services. This reflects the particular problems of those individuals who were at high risk of falling who, in the absence of community care, were likely to enter residential homes. Hearing difficulty appeared to exert a significant positive influence on costs for the elderly receiving standard services. It appeared that these people were more likely to enter residential care than others, perhaps because the difficulty of communication made care at home less manageable.

Other analyses found that high dependency exerted a significant positive effect on costs for the community care scheme. In the comparison group, higher levels of dependency were less costly. This suggests that resources were more closely tailored to needs in community care since, other things being equal, greater resources tended to be provided for the more frail.

The positive cost effect of loneliness in the community care group indicates the degree of importance placed on meeting the psychological as well as the more practical needs of elderly people. The more lonely individuals, often very isolated, were likely to prove additionally costly since their need for support was greater. Depressed mood appeared to reduce expenditure on those in receipt of standard services although at a low level of significance. At first sight this may seem surprising. However, depression is frequently undetected in the elderly (Goldberg *et al.*, 1970; Goldberg and Huxley, 1980); those with affective disorders are less likely to receive social services (Foster *et al.*, 1976). Depressed elderly people may well initially refuse help, and with less careful assessment and preparatory work with the elderly person there is a danger that this refusal may be accepted at face value.

(ii) Informal support

The influence of Social Support is of particular interest in view of concern about complementarity and substitution between formal and informal care (Abrams, 1977). For the group of elderly people receiving community care, two elements of informal support had a negative effect on costs: support from a spouse and support from relatives. So, the greater the level of informal care, the less costly the care of the elderly person. Other analyses indicated that improvements in Quality of Care were less costly for the very frail where informal carers were involved and that possibly improved Quality of Care enhanced the relationship of the elderly person with their carers. There was, however, no evidence that informal support influenced costs for those in receipt of standard services. This suggests that the community care scheme, by providing support to carers who in the absence of the scheme would receive relatively little help, was actually able to reduce costs in the longer run. If not given adequate support at a sufficiently early stage, carers can reach a breaking point beyond which they can become a powerful pressure group for an elderly person to enter residential care, which substantially increases costs. The evidence is therefore consistent with a relationship of complementarity between formal and informal care in the community care scheme, but there was no such evidence for those receiving standard services.

(iii) Personality and attitude to help

The evidence about the influence of attitudes to help and personality characteristics is not easy to interpret. There was a clear negative effect on costs of a 'rejecting-refusing' attitude to help in the community care scheme, reflecting the difficulty experienced with some of these individuals in enabling them to accept help. In part, the explanation for the lack of significance of this factor in the group receiving standard services may lie in their willingness to accept a small baseline level of care but not to accept a more intensive level of support. Consequently, they would be unlikely to differ greatly from many others in the community receiving the standard level of service. The 'passive-dependent' attitude appeared to make elderly people more costly when in receipt of standard services. Since one-half of these individuals were in institutional care at follow-up, one possible explanation is that these individuals are more likely to respond to pressure to enter residential care. Since this effect was not evident in community care, it may be that the emphasis on client choice and the wider range of options open to staff in the scheme made it more feasible for these individuals' wishes to be taken into account.

(iv) Other factors

The influence of age and sex on these relationships was tested by their addition once the final form of the equation had been estimated. For both the group receiving standard services and the group receiving community care, there was a significant positive age effect (community care 15.33, p=.059; standard services 26.55, p=.02) which would be expected. That is to say, the greater the age of an elderly person the more costly their care is likely to be. There was no real evidence of sex influencing costs, although there was a suggestion of a positive effect of male sex in both groups which might be expected, men often being admitted to residential care in a less dependent state than women, but this did not reach a satisfactory level of significance. The age/cost gradient which was found was not dissimilar for community care and standard services and was in the expected direction. Since the major interest was on other determinants of variations in cost, age was not used further in the analyses.

The cost of increasing survival appeared to be greater for the community care scheme than for the group receiving standard services. To some extent this must reflect the influence of the longer period of survival of the community care group, and their reduced likelihood of spending time in hospital care. However, it may also indicate how closer and longer contact with the elderly person, arising from the case-management responsibility, will tend to lead to the identification of further needs. It is only to be expected that matching services to need will mean the adjustment of services upward as health declines, particularly if people are less likely to enter hospital care.

(b) The costs of outputs for elderly people in different circumstances

The principal cost-effectiveness question was to identify the circumstances in which the community care project was most (or least) cost-effective. To answer this question, it is necessary to compare the differences in the cost of achieving outcomes between the two forms of care. This was done using the equations of the relationship between costs, client circumstances and outcomes described in the previous section to predict the cost of achieving different combinations of outputs for clients with a range of different characteristics.

(i) Costs of ten case types

Ten distinct groups of elderly people were identified. Six were types of case representative of a range of people likely to require domiciliary and residential services, and four were representative of the four Dependency Groups. In view of the relatively small number of cases on which the estimates were based, the predictions for the six types run the risk of extrapolation for which our relatively small number of cases provides insufficient evidence. The more aggregated estimates for the four Dependency Groups avoid this risk.

The characteristics of these ten different cases are described below, and are summarised in Table 9.4.

Table 9.4
Characteristics of the ten client types

	Types									
Characteristics	**A**	**B**	**C**	**D**	**E**	**F**	**DG1**	**DG2**	**DG3**	**DG4**
Health and dependency										
Dependency Group	4	3	3	3	2	1	1	2	3	4
Incontinence of urine	S	S	S	S	S	N	N	N	S	S
Breathlessness	V	S	N	N	S	N	S	S	S	S
Hearing difficulty	S	S	N	N	S	S	N	N	M	N
Giddiness	V	S	S	S	V	S	S	V	S	S
Mental health										
Confusion	V	N	V	V	N	N	N	N	M	M
Loneliness	H	L	L	L	M	M	L	M	M	L
Felt capacity to cope	H	L	H	H	L	L	M	M	M	M
Depressed mood	L	N	H	M	H	H	M	M	L	L
Social support										
Social support	P	P	P	N	N	N	-	-	-	-
Suppport from relatives	N	N	M	N	N	N	L	L	H	L

Key
N = None S = Some V = Severe L = Low M = Moderate H = High P = Present

Type A. Extremely physically frail people, who are also mentally impaired, with very poor health. A person in this group would be highly dependent, categorised in Dependency Group 4, reliant on their spouse but otherwise relatively isolated and lonely.

Type B. Physically frail, but less frail than cases categorised as Type A, and not suffering from dementia. This type of person is reliant on their spouse but has some doubt about their capacity to continue to cope with living in their own home.

Type C. Mentally frail, living with spouse, suffering from a degree of depression, unrealistic about their continued capacity to cope, and heavily reliant on support from other relatives as well as the principal carer.

Type D. As for Type C but less depressed and lacking in social support.

Type E. Lonely and depressed, living alone, and mentally well-preserved; but lacking social support and at considerable risk of falling.

Type F. Physically relatively unimpaired and no evidence of dementia, but very anxious about their ability to continue to cope, lacking social support and both depressed and lonely.

Dependency Group 1. In better physical health than most, no problem of incontinence or evidence of serious mental impairment. However, more isolated than most, and more likely to suffer from depression and anxiety. Difficulties particularly evident in meal preparation, care of home and some neglect of self and diet. They would be classified as the 'long interval need' group of Isaacs and Neville (1976).

Dependency Group 2. Tend to suffer from social isolation and live alone. Often suffer from giddiness and risk of falling at any time. Depression is likely to be associated with these problems. In addition to their security needs they have problems in meal preparation and home care. They would be classified as the 'short interval need' group of Isaacs and Neville (1976).

Dependency Group 3. These people are much more frail physically than those in Dependency Groups 1 or 2. They are more likely to suffer from problems of incontinence and mental frailty and have significantly more difficulties in Activities of Daily Living. They are likely to have a greater degree of informal support and would be classified as the 'critical interval need' group by the criteria of Isaacs and Neville (1976)

Dependency Group 4. These constitute the physically most frail subgroup of 'critical interval need'. They are less likely to exhibit mental frailty but are bedridden, chairbound or suffering from faecal incontinence.

The cost of care over a one-year period was estimated for each of these ten groups, for a range of different changes in output from no change to a 40 per cent improvement in Subjective Well-being (M) and 100 per cent improvement in Quality of Care (Q). These ranges were consistent with observed changes for individual cases. The initial level of well-being indicators of Subjective Well-Being and Quality of Care were set at the mean value for these estimates and it was assumed that the elderly person would survive over a full year. The estimated costs for the ten groups can be seen in Table 9.5. To interpret the Table it is helpful to examine four points: 'No change' (0,M,0,Q), 'Some improvement' (10%M, 20%Q), 'Considerable improvement' (20%M, 40%Q) and 'Substantial improvement' (30%M, 60%Q). These are marked in Table 9.5 overleaf.

Table 9.5
Annual costs of outcomes to the social services department for different types of case, £ at 1977 prices

GROUP	Degree of Improvement		'Some'			'Considerable'						'Substantial'		
	% improvement in Subjective Well-being													
	0		10			20			30			40		
	% improvement Quality Care													
	0	20	0	20	40	20	40	60	40	60	80	60	80	100
	£	£	£	£	£	£	£	£	£	£	£	£	£	£
Type A														
Community care	363	581	246	519	795	449	789	1,137	778	1,202	1,640	1,265	1,789	2,336
Standard provision	1,140	1,273	1,105	1,334	1,605	1,401	1,797	2,253	2,005	2,617	3,320	3,009	3,427	4,416
Type B														
Community care	194	296	132	278	424	251	451	659	472	743	1,216	827	1,152	1,535
Standard provision	516	765	481	826	1,213	893	1,404	1,976	1,612	2,340	3,158	2,733	3,733	4,832
Type C														
Community care	331	433	269	415	561	388	588	796	609	880	1,353	964	1,289	1,672
Standard provision	70	319	35	380	767	447	958	1,530	1,166	1,894	2,712	2,287	3,287	4,386
Type D														
Community care	725	825	663	809	955	782	982	1,190	1,003	1,274	1,747	1,358	1,683	2,066
Standard provision	214	463	179	524	911	591	1,102	1,674	1,310	2,038	2,856	2,431	3,431	4,530
Type E														
Community care	965	942	919	927	936	902	952	1,011	964	1,073	1,197	1,135	1,321	1,529
Standard provision	352	450	317	512	747	579	939	1,359	1,146	1,723	2,390	2,116	2,965	3,918
Type F														
Community care	751	834	626	741	858	640	797	961	731	947	1,178	931	1,224	1,539
Standard provision	310	444	275	505	776	572	967	1,423	1,175	1,787	2,490	2,180	3,063	4,052
Dependency Group 1														
Community care	367	450	242	357	474	256	413	577	347	563	794	547	840	1,155
Standard provision	174	308	139	369	640	436	831	1,287	1,039	1,651	2,354	2,044	2,927	3,916

Dependency Group 2														
Community care	296	273	250	258	267	233	283	342	295	404	528	466	652	860
Standard provision	264	362	229	424	659	491	851	1,271	1,058	1,635	2,302	2,028	2,877	3,830
Dependency Group 3														
Community care	510	612	448	594	740	567	767	975	788	1,059	1,532	1,143	1,468	1,851
Standard provision	156	405	121	466	853	533	1,044	1,616	1,252	1,980	2,798	2,373	3,373	4,472
Dependency Group 4														
Community Care	11	229	-106	167	443	97	437	785	426	850	1,288	913	1,437	1,984
Standard provision	313	446	278	507	778	574	970	1,426	1,178	1,790	2,493	2,182	2,067	4,056

Six case types. For the six hypothetical cases, the greatest advantage to the community care scheme was for Type A and Type B. These were cases of very severe frailty, where the scheme would focus on supporting a network of informal carers for an elderly person who, if entering institutional care, would be probably equally likely to enter hospital or a residential home. As might be expected there was a greater cost advantage to community care for those cases whose primary problem was dementia and where substantial informal care was available. This would be expected from the findings of Bergmann *et al.* (1978) who argued that it would be more cost-effective to focus domiciliary support on those cases with informal care than those living alone. Those cases living alone who suffered from dementia and who were successfully supported in their own homes tended to be relatively more expensive.

Four Dependency Groups. An examination of the predicted costs of the four Dependency Groups suggested that the greatest cost advantage lay in Dependency Groups 1 and 2, those whose difficulties were associated with depression, anxiety and low morale or for whom risk of falling and social isolation made institutional care likely.

These results suggest overall that for most cases throughout most of the range of outcomes there is a cost advantage to community care. This cost advantage appeared to be greater the higher the level of output achieved.

(ii) Effects for informal carers

The outcomes or 'outputs' considered in the analyses so far were benefits to the elderly person in terms of Quality of Care and Subjective Well-being. Although these are undoubtedly likely to be desirable from the point of view of informal carers, the effect on them is only an indirect one, although in an earlier chapter it was noted that both community care and standard services had tended to reduce the burdens experienced by carers.

It was not practicable to estimate the cost of different levels of improvement for carers in regression equations because of the small numbers of cases with principal carers. However some calculations were possible by examining the costs unexplained by the variables in the equation (residual costs).

Generally, cases with carers receiving standard provision tended to receive fewer resources than would be expected by their need characteristics. Cases with carers receiving standard services proved to be very inexpensive while living at home, but were very likely to enter residential care. Conversely, those receiving community care were more expensive while living at home, but proved less likely to require institutional care. Whereas 24 per cent of those with carers receiving community care had entered institutional care after one year, 60 per cent of those receiving standard services had done so. However, following a test of significance on the residuals (the amount of cost unexplained), there was no evidence of a significant difference between the cost of the two services in improving the well-being of carers. The slightly greater improvements achieved by community care do, however, indicate greater cost-effectiveness.

Nevertheless, this again supports the view that if informal carers are given help at an earlier stage, they are less likely to press family practitioners for the elderly person's admission to a residential home as the difficulties of caring increase. Some carers in the comparison group only reached this position with the greatest reluctance. For example, the son and daughter of one lady in the comparison group decided that their mother should enter a home. This happened, but after about a year they took their mother back home with them as she was clearly unhappy, although the only realistic assistance available to them was day care and they could confidently expect further difficulties for themselves.

3. Costs and Outcomes for the National Health Service

The cost which we sought to explain was total cost to the National Health Service and the outcome indicators were measures of General Health and performance of Activities of Daily Living. These are described in Section 1 of this chapter. The exploration of the forms of the cost relationships for the health service was not as exhaustive as that for social care. In the absence of independent medical assessments of the elderly people and therefore sensitive outcome measures, it was not possible to provide as good an explanation for cost relations in health as in social care. Therefore only a relatively simple form of the relationship was explored without the most complicated dependency-outcome interactions. The estimates of the relationships which proved best by statistical criteria are shown in Tables 9.6 and 9.7.

(a) Factors influencing variations in cost

(i) Health and dependency

The General Health indicator for the community care group had a positive and significant effect (Table 9.6), which suggested that the greater the degree of ill-health, the greater the level of health care expenditure on those individuals. This indicated that those cases receiving community care might be more likely to receive levels of resources appropriate to their needs. No such relationship was apparent for those in receipt of standard services; indeed the reverse proved to be the case.

Individual health and dependency characteristics also had significant influences on cost. Under the community care scheme, those incontinent of urine tended to be less costly, since they were managed in their own homes.

Table 9.6 Costs of outputs to the National Health Service in community care, £ at 1977 prices

Variable type	Variable	Cost effect £	p
Outputs			
	Activities of Daily Living (ADL)	12.31	.002
	General Health	9.47	.117
	G^2 (General Health)	-0.10	.067
	AG (ADL x General Health interaction)	0.09	.055
	$(AG)^2$ (ADL x General Health interaction)^2	-0.14*	.254
Quasi-inputs			
Dependency and health			
	Breathlessness	-763.92	.000
	Hearing difficulty	582.76	.018
	Risk of falling	-351.55	.169
	Incontinence of urine	-630.72	.020
	Dependency Group 4	-498.54	.170
Social support			
	Contact with children	-94.73	.006
	Contact with neighbours	-46.73	.100
Personality/attitudes			
	Dependent-demanding attitude	877.41	.041
	Rejection-refusing attitude	850.14	.003
Initial health status			
	General Health	180.09	.025
	ADL level	129.57	.291
	(Constant)	1343.85	.021
Equation		$R^2=.58$ Adj $F=5.25$	$R^2=.47$ $p<.000$

* coefficient multiplied by 10,000

Table 9.7 Costs of outputs to the National Health Service in standard provision, £ at 1977 prices

Variable type	Variable	Cost effect £	p
Outputs			
	Activities of Daily Living (ADL)	6.59	.003
	General Health	20.73	.000
	AG (ADL x General Health interaction)	-0.13	.000
	Survival	51.86	.139
Quasi-inputs			
Dependency and health			
	Incontinence of urine	1159.93	.000
	Breathlessness	246.54	.251
	Hearing difficulty	651.36	.047
	Dependency Group 1	-691.77	.141
	Dependency Group 4	620.91	.264
Social support			
	Contact with children	-58.12	.211
Initial health status			
	General Health	-265.36	.003
	ADL level	-251.22	.091
	(Constant)	571.82	.334
Equation		$R^2=.39$ Adj $F=3.15$	$R^2=.26$ $p<.002$

However, for the recipients of standard services, this condition tended to increase costs, reflecting a greater likelihood of long-term hospital care. Risk of falling appeared to reduce costs for the recipients of community care, since they were particularly likely to remain at home. In both community care and standard services, difficulties in hearing tended to lead to increased health service costs. Breathlessness appeared to be associated with increased costs for those receiving standard services but with reduced costs for those in receipt of community care. This can be explained most readily by shorter periods of inpatient care for the community care group. For those in Dependency Group 4 (the very frail), community care appeared to reduce the cost to the health service, whilst in the comparison group these individuals were particularly expensive. At first sight, the reduction in cost for this group in community care appears strange, but it is likely to reflect the possibility of substitution in care between the health service and social services. This has proved to be the case in other intensive social care services. For example, the Coventry Home Help project found that increased provision of home helps undertaking a wider range of tasks reduced costs to the community nursing service (Latto, 1980a,b). Whilst the very frail tended to receive less from social services and more from the health service with standard provision, under community care the reverse was often the case. Community care appeared therefore to have helped the NHS to provide better health care since it helpeded it in targeting on those with treatable conditions and enabled it to undertake more acute and less long-stay hospital care (Chapter 8).

(ii) Social support

Social support only appeared to exert a discernable effect on costs for elderly people receiving community care. For these, support from both children and neighbours had a negative effect on health service costs. This suggests that the higher the level of informal support, the greater the reduction in costs to the health service. It appears that the greater provision of support to carers in the community care scheme tends to reduce costs not just for the social services department but also for the National Health Service, by reducing the need for long-term care in hospital.

(iii) Personality and attitudinal characteristics

In the community care scheme two of the personality/attitudinal characteristics appeared to influence costs. The positive influence of the 'dependent-demanding' and 'refusing-rejecting' attitudes reflects the higher degree of physical frailty of individuals with these characteristics, and the efforts of the community care team to ensure that they received treatment which they otherwise were unlikely to receive.

(iv) Other factors

Age exerted a significant negative influence on costs to the health service in both community care ($p = .05$) and standard services ($p = .09$). Whilst this may appear to be at odds with accepted wisdom, it is likely to be explained by the fact that the more acutely physically ill individuals tended to be younger than the group as a whole. Sex did not appear to have a significant influence on costs.

(b) The costs of outputs for elderly people in different circumstances

In order to examine the characteristics of elderly people for whom the community care scheme made the provision of health care more cost-effective, the equations in Tables 9.6 and 9.7 were used to predict costs at different levels of health. As before, costs were predicted for the average case in each Dependency Group, from the relatively low degree of frailty represented by

Dependency Group 1 to the extreme frailty of Dependency Group 4. It was assumed that the elderly person survived for a whole year. The predicted cost is therefore the annual cost of achieving a given level of output for an elderly person of a certain dependency level. The results are shown in Table 9.8. For ease of interpretation it is helpful to examine the degrees of improvement, 'No change' in Activities of Daily Living or General Health (0 ADL, 0 GH), 'Some improvement' (10% ADL, 10% GH), 'Considerable improvement' (20% ADL, 20% GH) and 'Substantial improvement' (30% ADL and 30% GH). These are marked on Table 9.8.

It can be seen that it is only in Dependency Group 2 that the standard services appeared to be more cost-effective and even in this case only at lower levels of output. When in receipt of standard services these elderly people were particularly likely to enter residential care, which probably reduced their level of demand for health care. In the community care scheme, the social workers attempted to liaise more closely with NHS staff, particularly in the field of geriatric medicine, which led to increased use of acute hospital beds and day hospital treatment, and therefore increased costs. At times this involved attempts to improve an individual's mobility, but frequently admission was for other discomforting conditions suffered by elderly people, which made managing alone more difficult. Changes in some of these conditions would be unlikely to be reflected in the relatively crude output measures used, and as a consequence this might lead to apparent overstatement of the cost of producing other outputs. It may well be that this additional health care for the community care group influenced survival patterns.

The community care scheme appeared to be more cost-effective for the health service in the care of the remaining three groups. This was particularly so for Dependency Group 4 - the most frail - for whom, in the absence of the scheme, long-term hospital care would probably be required. Furthermore, as was the case for the costs of social care, the greater the improvement in health, the more cost-effective did community care appear to be in relation to standard services.

(c) The interdependence of health and social care

The incidence of costs on the health service or social services department may well be to some extent arbitrary, and costs borne by one agency could well lead to outputs which in principle are the goals of the other. Indeed, the same functions may at times be performed by either agency. For example, bathing or washing could be undertaken by either, and elderly people with similar characteristics may be found in a hospital, a residential home, at home, or living with relatives and receiving very little service from either agency (Kay *et al.*, 1964; Isaacs and Neville, 1976). For those elderly people receiving community

Table 9.8
Annual costs to the National Health Service of different levels of output for four Dependency Groups, £ at 1977 prices

Group	Degree of Improvement: 'Some'					'Considerable'			'Substantial'					
% improvement in ADL	0		10			20			30			40		
% improvement in Health Status	0	10	0	10	20	10	20	30	20	30	40	30	40	50
Dependency Group 1														
Community care	795	739	732	680	604	617	543	445	478	379	257	309	185	36
Standard provision	689	942	801	861	920	779	825	872	730	763	796	655	674	693
Dependency Group 2														
Community care	1,264	1,209	1,201	1,149	1,073	1,136	1,086	1,012	946	848	726	778	654	505
Standard provision	909	982	840	900	959	772	818	865	769	803	835	694	713	733
Dependency Group 3														
Community care	1,196	1,141	1,134	1,081	1,005	1,018	944	846	879	781	658	711	587	437
Standard provision	1,312	1,385	1,244	1,303	1,363	1,222	1,268	1,314	1,173	1,206	1,238	1,097	1,116	1,136
Dependency Group 4														
Community care	812	757	749	698	622	635	561	462	495	397	274	327	203	54
Standard provision	1,083	1,156	1,014	1,074	1,134	993	1,039	1,085	944	977	1,009	868	887	906

care, the costs to the health service of providing health care appeared to be reduced for the most frail, those in Dependency Group 4. One possible explanation of this finding would be that the costs of producing outputs in social care may depend on the inputs of health resources, and vice versa. It appeared that within the community care scheme those old people who were relatively costly to the social services department were less costly to the health service. Conversely, under standard provision, those with high health service costs were less costly to the social services department.

A more sophisticated analysis of this issue was attempted, in order to assess the degree of interdependence of the two agencies. The method involved re-estimation of the two best equations for NHS and social services department costs using the technique of the 'Seemingly Unrelated Regression Equation' (Zellner, 1962), and including an indicator to identify those cases with high expenditure. The results confirmed the previous observation of the influence of high spending in one agency on the other. In the comparison area it appeared that high spending by the NHS significantly reduced expenditure by the social services department; inevitably, since this was predominantly hospital inpatient care. Conversely, under the community care scheme, it appeared that high spending on elderly people by the social services department significantly reduced expenditure by the National Health Service. The evidence of enhanced collaboration as a result of the new scheme appeared to be in the care for the most frail. The analyses are further elaborated in Chapter 12 of *Matching Resources to Needs* (Davies and Challis, 1986), which also contains a similar analysis of costs to clients and their informal carers.

4. Costs and Outcomes for Society as a Whole

In this section the cost which we attempt to explain is total social cost, described in Section 1 of this chapter. The outcome indicators were the two social care outputs - Subjective Well-being and Quality of Care - since our concern was to consider the costs and benefits of a social care intervention and therefore of ways of improving social care outputs. The form of the relationship which was estimated was that which included interactions between outcome and dependency as in our estimation of costs to the social services department. The final forms of these equations are shown in Tables 9.9 and 9.10.

(a) Factors influencing the relationship between costs and outcomes

(i) Health and dependency

It can be seen that several health characteristics exerted a significant influence on costs. Incontinence of urine had a negative effect for those in the community care scheme (Table 9.9). In part this is likely to reflect an association with death, 25 per cent of those who had suffered from incontinence having died compared with only 12 per cent of those who did not suffer incontinence. However, it is also indicative of lower hospital and institutional costs for community care. This is clear since for those in receipt of standard services, incontinence of urine made care more costly. The negative effect of breathlessness in community care is most probably explained by the fact that people with this condition were able to remain in their own homes. Conversely, the positive cost effect of hearing difficulty is most readily explained by the greater likelihood of such people entering institutional care, whether in receipt of community care or standard services. The negative cost effect of loneliness for those in receipt of standard servies is probably explained by a relative

Table 9.9
Costs of outputs to society in community care, £ at 1977 prices

Variable type	Variable	Cost effect £	p
Outputs			
	MDG1 (Subjective Well-being x Dependency Group 1)	-33.64	.119
	MDG3 (Subjective Well-being x Dependency Group 3)	17.73	.043
	MDG4 (Subjective Well-being x Dependency Group 4)	54.78	.001
	QDG2 (Quality of Care x Dependency Group 2)	8.27	.110
	MQDG4 (Subjective Well-being x Quality of Care x Dependency Group 4 interaction)	-0.18	.035
	M^2 (Subjective Well-being)^2	-0.043	.312
	Q^2 (Quality of Care)^2	0.013	.147
	Survival	128.53	.018
Quasi-inputs			
Health and dependency			
	Breathlessness	-459.37	.010
	Hearing difficulty	872.65	.000
	Incontinence of urine	-745.29	.002
	Dependency Group 1	4410.43	.071
Social support			
	Support from relatives	78.18	.146
	Support from children	-70.64	.032
Personality/attitudes			
	Refusing-rejecting attitude to help	667.84	.024
	Dependent-demanding attitude to help	1061.14	.022
Environmental Factors			
	Housing unsuitability	213.88	.221
Initial Level of Need			
	Subjective Well-being	-93.41	.001
	Quality of Care shortfall	402.32	.154
	(Constant)	829.41	.493
Equation		$R^2=.68$ Adj $R^2=.57$	
		$F=5.92$	$p<.001$

Table 9.10
Costs of outputs to society in standard provision, £ at 1977 prices

Variable type	Variable	Cost effect	p
Outputs			
	M^2 (Subjective Well-being)^2	0.15	0.42
	Survival	218.11	.000
Quasi-inputs			
	Health and dependency		
	Incontinence of urine	484.71	.022
	Giddiness	203.61	.248
	Hearing difficulty	385.24	.124
	Loneliness	-159.37	.077
	Social support		
	Support from spouse	-99.65	.043
	Support from neighbours	56.93	.024
	Physical environment		
	Housing unsuitability	-317.86	.036
	Initial Level of Well-being		
	Subjective Well-being	99.31	.022
	Quality of Care shortfall	194.01	.481
	(Constant)	-3313.06	.025
Equation		$R^2=.61$ Adj $F=8.66$	$R^2=.54$ $p<.001$

unresponsiveness to psychological needs. There appeared to be no evidence of differential effects of dependency on the cost of improving outputs for those elderly people receiving standard services.

(ii) Social support

Social support from neighbours made cases receiving standard services more costly. It is likely that this positive cost effect can be explained by the greater likelihood of those with close social support entering residential care (Table 9.10). Thus, of those in close contact with neighbours, 34 per cent went into residential care compared with 15 per cent of those with little or no contact. Conversely, in the community care scheme, those with close contact with their children were less costly, since they were less likely to enter residential care, and those sharing a home with their children had lower housing costs. However, support from relatives appeared to raise costs. Support from a spouse, unsurprisingly, tended to reduce costs under standard services, in part due to shared housing costs.

(iii) Personality and attitudinal characteristics

Two of the personality-attitude characteristics proved to be significant for those cases in receipt of community care. The 'refusing-rejecting' group had a positive cost effect which can be explained by the fact that members of this group were particularly unlikely to die, only 8 per cent compared with 28 per cent of those with a more positive attitude towards the receipt of help. As a result, they tended to remain at home - 72 per cent compared with 51 per cent of the more positive group. They occupied housing for a longer period and, as shown in the analysis of the costs of the health service, were likely to require above-average amounts of hospital care. This finding is interesting in the light of suggestions that at times a hostile and rejecting attitude can be an adaptive response to the problems of dependency (Turner *et al.*, 1972; Bergmann, 1978). Community care appeared to have been more effective for these individuals for whom a straightforward response alone was insufficient, since a sensitivity to their particular difficulties was required. Those with 'dependent-demanding' characteristics also appeared to be more expensive than other cases in receipt of community care. This was discussed in Chapter 4.

(iv) Other factors

Unsuitable housing had a negative cost effect for those receiving standard services. This was most probably due to the association of this characteristic with entry to institutional care, and therefore lower housing costs.

The initial indicators of need - Subjective Well-Being and Quality of Care -suggested greater evidence of targeting resources in community care than standard services. The negative and significant cost effect of the first assessment of Subjective Well-being, suggests that the higher the person's Subjective Well-being at first assessment, the less the overall cost. The Quality of Care shortfall indicator, which was positive, is also indicative of tailoring care to needs, the greater the need for care the higher the cost (Table 9.9). No such relationship between level of need and level of resources was apparent in the comparison group; indeed, on the contrary, the significant and positive cost effect of the initial measure of Subjective Well-being, suggests that the higher the initial level of Morale, the greater the level of expenditure, which is the converse of effective targeting (Table 9.10).

Neither age nor sex had a significant effect on costs for elderly people in receipt of community care. However, for those in receipt of standard services, male sex had a negative cost effect, probably reflecting the reduced likelihood of survival of elderly men in the comparison group.

Finally, it can be seen that the cost of promoting survival itself appeared to be less for those in receipt of community care than for those receiving standard services.

(b) The costs of outputs for elderly people in different circumstances

(i) Costs of four case types

Using the equations in Tables 9.9 and 9.10, the costs of achieving a range of outputs for a representative case in each of the four Dependency Groups was estimated. The results are shown in Table 9.11 for a range of outcomes from 'no improvement' to a 40 per cent improvement in Subjective Well-being and a 100 per cent improvement in Quality of Care. Again, for ease of interpretation it is helpful to consider the degrees of improvement - 'some', 'considerable' and 'substantial' - marked in the Table.

First, it can be seen that the higher the level of output, the more cost-effective the community care scheme appeared. Second, it is clear that the greatest relative advantage to the community care scheme was for those elderly people with lower levels of dependency. Indeed, only at higher levels of output was there a clear cost advantage to the community care scheme for the most frail, in Dependency Group 4. Therefore, while the community care scheme appeared to have proved more cost-effective at higher levels of output for all cases, the advantage was most marked for those cases in the low dependency categories. This finding is similar to the conclusions drawn for costs to the social services department, where it was for those with low morale, depression and social isolation requiring the construction of care networks for whom the scheme was most cost-effective. However, the lesser cost advantage for the high dependency cases may be partly explained by patterns of survival and entry to institutions. The higher dependency cases (in Groups 3 and 4) were less likely to enter institutional care under the community care scheme (16 per cent compared with 24 per cent) and less likely to die (27 per cent compared with 42 per cent). Those elderly people who died or entered long-term institutional care would incur lower housing costs, whilst those remaining at home would incur both housing costs and periodic hospital admissions. This effect could have increased the apparent social opportunity costs for the high dependency groups receiving community care. In order to check the effect of housing costs, which in other studies have crucially influenced the differences between care at home and institutional care (Wager, 1972), separate analyses were undertaken both including and excluding housing costs. Housing costs made little or no difference to the relative cost-effectiveness of community care compared with standard services. However, it must be remembered that these comparisons are of costs and outcomes of alternative forms of care over a one-year period. During one year, whichever mode of care is adopted, an elderly person is likely to incur considerable housing costs; particularly so since admission to institutional care does not necessarily free an elderly person's housing for some weeks.

Table 9.11

Costs to society of different levels of output for four Dependency Groups, £ at 1977 prices

Group	Degree of improvement													
	'Some'					'Considerable'					'Substantial'			
	% improvement in Subjective Well-being													
	0		10			20			30			40		
	% improvement in Quality of Care													
	0	20	0	20	40	20	40	60	40	60	80	60	80	100
Dependency Group 1														
Community care	2,321	2,379	1,895	1,952	2,021	1,518	1,586	1,665	1,143	1,222	1,312	771	861	961
Standard services	2,347	2,347	2,665	2,665	2,665	3,013	3,013	3,013	3,391	3,391	3,391	3,799	3,799	3,799
Dependency Group 2														
Community care	2,451	2,674	2,361	2,584	2,818	2,486	2,720	2,964	2,613	2,858	3,112	2,742	2,997	3,263
Standard services	3,013	3,013	3,331	3,331	3,331	3,679	3,679	3,679	4,057	4,057	4,057	4,465	4,465	4,465
Dependency Group 3														
Community care	2,889	2,947	2,977	3,035	3,103	3,114	3,182	3,261	3,253	3,332	3,501	3,394	3,484	3,584
Standard services	3,446	3,446	3,764	3,764	4,111	4,111	4,111	4,111	4,489	4,489	4,489	4,898	4,898	4,898
Dependency Group 4														
Community care	4,716	4,419	4,997	4,665	4,344	4,902	4,546	4,200	4,739	4,358	3,987	4,507	4,101	3,706
Standard services	2,894	2,894	3,212	3,212	3,212	3,559	3,559	3,559	3,937	3,937	3,937	4,346	4,346	4,346

(ii) Effects for informal carers

As was explained previously, the small number of cases with carers did not make it practicable to estimate the costs of different levels of improvement for carers in the regression equations. As before, the residual or unexplained costs of the regression equations were examined as a guide to the different costs of outputs to informal carers. However, there was no evidence of a significant difference between the cost of community care and standard services in improving the well-being of carers despite our evidence that the lot of carers had improved more under community care.

5. Conclusions

(a) An important theme of recent debate has been the relationship between formal and informal care: whether formal services effectively complement or substitute for the activities undertaken by family, friends and neighbours (Abrams, 1977). The results from our study suggest that they do not. The analysis of costs and outcomes to the social services department suggests that, in certain circumstances, the two forms of care can act as effective complements. The results are consistent with the view that if informal carers are given adequate help at an earlier stage, the carers are less likely to press for an elderly person to be admitted to a residential home as the difficulties of caring increase.

(b) Dependency had different effects on costs to the social services department for cases receiving community care and standard services, there being a much clearer relationship of increasing costs with increasing dependency for those in receipt of community care. A closer relationship between dependency and level of provision is indicative of more effective matching of needs and resources.

(c) The community care scheme appeared more advantageous to the social services department than the alternative form of care for most cases at most levels of improvement. The relative cost advantage appeared greater, the higher the level of improvement. It was particularly cost-effective among those who were extremely physically deteriorated and perhaps also mentally impaired, but who received considerable informal help. These individuals are particularly heavy consumers of resources even within institutional care. They are very likely to be admitted to residential or hospital care when their carers reach breaking point, although they may receive relatively little support until this crisis is reached. Such an outcome is frequently one which generates distress in the elderly person and guilt and frustration in the carers. However, if sufficient support is given to carers at an earlier stage, as appeared to happen in the community care scheme, then it seems possible to achieve considerably

greater improvements in well-being of both elderly person and carer at no greater, and sometimes lower, cost (Bergmann *et al.*, 1978).

Of the four Dependency Groups, it appeared that community care was particularly more cost-effective for Dependency Groups 1 and 2 whose major difficulties were likely to be associated with depression, a psychotic illness or a problem of alcohol abuse, for whom social isolation and risk of falling made continued living at home very difficult. Failure to receive support of an appropriate kind, or to gain access to effective treatment, could well mean that such elderly people would enter residential care through apathy and apparent neglect, and become extremely costly. The careful assessment made in the community care scheme may more readily identify the problems and lead to an appropriate response, preventing admission to residential care. The opportunity to construct and monitor supportive and surveillance networks for isolated elderly people at risk of falling could relieve anxiety by reducing the risk of the 'long lie' (Hall, 1982), enabling them to remain at home (Chapter 4).

(d) The community care scheme appeared more cost-effective to the National Health Service for most cases at most levels of output. It appeared to be most effective for the very frail from the perspective of the NHS. It seemed that a different balance of service provision had begun to develop, a new form of service complementarity or even substitution, which reduced costs incurred by the health service. Perhaps this could justify the use of joint finance to further such developments in home care.

(e) The analysis of social opportunity cost suggested that the community care scheme was more cost-effective for all save the most severely frail. It was interesting that the equations were able to explain more of the variation in costs to society as a whole for the community care group than to the social services department. One possible explanation for this might be that the fieldworkers were taking a wider range of interests into account, including those of informal carers and the health service.

(f) However, the analysis of costs and outputs is only over a one-year period. As time passes, clients will become increasingly dependent and staff will tend to increase provision in response to need and jealously guard the elderly person's right to stay in their own home. Adequate monitoring built into service provision is necessary to detect such shifts (Challis and Chesterman, 1986). Housing costs could also be more influential over subsequent years, bearing more heavily on the costs of those not entering institutional care. It is possible that there could be a break-even point beyond which the aggregate costs of community care exceed the aggregate costs of alternative forms of care, although a four-year follow-up does not indicate this (Chesterman *et al.*, 1986; and see Chapter 8).

CHAPTER 10

CONCLUSIONS AND FUTURE PROSPECTS

The community care approach was designed to provide an organisational framework within which social work staff could develop more effective and efficient care at home as an alternative to residential and long-term hospital care. It involved the decentralisation of control of resources to individual fieldworkers, with defined caseload and expenditure limits to ensure accountability, so that more flexible and sensitive responses to need could be devised, and fragmented services integrated into a more coherent package of care. Let us review our initial expectations of that approach in the light of this study.

1. Expectations Reviewed

In the first chapter eight hypotheses or expectations of a fairly high level of generality were formulated concerning the possible impact of this, an experimental scheme in social care. We now recapitulate these in the light of the experience of our research.

(a) Admission to institutional care

It had been expected that a lower proportion of elderly people would enter institutional care.

There was very clear evidence of lower rates of admission to institutions. In Chapter 7 we saw that over a twelve-month period there was a lower rate of entry to residential homes and also a reduction in the use of hospital long-term care facilities for the very frail. The probability of entry to residential care remained lower over three subsequent years. In cost terms, however, this latter effect was partly counterbalanced by a greater use of acute hospital care facilities (Chapter 8).

(b) Cost-effectiveness

At least for some cases, the new approach should be more cost-effective than the usual range of services.

The analyses of the cost of achieving desired outcomes suggested that, on the whole, the scheme was a more cost-effective response to the needs of frail elderly people, particularly where marked improvement had taken place. The scheme was particularly cost-effective for the social services department in the care of physically and mentally frail old people who enjoyed considerable informal support and for people with moderate degrees of dependence. In these cases, problems of social isolation, psychiatric disorder and risk of falling were particularly prevalent. For the health service, the new scheme appeared to be most cost-effective for those who were the least and also the most dependent. There were also signs of a developing service complementarity, with the scheme providing care at home for individuals who would otherwise be likely to receive long-term hospital care. For society as a whole the scheme appeared more cost-effective for the cases of lower dependency, as we have seen in the case of the social services department. One factor likely to determine (in the longer term) the relative costliness of community and institutional care might be the cost of housing occupied by an elderly person. The analysis of costs was undertaken only over a one-year period and in the longer term there might be a crossover period when care at home could be less cost-effective due to the greater importance through time of housing costs for cases living at home. However, a four-year follow-up does not indicate this (Chesterman *et al.*, 1986; see also Chapter 8).

(c) Matching resources to needs

A closer relationship between levels of need and levels of resource provision should be evident than in the usual range of services.

There was some evidence in the new scheme that resources were more closely matched to needs. The analysis of costs and outcomes suggested that there was a clear relationship between dependency and costs. This was true for both costs to the social services department and costs to society. The more dependent received substantially higher levels of provision (Chapters 8 and 9). This was not found for the comparison group. In the group receiving community care, the provision of health care was also more closely associated with dependency, and good health and higher morale were associated with lower levels of expenditure (Chapter 9). Both these observations are compatible with a closer match of resources to needs. These findings are compatible with an improvement in the degree of 'input-mix' efficiency discussed in Chapter 1.

(d) Improved benefits

It was expected that elderly people and their carers would benefit more from the scheme than from the usual range of services.

Both elderly people and their carers appeared to benefit more from the scheme than from the usual range of services. Therefore the reduction in admission to institutional care did not appear to be achieved at the expense of quality of life. On a range of indicators of both Quality of Care and Subjective Well-being, improvements for those receiving the scheme were significantly greater than for those receiving the usual range of services. Whilst both the scheme and standard services reduced the practical difficulties experienced by carers, the scheme seemed to reduce mental stress and subjective burden to a greater extent (Chapter 7). This refers to the concept of 'market efficiency' (or output mix efficiency) discussed in Chapter 1.

(e) Social work roles and tasks

It was expected that the assumption of responsibility for the long-term care of frail elderly people would differentiate a more distinct role for social work with the elderly than is at present evident.

The activities of the social work team demonstrated the development of certain roles, particularly in aspects of 'indirect activity'. These were related to continuing case responsibility, coordinating care, and supporting and advising others in direct contact with the elderly person. The combination of these 'indirect' activities with the more usual aspects of 'direct' work, such as assessment, support and counselling, each of which were undertaken in the project, provides some clarification of the nature of an effective social work role with the elderly. As Goldberg and Connelly argue, these aspects of indirect work have rarely been developed and implemented. Our findings can only reinforce their conclusion that 'the role of case coordinator and resource person is coming more to the fore, as various combinations of statutory, voluntary and informal supports are being developed or strengthened and it is being recognised that these support networks can make their optimal impact only if they are coordinated and reviewed regularly' (1982, p.90).

This synthesis of roles and tasks is not a new one in aspiration. The idea of a more 'client-centred service package' (Cmnd 1973, 1963, para. 9) is some twenty years old (Goldberg *et al.*, 1970). Similarly, Wager (1972), noting that 'the greater provision of a range of accommodation and domiciliary services will not be sufficient in itself to provide satisfactory domiciliary care' (p.66), echoes Plank's (1979) argument about 'the comprehensive nature of need'. Thus, whilst the perception of these roles as central to effective social care is not new, the scheme would seem to have provided a framework within which the accepted norms of 'good practice' can flourish.

The synthesis is not just of roles and tasks but of social work and social care. In such an environment the frequently undervalued 'maintenance function' (Davies, 1981b) in care can be developed, through responsibility for coordination of the overall support system. Approaches to the care of the elderly which separate the tasks of care into levels such as basic care and social work (Hey, 1980) are perhaps less helpful, since with a long-term care population requiring frequent reassessment and monitoring, problems arise from an interaction of basic care needs with other difficulties and the need is for a holistic perception of need and the consideration of alternative solutions to problems. In community care, the unhelpful dichotomy between 'practical needs' and 'psychological needs' which has bedevilled services to the elderly was transcended. The case-management roles and tasks were undertaken within an environment where the social work approach was pervasive, crucially influencing the means adopted to achieve the objectives of care (Howe, 1979).

Our observations on the nature of the case-management process are pertinent to the search for a specification of clearer roles and tasks for social work practice (Barclay, 1982). Roles and tasks are more helpfully delineated in relation to particular care settings with specific client groups with varying needs than in the abstract. One form of this differentiation is between cases whose need is for relatively short-term intervention and those where the need is for long-term care (Morris, 1977). A considerable literature has developed focusing on more effective approaches in short-term interventions (Reid and Shyne, 1969; Reid and Epstein, 1972; Goldberg *et al.*, 1985). The community care approach can be seen as a contribution to the development of the case-management process in long-term care (Steinberg and Carter, 1983).

(f) Variations in responses to different problems

It was expected that the community care approach would lead to substantial variations in packages of care reflecting the nature of different types and combinations of problems.

Packages of care provided to elderly people varied considerably in relation to mixes of problems. The factor over which the team exerted most control was the budget, and its usage varied considerably according to circumstances. Cases with costs which were proportionately high in project expenditure, as opposed to other services, were those living with informal carers and those with serious mental disorders such as paranoid psychosis or dementia. Attempts to respond to the needs of informal carers were evident, trying to adapt care to their individual circumstances and needs. Problems which pose considerable management difficulties such as alcohol abuse and dementia were tackled with a degree of imagination and persistence beyond that which would be expected in normal circumstances (Chapters 4 and 5). Indeed, the work undertaken with demented elderly people suggested some possible approaches which could be taken up in a special study involving health personnel to illuminate further the ways in which individual care planning strategies can help in the management of this problem (Barrowclough and Fleming, 1984, 1986). These responses are indicative of the greater 'input mix efficiency' which was one of the aims of the project discussed in Chapter 1.

Nonetheless two kinds of obstacle appeared to impede attempts to respond more imaginatively to need. The first was perhaps an inevitable consequence of an innovation: limits to development were imposed by the workers themselves and their perception of the possible. Indeed there may come a point in a scheme which has developed a series of new responses to social need when the drive for innovation diminishes. For example, if implementation of a new approach requires considerable negotiation with agencies and individuals, then once sufficient compliance has been negotiated for effective day-to-day operation, the incentive may be to maintain that system in operation rather than attempt further innovation. Some evidence for this 'negotiation exhaustion' argument could perhaps be found in the way that subsequent projects have built on the early work in Kent and introduced new responses such as arrangements with voluntary agencies, localised day care, helper training and purchase of pre-packaged meals. These developments underline the need for peer review and support so that new ideas and approaches to care can stimulate staff and avoid routinisation. The other limitation which emerged arose from the organisational structure of the health and social services. In dealing with certain types of problems, such as incontinence and psychiatric disorder, effective home care required the involvement, if not complete team membership, of at least medical and nursing staff to improve the quality of assessment, care planning and case management. The involvement of psychologists in dealing with mentally disordered people would open further possible avenues for improved care.

(g) A heightened sensitivity to care networks and informal care

It was expected that the way in which resources were deployed would show a greater sensitivity to the care network as a whole. This would mean that care from a wide range of sources would be interwoven, closer support given to informal carers and new elements of community support introduced.

The social work team made deliberate attempts to manage the care network and effect better communication between its component parts. This was evident in the use of monitoring charts and their distribution to other key actors. Packages were devised in consultation with various people in the network, and new services were introduced with due regard to their possible effects on the existing network. The approach was concerned with the care network as a whole.

There was no evidence that the existence of the scheme had a negative impact on the extent or type of contribution by informal care. On the contrary, there was some evidence of greater complementarity between formal and informal care as a result of the scheme, as we saw in Chapters 5 and 9. The main additional way in which the team responded to the needs of informal carers, as to most clients, was by the recruitment of members of the local community as helpers. Whilst certain tasks could have been equally well undertaken by a small cadre of employees, the team believed that the use of local people provided an additional dimension to the scheme, particularly for companionship needs and such activities as 'check-up' visits. The use of helpers, matched with individual clients, attempted to ensure satisfaction for both helper and helped and was able to focus on social and companionship needs as well as the more practical. In so doing a new resource was brought to the care of the elderly. This higher than usual investment in home care proved to be less expensive than the alternative of residential care ('input mix efficiency').

(h) Meeting new needs

It was expected that attention would be given to needs which are not usually met. This referred both to certain groups of elderly clients, such as those with mental impairment, and to higher levels of need such as loneliness and subjective well-being, as well as more basic care needs.

The project tackled certain kinds of problem to which social services departments often only respond in a partial fashion. In Chapters 4 and 5 we noted that these tended to be cases with substantial levels of informal support, minor psychiatric disorder and high levels of frailty. The positive approach to the management of the demented elderly is also indicative of an attempt to meet needs previously unmet (Bergmann *et al.*, 1978). Some cases were only referred because of the existence of the project, which could tackle previously unmet needs. This indicates an increase in service uptake or 'horizontal target efficiency' which we discussed in Chapter 1.

A second way in which the scheme appeared to meet new needs was the attempt to move beyond the provision of 'basic services' (Hey, 1980) to prevent the onset of 'giving up', described as the 'pre-admission effects' of residential care (Tobin and Lieberman, 1976). This was evident in the deliberate focus on elderly people's subjective well-being, through contracts focused on therapeutic objectives such as reviving old interests, or in one case enabling an elderly man to accept loss by regular visits to his wife's grave. The attempts to provide for a wider range of needs are indicative of improvements in 'market efficiency' which we discussed in Chapter 1.

2. Future Issues for Policy and Practice

The relevance of these findings is, of course, dependent on replication of the approach and its organisational integration into the structure of social services departments. The extent to which such a project can be made to work elsewhere, and whether an approach which devolves control of resources to front-line staff can be successfully integrated into local authority structures without excessive routinisation and loss of flexibility, can only be resolved by time and observation. At the present time the evidence indicates that the scheme can be developed in widely disparate areas at not too dissimilar costs (Challis *et al.*, 1983; Challis and Chesterman, 1985).

Our study has not tackled the issue of integration and the scheme's effects on the organisation of the social services department. To do so would have risked drawing conclusions on the basis of the idiosyncratic experience of one divisional office in a large social services department. Hence, our concern has been at the level of field social work and the immediate impact of the scheme on elderly people and their carers. The organisational and 'system' effects should become more evident from observations of such projects developing across a number of different local authority districts. The project has been implemented in an urban city area, a rural area and other parts of Kent, and all are being evaluated in detail. The findings from these should help us to tease out these issues in greater detail. One of these projects, having operated for some three years with three social work staff, has begun a pilot health and social care approach in addition to continuing as a social care project. This was made possible by the provision of additional resources from the district health authority to appoint a nurse and part-time registrar as members of that team, sharing a common budget and providing for the most frail elderly clients in one group practice. Even at a relatively early stage, it is possible to see the benefits which can accrue from processes of mutual learning in the improved assessments and wider knowledge base brought to bear on problems.

However, it would be misleading to conceive of the approach as only relevant to the needs of the frail elderly and therefore perhaps insulated from the rest of the social services department. The implications of the scheme are broader than the social care of one client group and raise questions of central concern about such issues as social work practice and management, decentralisation, specialisation, multi-disciplinary working and long-term care of other client groups. It is only possible to make passing reference to each of these here.

(a) Social work and costs

It might have been expected that taking account of costs as well as welfare objectives could have caused difficulty for the social workers and perhaps distracted them from what they saw as their main objectives. However, this did not seem to be the case. Indeed, knowledge and recording of costs was the balancing element in the greater autonomy and flexibility given to fieldworkers and was recognised as such by them. Without exercising retrospective accountability through costs and setting limits to autonomy, it is hard to see how a public organisation could devolve responsibility for budgets and retain an acceptable level of control. For the individual fieldworker, control over resources was seen as essentially liberating, giving an incentive to undertake more precise assessments of need. Costs appeared to introduce a new dimension into their thinking. Normally, the only item a fieldworker is likely to weigh up as a cost to be spent in one way rather than another is their own time and the most appropriate allocation of visits to clients. However, one of the earliest observations made by one of the team was her perception of a client's relative valuation of two resources of equivalent cost, five hours home help or a visit to a day centre. These would not normally be considered so readily available as alternatives to meet need. The other evidence of social workers' lack of discomfort in dealing with costs has been the attitude expressed about other social work posts. These have been seen as frustrating and lacking sufficient autonomy by staff who had had the opportunity to control their own resources.

(b) Social work practice and management

In Chapter 2 we noted how social work and social care have suffered from a failure to develop a more 'clinically' focused base of knowledge. Underlying this is a belief in the indeterminacy of the world in which social care is provided. It is as if the focus on the individual, essential for a sensitive response to need, has led to a world where differences between cases are stressed to the neglect of lessons which may be learned from their common features. If in medicine criticisms have sometimes been voiced that the abstract generalisation of disease entity too often has permitted the obscuring of important differences between individuals (Wing, 1978), then in social work and social care the malaise has been the obverse of the same coin; at worst a 'tyranny of individualisation'. Yet, as we have noted elsewhere, even in the problematic area of family relationships, such a knowledge base is emerging (Brown *et al.*, 1972; Vaughn and Leff, 1976; Bergmann *et al.*, 1985). It is only on the basis of norms of the likely consequences of acting in one way rather than another that we can evaluate each specific individual case (Wing, 1978, Chapter 4). The lack of use made of this knowledge base was criticised in the Beckford child abuse enquiry (London Borough of Brent, 1985). Thus in social care the activity and knowledge base required to identify and generalise from aspects of effective care process or social work practice is poorly developed. However, it is fundamental to attempts to improve the effectiveness and efficiency of services.

Such a knowledge base would entail a move towards developing valid patterns of generalisations. These might be couched in the form of probability statements, that certain care strategies with certain probable costs have a reasonable probability of being effective for clients in certain situations. In our study certain aspects of care strategies were discussed in Chapters 3, 4 and 5 which contributed to the improvements in efficiency and effectiveness discussed in later chapters. It is through these linkages between process questions and cost-effectiveness questions that research may inform practice. The more structured approaches to individual care planning with elderly people developed by psychologists (Barrowclough and Fleming, 1986) could assist this process.

The same problem, at a more general level, afflicts the attempts of management to monitor the efficiency and effectiveness of care services, namely the perceived indeterminacy of social care. However, it can be seen, as demonstrated by the prediction equations in our study of the elderly, that evaluation research can produce more precise generalisations about strategies of care and the likely costs of care and resources required for certain kinds of client and the desirable target populations for different modes of care. From such observations more precise guidelines of the expected relationships between the characteristics of clients, the costs of care and different styles of intervention could be produced. These guidelines could then constitute parameters within which the delegated autonomy of fieldworkers could operate and the effectiveness of services be adequately monitored. There are important lessons from the American experience of the Professional Standards Review Organisation in medicine (Smits, 1981) and attempts at continuously linking quality control procedures in nursing to empirical research findings (Lang and Clinton, 1983) which could assist in the development of appropriate recording systems.

If we are to improve the efficiency and effectiveness of the provision of social care, it must come through the development of a greater degree of predictability in our knowledge about effective care processes. This predictability is relevant at all levels, from the need for more specific 'clinical' case norms which guide the practitioner in dealing with the individual case to more general operational norms and guidelines for managers which may enable them to ensure the better deployment of scarce resources. Chapters 2 and 13 of *Matching Resources to Needs* further explore the implications of greater determinacy in social care.

(c) Decentralisation and specialisation

A major issue concerning the organisation of social services departments has been the issue of decentralisation. This often appears to be understood in purely geographical terms - services located in smaller geographical areas - but in community care the focus has been on resource decentralisation - where decisions about the precise allocation of resources are formally located at a lower level in the organisation (Challis, 1985a). In community care we have observed resource decentralisation to individual fieldworkers specialising in work with elderly people, effectively balancing their greater autonomy considered as through mechanisms enhancing their accountability. Many of the effects are similar to those observed with geographical decentralisation -heightened sensitivity to, and understanding of, local networks; responsiveness to local needs, opportunities and constraints; reaching cases with previously unmet need; and improved staff morale (Hadley and McGrath, 1984). However, in addition, there was some evidence of the benefits of learning from specialisation in the management of some of the more intractable problems of mental disorder, and in establishing working relationships with other services which are also concerned with the elderly. The benefits of specialisation are of course difficult to achieve in a scheme based on very small geographical areas, which presupposes generic working of individual staff (Hadley and McGrath, 1984). As Glennerster (1985) has argued, liaison between agencies may be very difficult to achieve when different agencies are organised according to different criteria, and there may be relatively few clients requiring long-term care in any given small area.

It is hard to see how the benefits of improved assessment arising from improved knowledge and linkages with the health service could have occurred in a generic work setting. Indeed, an attempt to enable staff from an area team to work with a few community care cases, while continuing with their usual workload for the rest of the time, did not prove successful. It is even harder to see how issues of equity would be tackled when staff were deploying a budget not just between individuals with varying needs in a single client group, but also making decisions about the relative levels of expenditure between client groups, such as the elderly and children. At its worst, this could serve to reinforce the biases which have worked against the elderly.

In this context it is interesting to note that many local authorities are moving towards a specialist, client group mode of organisation. Many of those with a commitment to patch-based working have maintained a considerable number of specialist teams and staff. Others have attempted to integrate small area geographical deployment with client-based specialisation (Challis and Ferlie, 1986a,b). Overall, it is likely that in the current pattern of social care provision, the community care approach is most likely to thrive as a service specialising in the care of a single client group.

(d) Long-term care for other client groups

The focus of the scheme on a very clearly defined target group - the frail elderly -was reflected in the budget limit. Most of the elderly people were those living in their own homes who were on the margin of institutional care. More recently, the scheme has been used to rehabilitate people from long-term residential care and perhaps this could be extended to a proportion of those elderly people currently in long-term hospital care. The approach could also be considered as a means of organising domiciliary services for a wider range of elderly people with a spread of disability levels and similar variation in the budget limits. Perhaps this could bring to more elderly people some of the benefits of the scheme, such as a wider range of solutions to care problems and enhanced support for informal carers.

The younger physically handicapped require much support similar to that of the disabled elderly. The principles and practice of the approach could be extended to this group with probably least modification. Indeed, this has already occurred to a limited extent, for example the scheme has in one case provided care to a woman in her late 30s suffering from multiple sclerosis who has several children, thereby enabling her to remain at home.

Even in the field of child care, where the case-management role has been most clearly and explicitly developed, there are opportunities for improving effectiveness by decentralising resources to individual fieldworkers. Certainly the idea of more individually tailored packages of Intermediate Treatment is a possible development. More controversially, cases of possible child abuse raise serious problems of establishing an adequate support system for parents. As a consequence, intervention may prove to be rather more anxious surveillance than problem alleviation. Families where child abuse is suspected are often young and lack adequate social supports and parental role models. The community care approach might make more readily possible the development of support networks for such cases.

The authors of a study of mental illness in the community observed that: 'The social work role in relation to the mentally ill client has in most local authorities become stagnant, and the emphasis has remained on outdated methods of intervention which has led to the atrophy of skill development' (Goldberg and Huxley, 1980, p.147). This critique of social work with the mentally disordered, the chronically impaired of whom are another long-term care population, has much in common with the rationale for the development of the community care approach. The development of approved social worker training as a result of the 1983 Mental Health Act and the expectation of improved modes of intervention provides a basis for the development of the scheme with this client group. The approach is particularly relevant for the important maintenance function with the chronically impaired (Butler and Pritchard, 1983). Certain aspects of case management, in particular uptake and monitoring, have been neglected in the mental health field since the Seebohm reorganisation of social services departments. The shift in psychiatric services from large hospitals and the consequent need for new service models provides an opportunity for pursuing further such a development. Studies in the USA have indicated that a case-management approach to the chronically mentally ill is important in enhancing the accessibility of services, the comprehensiveness of their coverage and the quality of care planning (Ingliata, 1982). Similar arguments could be deployed for the development of services for the mentally handicapped.

3. Inter-agency Working

Glennerster (1985) has argued that some of the most productive developments in the field of community care are services such as community mental health teams and geriatric assessment teams where there are clear improvements in inter-professional working relationships. Our study suggested that the management of several types of problem would have benefited from the involvement of a range of health service staff. A joint agency approach with a single budget would broaden the span of control of any scheme covering health and social services resources, and reduce the danger of any one agency pursuing its own objectives with insufficient regard to those of the other. Furthermore, the potential for enhancing the efficiency of care would be greater since a wider range of costs would be taken into account. The lessons of the pilot health and social care project still being undertaken indicate that a wider range of knowledge can be deployed in assessment and care planning and that it is feasible to operate such a model with staff of several disciplines working from a social services office.

There are a number of possible benefits from the creation of a team whose members were drawn both from social services and the health service and whose budget covered the resources of both agencies. This should at least include medical staff, nursing staff, psychologists and social workers. Obvious gains could be made in areas such as the reduction of bed-blocking and improved assessment, but perhaps greater gains could be in cases of extreme frailty where aspects of ill-health or poor diet generate problems in physical and mental functioning as well as social distress. Here early ascertainment of physical and psychiatric disorders could prevent inappropriate admissions to hospital and residential care and result in more coordinated treatment and management. Even the limited joint working found in this study may well have been influential in its effect on survival.

The development of such a scheme also raises questions about the appropriate location or base. At first, it might seem that primary health care would provide the most suitable setting, so that early assessment of difficulties could be combined with effective treatment and management. However, it is the very frail who constitute the most demanding workload, and those on whom such a team might have greatest impact, and yet their prevalence is relatively low within any one general practice. Hence an alternative setting for a community care team might be a psychogeriatric or geriatric day hospital, particularly as these services become more community-oriented. The key-worker role has already been delineated in such service settings (Hemsi, 1980) and the community care approach could enhance the effectiveness of this.

Overall, we may conclude that our study of a new approach to social care has identified several ways in which improvements in service efficiency and effectiveness may be achieved. There appears to be considerable room, both through broadening client groups and by extending inter-agency collaboration, for wider experimentation with this approach, which seeks to enhance the matching of resources to needs in social care.

APPENDIX A

OUTCOME AND DESCRIPTOR INDICATORS

Throughout the study we have discussed a number of outcome or output indicators and descriptors of client state (or 'quasi-inputs') such as incontinence or depressed mood. In this Appendix we describe the basis of these indicators and provide evidence about the concurrent reliability of some of the ratings which we have used.

1. Outputs

These constituted our indicators of effectiveness: the changes in clients' and carers' states of well-being. As we noted earlier, outcomes can be at a 'final' stage in the production of welfare, that is they are effects valued in their own right, or they may be more intermediate effects, such as the receipt of needed services (Davies, 1977a). Final outputs may be highly general, such as indicators of subjective well-being, or very specific, such as receipt of an adequate diet. A number of different approaches to the measurement of different aspects of outcome in care of the elderly are reviewed in Challis (1981).

In the following sections we describe some of the main indicators used and, where appropriate, indicate their relationship with other measures.

(a) Final outputs

(i) Highly general factors

Morale. Three variables were derived from the Philadelphia Geriatric Center Morale Scale (Lawton, 1972). The version used was that consisting of seventeen items based on the work of Lawton (1975) and Morris and Sherwood (1975). Certain words were anglicised to make them intelligible to British elderly people; for example 'pep' was translated as 'energy' and 'mad' as 'angry'. This scale was chosen rather than the obvious alternative, the Life Satisfaction Index (Neugarten *et al.*, 1961), because of its greater relevance to a frail population. Respondents were restricted to a binary 'Yes/No' format. The scale is shown as an appendix to Goldberg and Connelly (1982).

'Morale' or 'Subjective Well-being' was conceived of as the aggregate score on this scale. Two sub-scales were also derived. 'General Dissatisfaction with Life' consisted of six items of the morale scale in the light of principal components analysis (Items 4, 6, 8, 15, 16, 17). These were items referring to negative evaluations of the present, lack of family contact, being easily upset and taking adversity badly.

'Dissatisfaction with Life Development' was also derived from this analysis and consisted of four items (1, 2, 6, 10) which implied that life satisfaction tended to diminish with age. A similar dimension was identified by both Lawton (1975) and Morris and Sherwood (1975), and also by Abrams (1982) using a different set of items.

Depression and anxiety. Other variables related to morale were 'Depression' and 'Anxiety'. The twelve-item General Health Questionnaire (GHQ) (Goldberg, 1972) was administered to most cases, although where respondent fatigue was evident this schedule was omitted to shorten the interview. Depression and Anxiety were also assessed on a four-point rating by the interviewer; the depressed mood rating being based on the relevant item in the scale devised by Hamilton (1960). This correlated .71 with the twelve-item GHQ score and the anxiety rating correlated .68 with the GHQ for 173 cases. Using the GHQ as a measure of 'caseness', that is of the probability of the degree of distress being clinically significant, is an alternative indicator of validity and reliability. With a cutting score of between one and two, only five individuals not rated as at least 'mildly depressed' reach this point. Ninety-three per cent of those rated as 'moderately depressed' reached this point as did all of those rated as 'severely depressed'. The only area of disagreement, as might be expected, was over the 'mildly depressed' state where only two-thirds reached a score of two or more. If 'moderate' and 'severe' are taken as equivalent to 'caseness', as in our analyses, then there is a 97 per cent degree of agreement between the two measures.

Loneliness. This was a composite variable based on the sum of two items, one tapping the frequency of the elderly person's subjective feelings of loneliness, the other an interview rating of the degree of satisfaction with social contacts.

Boredom. This was made up of the sum of two items, one about the frequency of boredom and the other about the extent to which time passed slowly.

Felt degree of control over own life. This was the sum of people's responses to five items covering issues of over reliance on others, degree of control over making decisions, whether they felt a burden on others and reactions to dependence.

Felt capacity to cope. This was based on elderly people's perceptions of the degree to which they could cope with four areas of daily living: rising and retiring, personal care, daily household care and weekly household care.

Family/carer relationships. Three items, each a three-point rating of carer difficulty, were used. These were 'subjective burden', 'health and strain' and 'mental health and anxieties'. 'Subjective burden' was the extent of burden felt by the carer (Hoenig and Hamilton, 1969).

In addition there are the outcome indicators used in Chapter 9.

Subjective Well-being. This was based on the Philadelphia Geriatric Centre Morale Scale (Lawton, 1975).

Quality of Care. This was made up from the sum of the standardised ratings of the shortfall in care provided in four areas: rising and retiring, personal care, daily household care and weekly household care.

General Health. This was the sum of self-rated health and ratings based on information from the elderly person about eyesight, hearing, breathlessness, giddiness, incontinence of urine and faeces.

Appendix A, Table 1
Distribution of Activities of Daily Living and General Health ratios for matched cases

	Community care £	Standard provision £
Activities of Daily Living		
Deterioration of 50% or more	7	29
Deterioration of 1% but not more than 50%	11	5
No change: improvement or decline of less than 1%	36	37
Improvement of 1% but not more than 50%	11	5
Improvement of 50% or more	35	23
Mean	118.69	68.57
Standard error	11.91	21.97
Variance	7800.79	16887.61
General Health		
Deterioration of 50% or more	9	28
Deterioration of 1% but not more than 50%	42	26
No change: improvement or decline of less than 1%	18	26
Improvement of 1% but not more than 50%	29	20
Improvement of 50%	2	0
Mean	85.44	63.64
Standard error	5.49	11.69
Variance	1661.41	4781.01

Activities of Daily Living. The number of key activities of daily living with which the elderly person required help (0-6) (Katz *et al.*, 1963).

Each of these variables was transformed into a measure of percentage improvement using the formula

$$\frac{02}{01} \times 100$$

where 02 was the score on the variable at follow up and 01 the score at initial interview. This yielded a possible range of scores from 0 to infinity, nearly all being in the range 0-200. 'Quality of Care', 'Activities of Daily Living' and 'General Health' were originally negative indicators, since they were measures of need for care, or poor health status. They were transformed into positive indicators by subtracting the score from 200.

The distributions are shown in Appendix Tables 1 and 2.

Appendix A Table 2
Distribution of Subjective Well-being and Quality of Care

Outcome	Community care %	Standard provision %
Subjective Well-being		
Decline of 20% or more	3	11
Decline of 10% and less than 20%	3	9
Decline of 1% and less than 10%	3	27
No change: improvement or decline of less than 1%	18	7
Improvement of 1% and less than 10%	30	44
Improvement of 10% and less than 20%	13	2
Improvement of 20% or more	33	-
Mean	111.91	98.41
Standard error	2.94	1.83
Variance	528.29	151.01
Quality of Care		
Decline of 20% or more	0	4
Decline of 10% and less than 20%	0	7
Decline of 1% and less than 10%	2	20
No change: improvement or decline of less than 1%	2	2
Improvement of 1% and less than 10%	29	20
Improvement of 10% and less than 20%	39	2
Improvement of 20% or more	28	45
Mean	174	134.83
Variance	2684.15	5987.29
Standard error	6.63	11.54

(ii) Less general factors

Care shortfalls. This set of items was based on the concept of need as a shortfall. Need is seen as a shortfall compared with a state of being which is generally acceptable. The effect of care services is to partially or wholly remove the shortfall (Davies, 1977a). The logic of the measures utilised was that the reduction of a given shortfall was equivalent to the provision of a certain level of care resources. The indicators were based both on interviewer ratings and the perceptions of the elderly person.

Interviewer-rated variables were devised from the product of two items: the amount of care time in hours required to close the shortfall and a judgement of the apparent importance of closing that shortfall in care. The responses of the individual old person to help received were conceived of as a measure of adequacy. Three aspects were considered: quantitative sufficiency, qualitative effectiveness and reliability. Each covered care both during the week and at weekends. Since these items proved in practice to be highly correlated, a composite measure of 'adequacy' was constructed as the sum of the responses to the individual items. These indicators of need for additional care were developed for four separate areas: rising and retiring, personal care, daily household care and weekly household care.

Social contacts. A measure of social contacts was used based on a count of weekly contacts as used by Tunstall (1966).

Family/carer relationships. Ratings were made on a three-point scale of severity of the extent of carers' difficulties in the areas of 'social life', 'household routine', 'employment', 'financial affairs' and 'child-related difficulties'. A count of the number of difficulties associated with the demands of the elderly person's ill-health and behaviour was also made, described as 'physical health difficulties'. Much of this was based on earlier work about carer stress (Grad and Sainsbury, 1968; Hoenig and Hamilton, 1969).

Effects on care network. At the follow-up interview it was ascertained whether different parts of the informal care network were more or less extensive and contributed as much help as they had done previously.

(b) Intermediate outputs

Other indicators were less 'final' and were concerned more with the actual receipt of services than with their benefits. A measure of 'reduction in need for extra services', a count of services needed but either not received or not received in sufficient quantity to be effective, was used, derived from Goldberg *et al.* (1970). Other items covered the receipt of state benefits and attendance allowance. However, this last aspect of the interview information proved insufficiently reliable to use, elderly people being frequently vague about benefits and income. A question was also asked about the elderly person's perceived income sufficiency, but the responses to this could not be realistically used since the variability was insufficient (Goldberg *et al.*, 1970; Abrams, 1982). Changes in satisfaction with housing or improved facilities were also considered as possible measures of outcome. However, these were not used, since relatively few individuals experienced substantive changes in their housing and therefore any observed change would be expected to be a function of changes in morale.

2. Quasi-inputs

As we described earlier, these consist of factors such as the circumstances and personal characteristics of elderly people which are determinants of outcome.

(a) Physical health and dependency

Activities of Daily Living. Assessments of the key activities of daily living, both personal and instrumental, were collected on a four-point scale, from unaided to fully dependent, for items in four different domains: rising and retiring, personal care, daily household care and weekly household care. These domains were derived from the work of Isaacs and Neville (1976). The individual items which were collected made it possible, with other additional information, to construct the Activities of Daily Living Index (Katz *et al.*, 1963) and other categories of dependency.

Symptomatic health. Items which covered specific health-related difficulties were derived from the screening schedule developed by Bergmann *et al.* (1975). These covered problems of eyesight, hearing, breathlessness, giddiness, urinary and faecal incontinence, and one item covering risk of falling was added. A question covering self-rated health was also included.

(b) Mental health

Non-psychotic disorders. Items rating the extent of depressed mood and anxiety have already been discussed under outcome measurement, as has the use of the GHQ (Goldberg, 1972).

Organic mental states. In assessing the presence or absence of organic symptomatology, nine items developed by Bergmann *et al.* (1975) which covered memory and behavioural characteristics were used. The memory test items were reduced to three: the date, the season and the year. This latter item has been demonstrated to be the most efficient discriminator and predictor of other memory items (Isaacs and Walkley, 1963). In addition a four-point interviewer rating of apparent disorientation and confusional state based on the evidence of the whole interview and other known details such as medical diagnosis was used.

The nine behavioural and memory items could be scored by the number of correct responses. In total there were 210 correct responses. Using a cut-off point between six and seven, of those not rated at least 'moderately confused' only eleven failed to reach this point. Of those rated as 'moderately confused', ten scored seven or more. There was thus 90 per cent concordance between the two indicators. The correctness of the elderly person's reply when asked the year could be taken on its own as a predictor of confusional state: only eight rated as less than moderately confused were incorrect in stating the year, but fifteen of those rated as moderately confused were correct in stating the year. The degree of agreement between these two indicators was 89 per cent.

(c) Informal support

Much of the detailed meticulous work on the influence of the quality of social relationships had not been published when this work commenced (Brown and Harris, 1978; Henderson *et al.*, 1978), and its construction was influenced by the one similar British study (Goldberg *et al.*, 1970). However, it would in any case have been very difficult to include indicators such as the Interview Schedule for Social Interaction (Henderson *et al.*, 1980), which could take the best part of one hour to administer, in a more general study.

Information about informal support was collected in the early part of the interview which covered living group, contacts with children, other relatives and neighbours, and the tasks which were undertaken. This information was necessary in order to make the ratings of shortfall in quality of care for the outcome measures. Consequently the focus was on the extensiveness of instrumental help and support from a range of different sources - spouse, children, relatives and neighbours. Social contacts were described in the section about outputs. Items devised to judge the quality of relationships from interviewing elderly people did not prove to be very effective.

When there were identified principal carers who could be interviewed, information was collected about particular difficulties and experiences of care for use as indicators of outcome. However, in addition, judgements about expressed warmth or hostility toward the elderly person were included since these might be expected to influence outcome through the medium of the carer/elderly person relationship (Brown and Rutter, 1966).

(d) Personality and attitude to help

It was expected that attitudes to residential care could influence outcome through the elderly person's determination to remain independent. Consequently questions were asked about attitude to entering a home and whether the person felt their entry likely within one year. Attitude to help was also important. A rating was derived of apparent attitude based on available information and interview content to identify those whose attitude to help was reasonably realistic from those who tended to refuse and reject, those who appeared dependent and demanding and those who appeared passive and dependent. Experience suggested that a more realistic categorisation would have been to subdivide the 'refusing-rejecting' into those who were the 'rejecting-hostile' (Bergmann, 1978) and those whose diffidence and refusal reflected simply a strong desire to maintain independence.

(e) Environmental and other factors

Housing. The early part of the interview was concerned with aspects of the physical environment. It covered the type and size of housing, the apparent adequacy of the home, furnishing, heating, satisfaction and dissatisfaction with housing and at the end of the interview a rating of suitability. Judgements of adequacy were based on the schedule developed by Sylph and Kedward (1974; see Clare and Cairns, 1978). Some of the housing information was of course necessary for the judgements of additional help required in outcome measurement, as well as in its own right. This domain also served as a relatively easy and logical lead into the interview.

Other factors. Age and sex were included in the questionnaire as basic descriptors. In view of the length of the interview, the minutiae of life events could not be explored, although the presence of two major events likely to affect the elderly were covered. These were whether the person had experienced a recent bereavement and whether the person had been a migrant to the area. Information on income and receipt of benefits was collected to guide the cost analysis and perceived adequacy of these was considered. However, this information appeared either rather unreliable or to vary little between individuals.

APPENDIX B
COMMUNITY CARE RECORDS

1. ASSESSMENT DOCUMENT

(Copies of the whole set of Documents are available from the authors)

COMMUNITY CARE SCHEME

Office Use		CCS Wkr	☐
Scheme	☐	Period	☐

ELDERLY CLIENT DESCRIPTION

(1) *Basic Details*

Surname ....

Christian names ....

....

Address ....

....

....

....

Tel. No ....

Date: ☐☐☐☐☐☐

Case Number: ☐☐☐☐

Area ☐☐

Sex: Male 1
Female 2

Date of Birth: ☐☐☐☐☐☐

Marital Status:

Single	1
Married	2
Widowed	3
Separated/Divorced	4

Referral Source

(i) *Non-departmental*

Self Referral	0 1
Household Member	0 2
Relative	0 3
Friend/Neighbour	0 4
G.P.	0 5
District Nurse	0 6
Health Visitor	0 7
Hospital	0 8
Housing Dept.	0 9
Police	1 0
Voluntary Agency	1 1
DHSS	1 2
Other (Specify)	1 3

....

(ii) *Departmental*

Area Team Social Worker	1
Hospital Social Worker	2
Home Help Service	3
Occupational Therapist	4
Local Authority Home	5

Comments

(2) *Formal and Informal Contacts*

Does client live alone? YES	1
OR with Spouse	2
Children	3
Other relative	4
Friend	5
Other (specify)	6

....

....

Comments

WHO is Principal Informal Carer?
(Code from above, Code 1 if none) 7 if neighbour ☐

Health of Principal Informal Carer	Good Fair Poor	1 2 3

Comments (Note: length of time helping, competing responsibilities, stress)

Principal Informal Carer's Need for Relief (in addition to existing relief)	None Occasional (e.g. Holidays) Regular (During Week) Urgent	1 2 3 4

Help and Support Received.

	Days Seen In Week	If Less Than Once Weekly-Times in Month
(a) Children		
(b) Other relatives		
(c) Spouse		
(d) Friends/Neighbours		
(e) Home Help		
(f) Social Worker		
(g) Meals on Wheels		
(h) Day Care		
(i) District Nurse		
(j) Health Visitor		
(k) Voluntary Visitor		
(l) Day Hospital		
(m) Social/Luncheon Club		
(n) Other (specify)		

(Note: if (a) to (d) visit several times daily code 8; if providing almost unlimited help code 9)

Comments

Does client seem to be lonely?	Never Occasionally Frequently	1 2 3

3. *Housing and Financial Circumstances*

Ownership

Owner Occupier	1
Local Authority	2
Private Landlord	3
Housing Association	4
Other (Specify)	5

Type of Dwelling

House	1
Bungalow	2
Single Room	3
Flat	4
Sheltered Accommodation with Warden	5
Other (Specify)	6

Facilities

Heating		*Cooking*
1	Cent.htg.	
2	Gas	2
3	Electric	3
4	Coal	4
5	Oil Stove	5
6	Other	6
7	None	7

(Code main source only)

Comments (Note: adequacy, accident hazards, privacy, cleanliness)

Access to Dwelling

Stairs	1
Incline	2
Lift	3
Level	4

Toilet (excluding commode)

Indoor—same level	1
Indoor—up or downstairs	2
Outside—same level	3
Outside—up or downstairs	4

Bathroom? Yes 1 No 2

Is Accommodation Suitable for Client? Yes 1 No 2

If No—State Why ....

Financial Needs:

Does client appear to have difficulty financially?	Yes	1
	No	2

Comments

Is there a need for Welfare Rights information?

	Yes	No
Supplementary Pension	1	2
Rate/Rent Rebates	1	2
Attendance Allowance	1	2
Invalid Care Allowance	1	2
Other	1	2

4. *Managing Daily Living*:

	Able alone with aids	Able with present help	Requires more help unable	*Comments*
(a) *Nocturnal Care*				
Attention during night	1	2	3	
(b) *Rising/Retiring*				
Getting in and out of bed	1	2	3	
Dressing	1	2	3	
(c) *Personal Care*				
Managing stairs/steps in home	1	2	3	
Getting in/out of home	1	2	3	
Getting in/out of chairs	1	2	3	
Using toilet	1	2	3	
Feeding	1	2	3	
Bathing/wash all over	1	2	3	
Chiropody/cutting toenails	1	2	3	
(d) *Home Care*				
Prepare meal	1	2	3	
Manage fire	1	2	3	
Housework	1	2	3	
Shopping	1	2	3	
Laundry	1	2	3	

5. *Physical Health*:

Mobility.	Independent	1
	Walks with aid	2
	Walks with other help	3
	Chairbound/bedbound	4

Risk of Falling:	None/slight	1
	Moderate	2
	Severe	3

Incontinence:		
Urine:	None	1
	Occasional	2
	Frequent/Always	3
Faeces:	None	1
	Occasional	2
	Frequent/Always	3

Speech Problems:	None	1
	Moderate	2
	Severe	3

Comments: (Note other difficulties—teeth, feet)

Visual Problems:	None	1
	Can see with glasses	2
	Partially sighted	3
	Blind	4

Hearing Problems:	None	1
	With Aid	2
	Some difficulty	3
	Very deaf	4

Giddiness:	None	1
	Moderate	2
	Severe	3

Breath-lessness:	None	1
	Moderate	2
	Severe	3

6. *Mental Health Problems*:

Evidence of disorientation/memory loss?

	No	Sometimes	Definite
In Time	1	2	3
In Place	1	2	3
Of Person	1	2	3
Loss of short-term memory	1	2	3

If evident: Is onset recent? Yes 1 No 2

Comments: (Note possible effects of drugs, alcohol, ill-health)

		Yes	No
Has there been abnormal behaviour?	Wandering	1	2
	Annoying others at night	1	2
	Annoying others during day	1	2
	Hoarding goods	1	2
	Self neglect	1	2

Comments:

Does client suffer depressed mood?	None	1
	Mild	2
	Moderate	3
	Severe	4

Does the client suffer anxiety?	None	1
	Mild	2
	Moderate	3
	Severe	4

Are there other mental health problems?	Yes	1
	No	2

If yes, specify:

Client's attitude to help:	Independent—rejecting/hostile: not receptive	1
	Independent—requires persuasion	2
	Accepting—able to accept	3
	Dependent—demanding	4
	Dependent—passive	5

Signed ....

COMMUNITY CARE SCHEME: CLIENT DESCRIPTION FORM

The purpose of the Client Description Form is to provide readily comparable information on clients in different areas who may be recipients of Community Care. Space has been left in the form for comments to illuminate the categories which are coded. This space will obviously be more important for some clients than others and the fieldworker must be the judge of what written information is necessary for clarification. If a case is closed and then re-opened it should then be treated as a fresh case.

These notes are to facilitate completion of the form. Please circle the coded response which is most appropriate for the client or enter the appropriate number in the box, according to your overall judgement on each issue. The date refers to the initial visit of the C.C.S. fieldworker to the client.

1. *Date of Birth*: Please complete in pairs of digits, i.e., 19th January 1902 would be 19/01/02.

2. *Principal Informal Carer*: is the person who provides the bulk of everyday informal care/supervision for the client. It refers to regular sustained help.

   Health of Principal Informal Carer: Good—refers to absence of ill health or disability.
   Fair—health status may be low but able to cope adequately.
   Poor—carer has difficulties with own health which make caring more difficult.

   Help and Support Received: Code the number of days on which the person is seen during the week. In the event of a person visiting several times daily code 8 and if this help is almost unlimited code 9. If living with a person who, although seen daily, gives little or no help, code as 7; but if that person provides substantial help code as 8 or 9.

3. *Suitability of Accommodation*: Reflects judgement of worker of client's overall situation.

4. *Managing Daily Living*:

   Able alone/with aids: can manage task competently and without serious risk.

   Able with present help: needs help to manage task but present help adequate. If help received is not essential code as 1.

   Requires more help/unable: needs additional help or help if receiving none.

   Risk of falling: *none/slight*—average for elderly person.

	moderate—a risk greater than that of average elderly person but not severe. *severe*—serious risk of falling at any time.
5. *Physical Health* *Incontinence*:	Often this is a source of great embarrassment to the elderly person. Ask about difficulty and pain, then enquire about 'slip-up's'; finally ask about frequency. Often the difficulty may be evident from smell. *Occasional*—slip-ups occur from time to time; perhaps due to medication. *Frequent*—evident by smell; a regular difficulty; including those where complete loss of control has occurred. If urinary incontinence is effectively controlled by a catheter, code as 1 and comment 'catheter'.
Visual Problems:	The criteria for being classed as partially sighted or blind are the same as those used in registration, though a client does not have to be registered in order to be included in one of these categories.
Hearing Problems:	
Some difficulty:	If it is possible to have, albeit with difficulty, a reasonable conversation; speaking in a low clear voice.
Very deaf:	If communication almost impossible: has to be written or a communicator used.
Giddiness—Moderate:	Evidence of discomfort, serious difficulties in bending down due to this; very high blood pressure—but less disabling than severe.
Severe:	Unsteadiness which makes the old person stagger and fall unless helped; or can just travel from one piece of furniture to another.
Breathlessness—Moderate:	Perceived by the old person as a limitation; evident when they move.
Severe:	Crippling breathlessness, often present even when sitting at rest in an armchair.
Speech Problems—Moderate:	Speech obviously impaired, being slurred or extremely slow, but intelligible with care.
Severe:	Substantial impairment; almost unintelligible.
6. *Mental Health Problems*	
Disorientation:	People will tend to lose their sense

	of time before place or person. Check whether they are aware of the date, of where they are and who they are. Some elderly people will believe their parents are still alive and that they themselves are quite young.
Recent onset:	Recent onset is defined as within the last six months.
Abnormal Behaviour:	*Self neglect*—should be included even if it would only become apparent on withdrawing present support.
Depressed mood:	*Mild*—gloomy attitude, sadness. *Moderate*—tendency to weep, considerable pessimism. *Severe*—extreme symptoms of depression.
Anxiety:	*Mild*—complains of worrying over minor matters. *Moderate*—complains of loss of sleep due to worry: displays apprehensive attitude; expresses fears. *Severe*—Extreme symptoms, tending to incapacitate person from managing adequately.

COMPLETION OF A CASE REVIEW FORM

Descriptive data: For a reopened case, review numbers should start back at 01.

Case number: This is the number by which the client is known in the Social Work Office. Please put each figure separately in one of the boxes. Start from the left-hand side and enter the first figure in the first box (e.g. 0102). If a husband and wife are both clients, they should have separate case numbers.

Referral source: If a first review or a new or reopened case please code referral agent: (i) non-departmental (if known), (ii) departmental (if applicable), e.g. if a client was referred to the SSD area team by a GP and re-referred by a social worker to the CCS worker a year later, code (i) as 05 and (ii) as 1.

REFERRAL SOURCE:

(i) *Non-departmental*		(ii) *Departmental*	
01	Self Referral	1	Area Team Social Worker
02	Household Member	2	Hospital Social Worker
03	Relative	3	Home Help Service
04	Friend/Neighbour	4	Occupational Therapist
05	GP	5	Local Authority Home
06	District Nurse	6	Local Authority Day Centre
07	Health Visitor	7	CCS Helper
08	Hospital	9	Other
09	Housing Department		
10	Police		
11	Voluntary Agency		
12	DHSS		
13	Other		

Last review date: Please enter the date to the best of your knowledge; all dates to be entered numerically (e.g. 9 January 1979 becomes 09 01 79).

This review date: Please enter the date of the present review.

Review number: Please enter if known.

Area:

Thanet = 01	Shepway = 02	Sheppey = 03
Tonbridge = 04	Gravesham = 05	Dover = 06

1. Client problems

In the first column please tick the major problems you have tackled since the last review. If the review is a first review please consider the first column as if it were headed 'Since referral'.

In the second column please tick the major problems present at this review. Also the second column should be considered when closing a case since problems may still be present.

01 *Physical disability/illness*: in this category are included all kinds of disability, physical handicap and chronic sickness; with the exception of sensory difficulties (02, 03).
02 *Visual difficulties*: problems arising from blindness or partial sight.
03 *Hearing difficulties*: problems arising from deafness or being hard of hearing.
04 *Incontinence*: either of urine or faeces.
05 *Difficulties arising a.m./p.m.*: problems in coping with rising and retiring, getting in and out of bed, washing and dressing self.
06 *Personal care problems*: includes problems of self-neglect, liability to fall, difficulties in getting to and from toilet, general 'risk' factors.
07 *Daily household problems*: difficulties in coping with household tasks which of their nature arise more than once a day, e.g. making fires, making hot drinks, preparing adequate meals, washing up.
08 *Weekly household problems*: difficulties in coping with household problems which arise once daily or less, e.g. shopping, heavy housework, laundry.
09 *Psychological/emotional disorder*: includes disturbances of emotion and behaviour not amounting to overt mental disorder, e.g. anxiety, grief, drinking problems, transient emotional distress, 'difficult personality'.
10 *Mental confusion*: include here problems caused by loss of short-term memory, disorientation, unless obviously a very short transient episode following an acute illness.
11 *Behavioural problems*: abnormal behaviour such as agression or accusations, such as wandering, leaving gas taps lit; often found in association with confusion.
12 *Other mental disorder*: refers to mental illness; overt and usually diagnosed episodes of mental disorder.
13 *Social isolation/loneliness*: referring both to the objective state of people being isolated in the community and/or from their families; and to the subjective feelings of loneliness.
14 *Family relations problems*: difficulties arising between clients and their family or close informal carers leading to tension, etc.

15 *Accommodation problems*: may include overcrowding, homelessness, problems due to inadequate facilities and unsuitability, e.g. damp, difficult to heat, steps to toilet, etc.
16 *Transport difficulties*: self-explanatory.
17 *Financial difficulties*: problems arising from inadequate finance, requiring welfare benefits.
1 8 *Managing affairs*: difficulties in handling financial details, paying bills, etc.
19 *Residential care problems*: includes support to carers where person boarded out, difficulties in settling into residential accommodation.
20 *Other*: please name the problem if none of the categories are appropriate.

Most important problem: In the first column code the most important problem that was the focus of intervention since the last review. In the second column, indicate the most important present problem.

Changes achieved: In this section please give a very short description of the actual changes you have brought about or progress that has been made: for example, partial relief of isolation and loneliness, improved nutrition.

Change areas

1. *None*: this applies to cases where no change is anticipated. In some cases where a stable equilibrium has been achieved (e.g. a steady pattern of reliable effective domiciliary care) the aim may be to preserve the status quo. In others it may not have been possible to make progress.
2. *Major environmental changes*: a complete change of the physical environment, e.g. admission to residential home.
3. *Social/personal environment*: denotes changes in the immediate environment brought about by a variety of services (home help, clubs, holidays, aids), which are intended to enable clients to lead fuller and more satisfying lives.
4. *Social role*: here the aim of social work is to help people in their transition and adjustment to role changes; for example adjustment to widowhood, to disability, to giving up one's home, etc.
5. *Behaviour/attitudes/relationships*: here the aim may be to help clients to a better relationship with their family, to become more active socially, to behave in a more acceptable fashion, etc.

Present situation/reason for closure: self-explanatory. If client died or moved into residential care/hospital, please give date.

2. Open cases

What changes are you aiming for?: as in the section on changes achieved, please give a very short description of the changes you wish to bring about, or progress you wish to make before the next review.
Change areas: the changes you wish to bring about in the future are categorised similarly to changes achieved since the last review.

Time before case likely to be closed: sometimes community care is planned for as long as the client can survive in the community but it is sometimes impossible to estimate even roughly how long this is likely to be. Then code as 6. If a client is, say, in hospital and unlikely to return home, it is left to the discretion of the CCS worker as to when the case is regarded as closed.

Closed cases: reasons for closure

1. *Aims achieved*: social work intervention has enabled the client/family to function adequately without further social work support. Aims will also be achieved when a social worker successfully carries out a piece of work such as referring a client to another agency or supplying a client with relevant information.
2. *Aims partially achieved*: no further change expected. Social work intervention has enabled the client/family to improve their functioning to a level where further improvements, although desirable, cannot be expected.
3. *Aims cannot be effected*: social work intervention has not had the desired effect and goals have not been achieved. Alternatively, a client's problems may be intractable or the department has not got the appropriate resources to effect change.
4. *No priority*: relates to referrals which receive no social work response and may be immediately directed on referral to other facilities/agencies.
5. *Contact not achieved*: social worker unsuccessfully attempts to make contact with client by home visits, letters and telephone calls.
6. *Client withdrew*: includes instances where a client requests a service to be discontinued, a client refuses help or resources offered, a client acknowledges his ineligibility for a service, and so on.
7. *Client left area*: client moves out of this local authority.
8. *Client died*: self-explanatory.
9. *Other*: if none of the above reasons for closure seem to fit, describe very briefly in your own words why you closed the case.

Since last review/before next review: On the right-hand side of the form you will find two columns for:

Social work activities
Outside agencies in contact with social worker
Practical services

If the review is a first review, please consider the first column as if it were headed 'Since referral' or 'Since allocation'.

If you are reviewing a case for the second time or thereafter, we would like you to put in the first column what actually happened since you last reviewed, what social work activities you engaged in, and what agencies you were in contact with. Under the second column 'Before next review', tick what social work activities you intend to engage in and what outside agencies you plan to contact; but for practical services, please indicate which would ideally be needed.

If the review is your last review on closure then you *should not* fill in the column 'Before next review'. If a box in the first column applied after the last review but is no longer applicable - e.g. client died -still tick that box.

3. Social worker activities

These categories attempt to describe the content of the social work practice. Again you are asked to tick what happened in the preceeding period in the first set of boxes and what you intend to do in the future in the second. In order for a category to be ticked, it does not have to apply for the full three-month period.

01 *None*: no one may have been engaged in or intended to be engaged in any of the following activities.

02 *Exploratory/re-assessment activity*: largely concerned with exploration of current and past situations in order to gain an understanding of the present issues and to re-assess possibilities and constraints of future work.

03 *Information/advice*: providing clients with information or advice to make applications, obtain welfare benefits, etc.

04 *Mobilising resources*: activities concerned mainly with arranging practical help such as aids, holidays, clubs, voluntary help, home helps, and help from other formal organisations.

05 *Coordinating Resources*: activities concerned with juggling resources to meet needs more effectively; e.g. ensuring that visitors go on different days of week, negotiating with other service providers to change roles.

06 *Check-up/review visits*: short popping in visits to ensure that everything is OK.

07 *Social skills education*: e.g. showing the disabled person how to use aids or other environmental supports to daily living; working with client to overcome speech difficulties.

08 *Facilitating problem-solving/decision-making*: various forms of counselling or casework, e.g. helping clients to ventilate feelings, to discuss, sort out and try to solve problems, make choices, become aware of their behaviour and its effect upon others, etc.

09 *Sustaining/nurturing client*: mainly friendly encouragement, caring and support rather than activities directed towards problem-solving or change. This activity directed at the client/patient.

10 *Sustaining/nurturing family or informal carers*: as before, but the focus of this activity is upon the family or the client's immediate support network, such as neighbours.

11 *Sustaining/nurturing - CCP helpers*: as before, but the focus of this activity is upon individual helpers and the difficulties they experience.

12 *Advocacy*: activities where social workers represent their client's cause to formal organisations such as housing departments, DHSS, and with other professionals.

13 *Group work/activities*: engaging in group work with clients or their carers either as a group leader or as an active member of a group.

14 *Other*: an activity not readily defined in the listed groups. (Please specify on the form.)

Code priority activity: always code the most important activity, both past and future, even if you have or intend to engage in one activity only.

Estimate number of contacts:
a) *With client/family*: consider the past and future and make approximate estimates of contacts with client and immediate family or very close informal carers. A contact can range from a brief chat on the telephone to a face to face interview. Please note that letters, with the exception of appointment letters, should be counted.
b) *With all others*: again consider the past and future and estimate the number of contacts with members of the extended family, community helpers, outside agencies and other personnel you have had on behalf of the client. These include contacts with helpers prior to introduction to the client, provided they were specifically for the purpose of helping that client, and even if they withdrew subsequently before meeting the client.

4. Outside agencies in contact with social worker

Please code those agencies with whom you have been, or plan to be in contact with on behalf of the client.

01 *None*: as before the coding of this negative category is as important as the positive categories.
02 *General practitioner*: self-explanatory.
03 *Psychiatric hospital/OPD*: self-explanatory.
04 *Geriatric hospital/OPD*: self-explanatory - include geriatricians.
05 *Other hospital/OPD*: self-explanatory
06 *Housing department*: self-explanatory
07 *DHSS (Social Security, etc.)* self-explanatory
08 *Probation*:
09 *Police*:
10 *Court*:
11 *Solicitor*:
12 *Other social services department*:
13 *Age Concern*:
14 *WRVS*:
15 *Red Cross*:
16 *Volunteer Bureau*:
17 *Other Volunteer Agency*: (specify on form)
18 *Other*: (specify on form) - include District Nurse here.

5. Practical services

01 *None*: coding this negative category is as important as coding the positive care given.

DOMICILIARY AND COMMUNITY RESOURCES

02 *Home help*: self-explanatory
03 *Night sitter*: paid by social services department.
04 *Private help*: including private night sitter and contractual arrangements with a neighbour.
05 *Private nursing*: self-explanatory.
06 *Volunteer involvement*: self-explanatory and including unpaid contracted helpers.
07 *Paid Helper*: where a neighbour, friend or other person is paid by social worker to perform tasks for the client.
08 Laundry service: laundry provision for incontinence.
09 *Occupational therapy*: Assessment services by departmental OT.

10 *Specialist social worker blind/deaf*: Assessment/services by specialist social workers for the blind or deaf, including home teachers.
11 *Financial application/assistance*: help related to income maintenance or connected with raising grants, etc.
12 *Accommodation applications/assistance*: help with problems arising from housing difficulty, e.g. overcrowding, inadequate facilities, inaccessible toilet, housing transfer, etc.
13 *Help with applications*: other - assistance with other form filling.
14 *Material improvements*: e.g. furniture or other improvements in home decoration, improved heating system, better amenities, or money for specific material improvements (not including adaptions where required due to disability).

Aids: Tick for each review period where aid is present or planned to continue.
15 *Aids for mobility*: e.g. walking frame, stick, tripod.
16 *Aids for toileting*: e.g. raised toilet seat, commode.
17 *Aids for bathing*: e.g. bath seat, mat, lever taps.
18 *Aids for household use*: e.g. special cups and cutlery, long-handled dustpan, helping hand, can opener.
19 *Aids for dressing*: e.g. long-handled shoehorn, stocking aid.
20 *Aids for blind/partially sighted*: e.g. talking book, white stick.
21 *Aids for deaf/hard of hearing*: e.g. visual bell, loud speaking telephone.
22 *Aids - other*: specify, e.g. alarm system, hoists, bed blocks, other recreational aids not included above.
23 *Adaptations*: e.g. ramp, handrails, door widening.
24 *Telephone*: provision of LA telephone.
25 *Day centre*: when attending a local authority purpose-built day centre.
26 *Day care*: OPH - day care in an old people's home.
27 *Luncheon club*: self-explanatory.
28 *Meals on wheels*: self-explanatory.
29 *Social clubs/outings*: self-explanatory.
30 *Other* where not included above, please specify.
31 *Other*: where not included above, please specify.

RESIDENTIAL CARE
32 *Group homes*: a group residence for several elderly clients where mutual support is encouraged to maximise independent living.
33 *Boarding out*: where client placed in a foster care or family setting.
34 *Sheltered housing*: self-explanatory.
35 *Part III - short-term*: short-term care (less than two months) in LA home.

36 *Part III - EMI*: short-term care (less than two months) in LA home for the mentally confused.
37 *Part III - long-term*: self-explanatory - local authority care.
38 *Part III - EMI - long-term*: care in LA home for mentally confused.
39 Voluntary home - short-term: a stay of less than two months in a home run by charitable trust or voluntary society; non profit making.
40 *Voluntary home - long-term*: long-term care in voluntary home.
41 *Private home - short-term*: less than two month stay in a home run for profit by a private concern, e.g. ex-boarding home.
42 *Private home*: long-term care in private home.
43 *OPH discharge*: discharge from short or long-term care in any old person's home, but excluding transfers between OPH's.
44 *Other (specify)*: a residential resource not specified above.
45 *Other (specify)*: a residential resource not specified above.

NHS ACTIVITIES

46 *District nurse*: self-explanatory.
47 *Bath attendant*: self-explanatory.
48 *Chiropody*: self-explanatory. Include private chiropody, if introduced by CCS worker. If treatment is continual but less frequent than quarterly, still tick, though include as well under resources required but unavailable, if appropriate.
49 *Community psychiatric nurse*: self-explanatory.
50 *Health visitor*: self-explanatory.
51 *Day hospital - geriatric*: including day care on geriatric ward and outpatient treatment/rehabilitation.
52 *Day hospital - psychiatric*: including day care on psychiatric ward.
53 *Geriatric hospital admission*: short-term admission for treatment/care.
54 *Psychiatric hospital admission*: short-term admission for treatment/care.
55 *General hospital admission*: to non-geriatric or psychiatric bed for treatment.
56 *Geriatric hospital - long-term*: admission for long-term care.
57 *Psychiatric hospital - long-term*: admission for long-term care.
58 *Hospital discharge*: discharge from any hospital.
59 *Other (specify)*: NHS resource not mentioned above.
60 *Other (specify)*: NHS resource not mentioned above.

6. Resource required but unavailable:

Please code in the available boxes resources listed in section 5 which are required but unavailable, or insufficient in quantity. If the unavailable resource is not listed please specify in the available space.

Other aspects of importance: any other relevant material relating to case management or planning.

COMMUNITY CARE OF THE ELDERLY

CASE REVIEW

Client Name..

Case Number [ ]

Reviewed by..

Referral Source (i)non-departmental [ ] (ii)Departmental [ ]

Last Review Date [ ] Area [ ]

This Review Date [ ] Sex: Male 1 [ ]

Review Number [ ] Female 2 [ ]

Office Use CCS wkr [ ]

Scheme [ ] Period [ ]

Date of Birth: [ ]

1. Client Problems

		Tackled since last review		Present at this review
01	Physical disability/illness	[ ]	01	[ ]
02	Visual difficulties	[ ]	02	[ ]
03	Hearing difficulties	[ ]	03	[ ]
04	Incontinence	[ ]	04	[ ]
05	Difficulties arising a.m./p.m.	[ ]	05	[ ]
06	Personal care problems	[ ]	06	[ ]
07	Daily Household problems	[ ]	07	[ ]
08	Weekly Household problems	[ ]	08	[ ]
09	Psychological/emotional disorder	[ ]	09	[ ]
10	Mental confusion	[ ]	10	[ ]
11	Behaviour problems	[ ]	11	[ ]
12	Other mental disorder	[ ]	12	[ ]
13	Social isolation/loneliness	[ ]	13	[ ]
14	Family relations problems	[ ]	14	[ ]
15	Accommodation problems	[ ]	15	[ ]
16	Transport problems	[ ]	16	[ ]
17	Financial difficulties	[ ]	17	[ ]
18	Managing affairs problems	[ ]	18	[ ]
19	Residential care problems	[ ]	19	[ ]
20	Other(specify)......................	[ ]	20	[ ]
21	Other(specify)......................	[ ]	21	[ ]

Code most important problem [ ] [ ]

Describe changes achieved....................................

....

....

....

....

....

....

Tick Change areas

1 None [ ]
2 Major environmental [ ]
3 Social/personal environment [ ]
4 Social role [ ]
5 Behaviour/attitude/relationships [ ]

Describe present situation/reasons for closure................

....

....

....

....

....

....

2 OPEN CASES What changes are you aiming for?...............

....

....

....

....

....

....

2. (continued)

Tick Change areas

1 None [ ]
2 Major environmental [ ]
3 Social/personal environment [ ]
4 Social role [ ]
5 Behaviour/attitude/relationships [ ]

Code Time before case likely to be closed. [ ]

1 Up to 3 months
2 6 months
3 1 year
4 3 years
5 More than 3 years
6 Until client leaves community

CLOSED CASES Code Reason for closure by CCS Worker [ ]

1 Aims achieved
2 Aims partially achieved
 - no further change expected
3 Aims cannot be effected
4 No priority
5 Contact not achieved
6 Client withdrew
7 Client left area
8 Client died
9 Other (.............
......................)

3. Social Worker activities

		Since last Review Actual		Before Next Review Planned
01	None	[ ]	01	[ ]
02	Exploratory/(re-)assessment	[ ]	02	[ ]
03	Information/advice	[ ]	03	[ ]
04	Mobilising resources	[ ]	04	[ ]
05	Co-ordinating resources	[ ]	05	[ ]
06	Check-up/review visits	[ ]	06	[ ]
07	Social skills education	[ ]	07	[ ]
08	Facilitating problem solving/decision making	[ ]	08	[ ]
09	Sustaining/nurturing-client	[ ]	09	[ ]
10	Sustaining/nurturing-family/informal carers	[ ]	10	[ ]
11	Sustaining/nurturing-CCP	[ ]	11	[ ]
12	Advocacy	[ ]	12	[ ]
13	Group work activities	[ ]	13	[ ]
14	Other (specify)............	[ ]	14	[ ]
15	Other (Specify)............	[ ]	15	[ ]

Code Priority activity [ ] [ ]

Estimate No. of contacts (with client/family) [ ] [ ]

(with others) [ ] [ ]

4. Outside Agencies in contact with Social Worker

		Actual		Planned
01	None	[ ]	01	[ ]
02	General Practitioner	[ ]	02	[ ]
03	Geriatric Hosp./O.P.D.	[ ]	03	[ ]
04	Psychiatric Hosp./O.P.D.	[ ]	04	[ ]
05	Other hosp./O.P.D.	[ ]	05	[ ]
06	Housing Department	[ ]	06	[ ]
07	DHSS (Soc.Sec. etc.)	[ ]	07	[ ]
08	Probation	[ ]	08	[ ]
09	Police	[ ]	09	[ ]
10	Court	[ ]	10	[ ]
11	Solicitor	[ ]	11	[ ]
12	SSD in another authority	[ ]	12	[ ]
13	Age Concern	[ ]	13	[ ]
14	WRVS	[ ]	14	[ ]
15	Red Cross	[ ]	15	[ ]
16	Volunteer Bureau	[ ]	16	[ ]
17	Other Voluntary Agency	[ ]	17	[ ]
18	Other (specify)............	[ ]	18	[ ]
19	Other (specify)............	[ ]	19	[ ]

5. Practical Services

Other aspects of importance (please describe below)

(i) Domiciliary and Community Resources

		Actual		Planned
01	None		01	
02	Home Help		02	
03	Night Sitter		03	
04	Private Help		04	
05	Private Nursing		05	
06	Volunteer Involvement		06	
07	Paid helper		07	
08	Laundry Service		08	
09	Occupational therapy		09	
10	Specialist S.W. blind/deaf		10	
11	Financial applications/assistance		11	
12	Accommodation applications/assistance		12	
13	Help with applications-other		13	
14	Material improvements		14	
15	Aids for mobility		15	
16	Aids for toileting		16	
17	Aids for bathing		17	
18	Aids for household use		18	
19	Aids for dressing		19	
20	Aids for blind/partially sighted		20	
21	Aids for deaf/hard of hearing		21	
22	Aids-other (specify)		22	
23	Adaptations		23	
24	Telephone		24	
25	Day Centre		25	
26	Day Care - OPH		26	
27	Luncheon Club		27	
28	Meals on wheels		28	
29	Social clubs/outings		29	
30	Other (specify)		30	
31	Other (specify)		31	

(ii) Residential

		Actual		Planned
32	Group Home		32	
33	Boarding Out		33	
34	Sheltered Housing		34	
35	Part III - short term		35	
36	Part III - E.M.I. short term		36	
37	Part III - long term		37	
38	Part III - E.M.I. long term		38	
39	Voluntary home - short term		39	
40	Voluntary home - long term		40	
41	Private home - short term		41	
42	Private home - long term		42	
43	O.P.H. discharge		43	
44	Other (specify)		44	
45	Other (specify)		45	

(iii) NHS Activities

		Actual		Planned
46	District Nurse		46	
47	Bath attendant		47	
48	Chiropody		48	
49	Community Psychiatric Nurse		49	
50	Health visitor		50	
51	Day hospital - geriatric		51	
52	Day hospital - psychiatric		52	
53	Geriatric hospital admission		53	
54	Psychiatric hospital admission		54	
55	General hospital admission		55	
56	Geriatric hospital - long term		56	
57	Psychiatric hospital - long term		57	
58	Hospital discharge		58	
59	Other (specify)		59	
60	Other (specify)		60	

6. Resources Required but unavailable

Code from Section 5 [ ][ ] [ ][ ] [ ][ ] [ ][ ] [ ][ ]

[ ][ ] [ ][ ] [ ][ ] [ ][ ] [ ][ ]

Others (specify)..

....

....

....

....

....

MONITORING CHART

The purpose of the monitoring chart is both for care-planning and for providing a readily available summary of care to an individual elderly person. It can provide an easily assimilated overview of the pattern of care, of who does what at what times, so that other staff can quickly familiarise themselves with the case in the event of the absence of the key worker.

MONITORING CHART

	Getting up/ dressing	Breakfast	Morning	Lunch	Afternoon	Teatime	Evening	Getting undressed/ into bed	Night Time
Monday									
Tuesday									
Wednesday									
Thursday									
Friday									
Saturday									
Sunday									

KENT COUNTY COUNCIL - SOCIAL SERVICES DEPARTMENT | COMMUNITY CARE SCHEME | CLIENTS COSTING SHEET

NAME:

DATE CASE RESPONSIBILITY ASSUMED: ____________ | ____________ QUARTER

ADDRESS:

DATE CASE RESPONSIBILITY CEASED: ____________

CLIENT CASE NO: ____________

COMMUNITY CARE ORGANISER: ____________

							TRAVELLING EXPENSES				
1. HELPERS NAME	2.CONTRACT NUMBER	3.CLAIM PERIOD	4.NO.OF VISITS	5.AMOUNT OF CLAIM	6.CUMULATIVE TOTAL	7.SENT TO C.T.	8.CLAIM PERIOD	9.AMOUNT OF CLAIM	10.CUMULATIVE TOTAL	11.SENT TO C.T.	12.HELPERS COSTS ADD 6 + 10
				TOTAL FEES COL. 6	______			TOTAL EXPENSES COL. 10	______	HELPERS COSTS 6 + 10	______

CLIENTS OTHER SOCIAL SERVICES DEPARTMENT COSTS

DATE	A. DAY CARE		B. HOME HELP		C. MEALS-ON-WHEELS		D. PERIODS IN RES. CARE		E. OTHER SERVICES (Specify)		F. CUMULATIVE COSTS (A+B+C+D+E)	G. HELPERS COSTS (12 Overleaf)	H. TOTAL (F+G)
	NUMBER	COST	NUMBER	COST	NUMBER	COST	NUMBER	COST	NUMBER	COST			
1.													
2.													
3.													
4.													
5.													
6.													
7.													
8.													
9.													
10.													
11.													
12.													
13.													
TOTAL													

Average Weekly Cost = H / No. of weeks in quarter during which Community Care Organiser holds case responsibility = £ ______

PDR19/DGAM247

Dear

Kent Community Care Scheme

Thank you for agreeing to take part in this scheme which is aimed at enabling elderly people to continue living in their own home when it is becoming increasingly difficult for them to do so without receiving the kind of help and support which you are willing to provide.

As from ... you will be asked to fulfil the following duties with ...

Description of duty Days Times

Although the estimated time involved in these duties is shown, the contract is for the performance of the duties rather than the amount of time spent on the duties.

This particular form of community care makes use of a different approach to the care of the elderly. The scheme therefore is being studied closely, both to assess its effectiveness in helping elderly people at this time, and also to see whether it may serve as a pattern for the further development of services. In order to help judge the success of the scheme, information will be sought from many sources including both the elderly person and the helper, which means there will be some degree of supervision of all activities carried out in connection with the project.

The terms of your engagement will be reviewed every two months or more frequently if necessary to ensure that both you and the staff of the project are satisfied that the Community Care Project is meeting the needs of the recipients of the services you are providing.

You will be regarded as an agent of Kent County Council, and as such you will not be an employee of the County Council and will not qualify for sick or holiday payments from the Council. You will be subject to the Council's existing cover for third party liability and, in the case of injury occurring in the course of the provision of community care service, the Council's liability will be met in accordance with Kent County Council's arrangements in respect of employer's liability. Details are available at this office.

You will receive a payment of £... per week for your services, and agreed travelling expenses of £... per week. Payment will be made by cheque/cash, on receipt of claims weekly/fortnightly/monthly, as agreed.

The following provisions also apply.

1. Income tax will only be deducted if your payments bring your total income above the limit of your allowances against tax. The County Treasurer will apply to H.M. Inspector of Taxes for your tax code. Expenses are not taxed.

2. National Insurance contributions will only be deducted if your total payments from this and other concurrent contracts with the Project are more than the limit for part-time earnings currently in force.

This engagement can be terminated either way at three days' notice.

Will you please confirm your acceptance of these conditions by signing and returning the attached copy of this letter.

I would like to take this opportunity to welcome you to this new form of community service, and wish you every success.

Yours sincerely,

Director of Social Services

National Insurance No. ...
Signature ....
Date ....

CONFIDENTIAL

Dear

The above named has applied to be a helper in the Community Care Scheme for the Elderly, and has given your name for reference.

Helpers are involved in looking after frail elderly people at home, by providing a range of services which will help them to stay in their own home rather than having to enter residential care.

The helper must be honest, trustworthy and reliable, as well as sympathetic and understanding towards elderly people. Although helpful, previous experience in caring for old people is not essential.

It would be much appreciated if you would give your opinion in confidence on ... suitability for this type of work.

Yours sincerely,

Community Care Organiser (Elderly)

BIBLIOGRAPHY

Abrams, M. (1982)
People in their Later Sixties, Age Concern, Mitcham, Surrey.

Abrams, P. (1977)
'Community care: Some research problems and priorities', *Policy and Politics*, 6, 125-51.

Allen, I. with Levin, E., Siddell, M. and Vetter, N. (1983)
'The elderly and their informal carers', in Department of Health and Social Security, *Elderly People in the Community: Their Service Needs*, HMSO, London.

Applebaum, R., Seidl, F.W. and Austin, C.D. (1980)
'The Wisconsin Community Care Organisation: Preliminary findings from the Milwaukee Experiment', *The Gerontologist*, 20, 350-55.

Audit Commission (1985)
Managing Social Services for the Elderly More Effectively, HMSO, London.

Audit Commission (1986)
Managing Social Work More Effectively: A Pilot Report, Audit Commission, London.

Barclay, P. (1982)
Report of the Committee of Enquiry into the Roles and Tasks of Social Workers, Bedford Square Press, London.

Bamford, T. (1984)
Managing Social Work, Tavistock, London.

Barrowclough, C. and Fleming, I. (1984)
'Not too old to learn', *Community Care*, 23 February, 16-17.

Barrowclough, C. and Fleming, I. (1986)
Goal Planning with Elderly People, Manchester University Press, Manchester.

Bayley, M. (1973)
Mental Handicap and Community Care, Routledge and Kegan Paul, London.

Bebbington, A.C. (1979)
'Changes in the provision of social services to the elderly in the community over fourteen years', *Social Policy and Administration*, 13, 111-23.

Bergmann, K. (1973)
'Psychogeriatrics', *Medicine*, 9, 643-52.

Bergmann, K. (1978)
'Neurosis and personality disorder in old age', in A. Isaacs and F. Post (eds) *Studies in Geriatric Psychiatry*, Wiley, Chichester.

Bergmann, K. (1979)
'How to keep the family supportive', *Geriatric Medicine*, August, 53-7.

Bergmann, K. and Jacoby, R. (1983)
'The limitations of community care for the elderly demented', in Department of Health and Social Security, *Elderly People in the Community: Their Service Needs*, HMSO, London.

Bergmann, K., Gaber, L.B. and Foster, E.M. (1975)
'The development of an instrument for early ascertainment of psychiatric disorder in elderly community residents: A pilot study', *Gerontopsychiatric*, 4, 84-119.

Bergmann, K., Foster, E.M., Justice, A.W. and Matthews, V. (1978)
'Management of the demented elderly patient in the community', *British Journal of Psychiatry*, 132, 441-9.

Bergmann, K., Manchee V. and Woods R.T. (1984)
'Effect of family relationships on psychogeriatric patients', *Journal of the Royal Society of Medicine*, 77, 840-44.

Berkmann, L.F. and Syme, S.L. (1979)
'Social networks, host resistance and mortality: A nine-year follow-up of Alameda County Residents', *American Journal of Epidemiology*, 109, 186-204.

Berman, S. and Rappaport, M.B. (1984)
'Social work and Alzheimer's disease: Psychosocial management in the absence of medical cure', *Social Work in Health Care*, 10, 53-70.

Biestek, F.P. (1961)
The Casework Relationship, Allen and Unwin, London.

Black, J., Bowl, R., Burns, D., Critcher, C., Grant, G. and Stockford, D. (1983)
Social Work in Context: A Comparative Study of Three Social Service Teams, Tavistock, London.

Blazer, D. (1981)
Social Support and Mortality in an Elderly Community Population, Unpublished Paper, Department of Psychiatry and Centre for the Study of Ageing and Human Development, Duke University Medical Center, Durham, N. Carolina.

Boyd, R.V. (1981)
'What is a "social problem" in geriatrics?', in T. Arie (ed.) *Health Care of the Elderly*, Croom Helm, London.

Brearley, C.P. (1975)
Social Work, Ageing and Society, Routledge and Kegan Paul, London.

Brent, London Borough of (1985)
A Child in Trust: The report of the panel of inquiry into the circumstances surrounding the death of Jasmine Beckford, London Borough of Brent, London.

British Association of Social Workers (1977)
'Guidelines: Social work with the elderly', *Social Work Today*, 8, 27, 8-15.

Brocklehurst, J.C. (1978)
'The investigation and management of incontinence', in B. Isaacs (ed) *Recent Advances in Geriatric Medicine*, Churchill Livingstone, London.

Brocklehurst, J.C., Carty, M.H. and Leeming, J.T. (1978)
'Care of the elderly: Medical screening of old people accepted for residential care', *Lancet*, ii, 141-2.

Brotherton, J. (1975)
The Need for Meals-on-Wheels and Luncheon Clubs in the Dover District of Kent, Kent County Council Research and Intelligence Unit, Maidstone.

Brown, G.W., Birley, J.L.T. and Wing, J.K. (1972)
'Influence of family life on the course of schizophrenic disorders: A replication', *British Journal of Psychiatry*, 121, 241-58.

Brown, G.W. and Rutter, M. (1966)
'The measurement of family activities and relationships', *Human Relations*, 19, 241-63.

Brown, G.W. and Harris, T. (1978)
Social Origins of Depression, Tavistock, London.

Butler, A. and Pritchard, C. (1983)
Social Work and Mental Illness, Macmillan, London.

Cahalen, D., Cisin, I.H. and Crossley, H.M. (1969)
American Drinking Practices, Rutgers Center of Alcohol Studies, New Brunswick, New Jersey.

Campbell, D.T. and Stanley, J.C. (1966)
Experimental and Quasi-experimental Designs for Research, Rand McNally, Chicago, Illinois.

Carter, K. and Evans, T.N. (1978)
'Intentions and achievements in admissions of the elderly to residential care', *Clearing House for Local Authority Social Services Research*, 9, 71-99.

Carver, V. and Edwards, J.L. (1972)
Social Workers and their Workloads, National Institute for Social Work, London.

Castledene, C.M. and Duffin, H.M. (1981)
'Guidelines for controlling urinary incontinence without drugs or catheters', *Age and Ageing*, 10, 186-90.

Challis, D.J. (1981);
'The measurement of outcome in social care of the elderly', *Journal of Social Policy*, 10, 179-208.

Challis, D.J. (1985a)
'The community care scheme: An alternative approach to decentralisation', in S. Hatch (ed.) *Decentralisation and Care in the Community*, Policy Studies Institute, London.

Challis, D.J. (1985b)
The Evaluation of Cost-effectiveness in Social Care Services, Northern Ireland Office/University of Ulster.

Challis, D.J. and Chesterman, J. (1985)
'A system for monitoring social work activity with the frail elderly', *British Journal of Social Work*, 15, 115-32

Challis, D.J. and Chesterman, J. (1986)
'Facilitating caseload and workload management through feedback from computerised case records', *Social Services Insight*, June, 15-18.

Challis, D.J. and Davies, B.P. (1980)
'A new approach to community care for the elderly', *British Journal of Social Work*, 10, 1-18.

Challis, D.J. and Ferlie, E. (1986a)
'All change, but which way?', *Community Care*, 13 February, 19-21.

Challis, D.J. and Ferlie, E. (1986b)
'Changing patterns of fieldwork organisation: I. The headquarters' view', *British Journal of Social Work*, 16, 181-202.

Challis, D.J., Chessum, R. and Luckett, R. (1983)
'A new life at home', *Community Care*, 24 March, 21-23.
Challis, D.J., Knapp, M.R.J. and Davies, B.P. (1984)
'Cost-effectiveness analysis in social care', in J. Lishman (ed.) *Research Highlights: Evaluation*, University of Aberdeen Press, Aberdeen.
Charlesworth, A., Wilkin, D. and Durie, A. (1984)
Carers and Services: A Comparison of Men and Women Caring for Dependent Elderly People, Equal Opportunities Commission, London.
Chartered Institute of Public Finance and Accountancy (1978)
Personal Social Services Statistics: 1976-77 Actuals, CIPFA, London.
Chernesky, R.H. and Lurie, A. (1976)
'The functional analysis study: A first step in quality assurance', *Social Work in Health Care*, 1, 213-24.
Cheshire County Council (1981)
'Home help service in Cheshire: Clients and their needs', *Clearing House for Local Authority Social Services Research*, 1, 67-94.
Chesterman, J., Challis, D.J. and Davies B.P. (1985)
Follow-up Evaluation after Four Years of the Community Care Scheme for the Elderly, Discussion Paper 399, Personal Social Services Research Unit, University of Kent, Canterbury.
Clare, A. and Cairns, V. (1978)
'Design development and the use of a standardised interview to assess social maladjustment and dysfunction in community studies', *Psychological Medicine*, 8, 589-604.
Cmnd 1973 (1963)
Health and Welfare: The Development of Community Care, HMSO, London.
Cmnd 3703 (1968)
Report of the Committee on Local Authority and Allied Personal Social Services, HMSO, London.
Collins, A.H. and Pancoast, D.L. (1977)
Natural Helping Networks: A Strategy for Prevention, National Association of Social Workers, Washington DC.
Cormican, E.J. (1977)
'Task-centred model for work with the aged', *Social Casework*, October, 490-94.
Craig, J. (1983)
'The growth of the elderly population', *Population Trends*, 32, 28-33.
Crosbie, D. (1983)
'A role for anyone? A description of social work activity with the elderly in two area offices', *British Journal of Social Work*, 13, 123-48.
Culyer, A.J. (1976)
Need and the National Health Service, Martin Robertson, London.
Davies, B.P.(1977a)
'Needs and outputs', in H. Heisler (ed.) *Fundamentals of Social Administration*, Macmillan, London.

Davies, B.P. (1981a)
'Strategic goals and piecemeal innovations: Adjusting to the new balance of needs and resources', in E.M. Goldberg and S. Hatch (eds) *New Look at the Personal Social Services*, Policy Studies Institute, London.
Davies, B.P. (1986)
The Production of Welfare Approach, Discussion Paper 400, Personal Social Services Research Unit, University of Kent, Canterbury.
Davies, B.P. and Challis, D.J. (1981)
'A production-relations evaluation of the meeting of needs in the community care projects', in E.M. Goldberg and N. Connelly (eds) *Evaluative Research in Social Care*, Heinemann, London.
Davies, B.P. and Challis, D.J. (1986)
Matching Resources to Needs in Community Care: An Evaluated Demonstration of a Long-term Care Model, Gower, Aldershot.
Davies, B.P. and Knapp, M.R.J. (1981)
Old People's Homes and the Production of Welfare, Routledge and Kegan Paul, London.
Davies, M. (1977b)
Support Systems in Social Work, Routledge and Kegan Paul, London.
Davies, M. (1981b)
The Essential Social Worker, Heinemann, London.
Davies, R.M. and Duncan, I.B. (1975)
Allocation and Planning of Local Authority Residential Accommodation for the Elderly in Reading, Operational Research (Health Services) Unit, University of Reading.
Department of Employment (1978)
Family Expenditure Survey 1977, HMSO, London.
Department of Health and Social Security (1978)
Social Security Statistics 1976, HMSO, London.
Department of Health and Social Security (1979)
Health Services Costing Returns: Year ended 31 March 1977, HMSO, London.
Department of Health and Social Security (1981)
Community Care, HMSO, London.
Department of the Environment (1978)
Housing and Construction Statistics 1977, 24, HMSO, London.
Dexter, M. and Harbert, W. (1983)
The Home Help Service, Tavistock, London.
Dimond, E., Challis, D.J., Davies, B.P., Grant, G. and Missiakoulis, S. (1987)
Community Care in Gwynedd: An Evaluation of the Approach in a Rural Area, Discussion Paper 444, Personal Social Services Research Unit, University of Kent, Canterbury.
Dowd, J.J. (1975)
'Ageing as exchange: A preface to theory', *Journal of Gerontology*, 30, 584-94.
Droller, M. (1964)
'Some aspects of alcoholism in the elderly', *Lancet*, ii, 137-9.

Dunnachie, N. (1979)
'Intensive domiciliary care of the elderly in Hove', *Social Work Service*, 21, 1-3.

Eason, D. (1982)
'Computerising clients' records', *Community Care*, 10 June, 18-20.

Edwards, C., Sinclair, I. and Gorbach, P. (1980)
'Day centres for the elderly: Variations in type, provision and user response', *British Journal of Social Work*, 10, 419-30.

Evans, J. Grimley (1982)
'The psychiatric aspects of physical disease', in R. Levy and F. Post (eds) *The Psychiatry of Late Life*, Blackwell, Oxford.

Family Policy Studies Centre (1984)
The Forgotten Army, FPSC, London.

Fennell, G., Emerson, A.R., Sidell, M. and Hague, A. (1981)
Day Centres for the Elderly in East Anglia, Centre for East Anglian Studies,University of East Anglia, Norwich.

Ferlie, E. (1982)
Sourcebook of Innovation in Community Care of the Elderly, Discussion Paper 271, Personal Social Services Research Unit, University of Kent, Canterbury.

Foster, E.M., Kay, D.W.K. and Bergmann, K. (1976)
'The characteristics of old people receiving and needing domiciliary services: The relevance of diagnosis', *Age and Ageing*, 5, 245-55.

Fox, R.M., Woodward, P.M., Exton-Smith, A.N., Green, M.F., Donnison, D.V. and Wicks, M.H. (1973)
'Body temperatures in the elderly: A national study of physiological, social and environmental conditions', *British Medical Journal*, i, 200-206.

Fuller, J., Ward, E., Evans, A., Massam, K. and Gardner, A. (1979)
'Dementia: Supportive groups for relatives', *British Medical Journal*, i, 1684-5.

Garraway, W.M., Akhtar, A.J., Prescott, R.J. and Hockey, L. (1980)
'Management of acute stroke in the elderly: Preliminary results of a controlled trial', *British Medical Journal*, i, 1040-43.

Gibbins, F.J., Lee, M., Davison, P.R., O'Sullivan, P., Hutchinson, M., Murphy, D.R. and Ugwu, C.N. (1982)
'Augmented home nursing as an alternative to hospital care for chronic elderly invalids', *British Medical Journal*, 284, 330-33.

Gilmore, A.J.J. (1975)
'Some characteristics of non-surviving subjects in a three-year longitudinal study of elderly people living at home', *Gerontologica Clinica*, 17, 72-9.

Gilroy, D. (1982)
'Informal care: Reality behind the rhetoric', *Social Work Service*, 30, 9-18.

Glendenning, C. (1984)
'The resource worker project: Evaluating a specialist social work service for severely disabled children and their families', *British Journal of Social Work*, 14, 103-16.

Glennerster, H. (1985)
'Decentralisation and inter-service planning', in S. Hatch (ed.) *Decentralisation and Care in the Community*, Policy Studies Institute, London.

Goldberg, D.P. (1972)
The Detection of Psychiatric Illness by Questionnaire, Oxford University Press, Oxford.

Goldberg, D.P. and Huxley, P. (1980)
Mental Illness in the Community: The Pathway to Psychiatric Care, Tavistock, London.

Goldberg, E.M. and Connelly, N. (1982)
The Effectiveness of Social Care for the Elderly, Heinemann, London.

Goldberg, E.M. and Warburton, R.W. (1979)
Ends and Means in Social Work, Allen and Unwin, London.

Goldberg, E.M., Gibbons, J. and Sinclair, I. (1985)
Problems, Tasks and Outcomes: The Evaluation of Task-centred Casework in Three Settings, Allen and Unwin, London.

Goldberg, E.M., Mortimer, A. and Williams, B. (1970)
Helping the Aged, Allen and Unwin, London.

Goldfarb, A. (1968)
'Clinical perspectives', in A. Simon and L.J. Epstein (eds) *Ageing in Modern Society*, American Psychiatric Association, Washington DC.

Grad, J. and Sainsbury, P. (1968)
'The effects that patients have on their families in a community care and a control psychiatric service in a two-year follow-up', *British Journal of Psychiatry*, 114, 265-78.

Gray, B. and Isaacs, B. (1979)
Care of the Elderly Mentally Infirm, Tavistock, London.

Greengross, S. (1982)
'Caring for the carers', in F. Glendenning (ed.) *Care in the Community: Recent Research and Current Projects*, University of Keele/Beth Johnson Foundation, Stoke.

Gwynedd Social Services Department (1977)
A Research Review of the Operation of the Home Help Service in Gwynedd, Gwynedd County Council Social Services Department, Caernarfon.

Gwynne, D. (1980)
'Home help service in Cumbria', in Social Services Research Group, *Research and Policy-making in the Home Help Service*, SSRG, London.

Gwynne, D. and Fean, L. (1978)
'The home help service in Cumbria', Cumbria Social Services Department, Carlisle.

Hadley, R. and McGrath, M. (1980)
Going Local, Bedford Square Press, London.

Hadley, R. and McGrath, M. (1984)
When Social Services are Local, Allen and Unwin, London

Hall, M.R.P. (1982)
'Risk and health care', in C.P. Brearley (ed.), *Risk and Ageing*, Routledge and Kegan Paul, London.

Hamdy, R.C. (1980)
'Remediable causes of incontinence', *Geriatric Medicine*, March, 56-8.

Hamilton, M. (1960)
'A rating scale for depression', *Journal of Neurology, Neurosurgery and Psychiatry*, 23, 56-62.

Hedley, R. and Norman, A. (1982)
Home Help: Key Issues in Service Provision, Centre for Policy on Ageing, London.

Hemsi, L. (1980)
'Psychogeriatric care in the community', *Health Trends*, 12, 25-9.

Henderson, S., Duncan-Jones, P., McAuley, H. and Ritchie, K. (1978)
'The patient's primary group', *British Journal of Psychiatry*, 132, 74-86.

Henderson, S., Duncan-Jones, P., Byrne, D.G. and Scott, R. (1980)
'Measuring social relationships: The interview schedule for social interaction', *Psychological Medicine*, 10, 723-34.

Hendriksen, C., Lund, E. and Strongard, E. (1984)
'Consequences of assessment and intervention among elderly people: A three-year randomised control trial', *British Medical Journal*, 289, 1522-4.

Hey, A. (1980)
'Providing basic services at home', in D. Billis, G. Bromley, A. Hey and R. Rowbottom (eds) *Organising Social Services Departments*, Heinemann, London.

Hillingdon, London Borough of (1975)
Organisation of the Home Help Service in Hillingdon, Hillingdon Social Services Department, London.

Hirsch, F. (1977)
Social Limits to Growth, Routledge and Kegan Paul, London.

Hoenig, J. and Hamilton, M. (1969)
The Desegregation of the Mentally Ill, Routledge and Kegan Paul, London.

Holme, A. and Maizels, J. (1978)
Social Workers and Volunteers, Allen and Unwin, London.

Howe, D. (1979)
'Agency function and social work principles', *British Journal of Social Work*, 9, 29-47.

Howe, D. (1980)
'Division of labour in the area teams of social services departments', *Social Policy and Administration*, 14, 133-49.

Howell, N., Boldy, D. and Smith, B. (1979)
Allocating the Home Help Service, Bell, London.

Hunt, A. (1978)
The Elderly at Home, HMSO, London.

Huntington, J. (1981)
Social Work and General Medical Practice: Collaboration or Conflict?, Allen and Unwin, London.

Hurley, B. and Wolstenholme, E. (1979)
The Home Help Study, Bradford Metropolitan District Social Services Department, Bradford.

Ingliata, J. (1982)
'Improving the quality of community care for the chronically mentally disabled: The role of case management', *Schizophrenia Bulletin*, 8, 655-74.

Isaacs, B. and Walkley, F.A. (1963)
'The assessment of the mental state of elderly hospital patients using a simple questionnaire', *American Journal of Psychiatry*, 120, 173-4.

Isaacs, B. and Walkley, F.A. (1964)
'A survey of incontinence in elderly hospital patients', *Gerontologica Clinica*, 5, 8-22.

Isaacs, B., Livingstone, M. and Neville, Y. (1972)
Survival of the Unfittest, Routledge and Kegan Paul, London.

Isaacs, B. and Neville, Y. (1976)
'The measurement of need in old people', *Scottish Health Services Studies*, 34, Scottish Home and Health Department, Edinburgh.

James, O.F.W. (1981)
'Alcoholism in the elderly', in N. Krasner, S. Madin and R. Walker (eds) *Alcohol-related Problems:- Room for Manoeuvre*, Wiley, Chichester.

Johnson, M.L., di Gregorio, S. and Harrison, B. (1981)
Ageing, Needs and Nutrition: A Study of Voluntary and Statutory Collaboration in Community Care for Elderly People, Policy Studies Institute, London.

Jones, D.A., Victor, C.R. and Vetter, N.J. (1983)
'Carers of the elderly in the community', *Journal of the Royal College of General Practitioners*, 33, 707-10.

Karn, V. (1977)
Retiring to the Seaside, Routledge, London.

Kastenbaum, R. and Kastenbaum, B.S. (1971)
'Hope, survival and the caring environment', in E. Palmore and F. Jeffers (eds) *Prediction of life Span*, Heath, Lexington, Massachusetts.

Katz, S., Ford, A.B., Moskowitz, R.W., Jackson, B.A. and Jaffe, M.W. (1963)
'Studies of illness in the aged', *Journal of the American Medical Association*, 185, 914-19.

Kay, D.W.K., Beamish, P. and Roth, M. (1962)
'Some medical and social characteristics of elderly people under state care', *Sociological Review Monograph*, 5, 173-93.

Kay, D.W.K., Beamish, P. and Roth, N. (1964)
'Old age mental disorders in Newcastle-Upon-Tyne, Part I: A study of prevalence', *British Journal of Psychiatry*, 110, 146-58.

Kay, D.W.K., Garside, R.F. and Roth, M. (1966)
A four-year follow-up study of a random sample of old people originally seen in their own homes: A physical, social and psychiatric enquiry, Communication to the 4th World Congress of Psychiatry, Madrid.

Knapp, M.R.J. (1984)
The Economics of Social Care, Macmillan, London.

Lang, N.M. and Clinton, J.F. (1983)
'Assessment and assurance of the quality of nursing care', *Evaluation and the Health Professions*, 6, 211-32.

Lask, J. and Lask, B. (1981)
Child Psychiatry and Social Work, Tavistock, London.
Latto, S. (1980a)
'Help begins at home', *Community Care*, 24 April, 15-16
Latto, S. (1980b)
'Help begins at home', *Community Care*, 12 June, 20-21
Law, E. (1982)
'Light on hospital social work: A major study in Manchester', *Social Work Service*, 29, 20-29.
Lawton, M.P. (1972)
'The dimensions of morale' in D.P. Kent, R. Kastenbaum and S. Sherwood (eds) *Research, Planning and Action for the Elderly*, Behavioural Publications, New York.
Lawton, M.P. (1975)
'The Philadelphia Geriatric Centre Morale Scale: A revision', *Journal of Gerontology*, 30, 85-9.
Levin, E. (1982)
The Supporters of Confused Elderly People in the Community, National Institute for Social Work, London.
Lieberman, M.A. (1971)
'Some issues in studying psychological predictors of survival', in E. Palmore and F. Jeffers (eds) *Prediction of Life Span*, Heath, Lexington, Massachusetts.
Lohmann, N. (1977)
'Correlations of life satisfaction, morale and adjustment measures', *Journal of Gerontology*, 32, 73-5.
Lowenthal, M.F. and Haven, C. (1968)
'Intervention and adaptation: Intimacy as a critical variable', *American Sociological Bulletin*, 33, 20-30.
Luker, K.A. (1981)
'Health visiting and the elderly', *Nursing Times*, 77, 137-40.
Mayer-Gross, W., Slater, E. and Roth, M. (1977)
Clinical Psychiatry, Bailliere-Tindall, London.
Means, R. (1981)
Community Care and Meals-on-Wheels, Working Paper 21, University of Bristol School for Advanced Urban Studies, Bristol.
Merry, J. (1980)
'Alcoholism in the aged', *British Journal of Alcohol and Alcoholism*, 15, 56-7.
Merton, London Borough of (1976)
'The home help service in the London Borough of Merton', *Clearing House for Local Authority Social Services Research*, 6, 3-92.
Miller, P. and Ingham, J.G. (1976)
'Friends, confidants and symptoms', *Social Psychiatry*, 11, 51-8.
Mishara, B.L. and Kastenbaum, R. (1981)
Alcohol and Old Age, Grune and Stratton, New York.
Moroney, R.M. (1976)
The Family and the State, Longman, London.

Morris, J.N. and Sherwood, S. (1975)
'A retesting and modification of the Philadelphia Geriatric Centre Morale Scale', *Journal of Gerontology*, 30, 77-84.
Morris, R. (1977)
'Caring for vs caring about people', *Social Work*, 22, 353-9.
Mullen, E.J. and Dumpson, J.R. (1972)
'Is social work on the wrong track?', in E.J. Mullen and J.R. Dumpson (eds) *Evaluation of Social Intervention*, Jossey-Bass, San Francisco.
Murphy, E. (1982)
'Social origins of depression in old age', *British Journal of Psychiatry*, 141, 135-42.
National Foster Care Association (1981)
Foster Care Allowances and Income Tax, London.
Neill, J. (1982)
'Some variations in policy and procedure relating to Part III applications in the GLC area', *British Journal of Social Work*, 12, 229-45.
Neugarten, B.L., Havighurst, R.J. and Tobin, S.S. (1961)
'The measurement of life satisfaction', *Journal of Gerontology*, 16, 134-43.
Nissel, M. and Bonnerjea, L. (1982)
Family Care of the Handicapped Elderly: Who Pays?, Policy Studies Institute, London.
Office of Population Censuses and Surveys (1971)
Census 1971, HMSO, London.
Palmore, E. (1969)
'Physical, mental and social factors in predicting longevity', *The Gerontologist*, 9, 103-8.
Parkes, C.M. (1971)
'Psycho-social transitions: A field for study', *Social Science and Medicine*, 5, 101-15.
Payne, M. (1977)
'Integrating domiciliary care into an area team', *Social Work Service*, 14, 54-8.
Pinker, R. (1985)
'Against the flow', *Community Care*, 18 April, 20-22.
Plank, D. (1977)
Caring for the Elderly, Greater London Council Research Memorandum, 512, London.
Plank, D. (1978)
The Policy Context, Paper given at the conference on *Evaluating New Domiciliary and Day Interventions for the Elderly*, University of Kent, May.
Plank, D. (1979)
An Overview of the Position of Elderly People in Society, Paper given at the MIND conference on *Positive Approaches to Mental Infirmity in Elderly People*, Westminster, May.
Porter, R. (ed.) (1984)
Child Sexual Abuse Within the Family, CIBA Foundation/Tavistock, London.

Post, F. (1962)
The Significance of Affective Symptoms in Old Age, Maudsley Monograph 10, Oxford University Press, Oxford.

Post, F. (1966)
Persistent Persecutory States of the Elderly, Pergamon, Oxford.

Qureshi, H., Challis, D.J. and Davies, B.P. (1983)
'Motivations and rewards of helpers in the Kent community care scheme', in S.Hatch (ed.) *Volunteers: Patterns, Meanings and Motives*, Volunteer Centre, Berkhamstead.

Qureshi, H., Challis, D.J. and Davies, B.P. (1986)
Why Help?, Gower, Aldershot (forthcoming).

Ratna, L. (1982)
'Crisis intervention in psychogeriatrics: A two-year follow-up study', *British Journal of Psychiatry*, 141, 296-301.

Ratna, L. and Davis, J. (1984)
'Family therapy with the elderly mentally ill: Some strategies and techniques', *British Journal of Psychiatry*, 145, 311-15.

Rees, S. (1978)
Social Work Face to Face, Edward Arnold, London.

Reid, W. and Epstein, L. (1972)
Task-centered Casework, Columbia University Press, New York.

Reid, W. and Shyne, A. (1969)
Brief and Extended Casework, Columbia University Press, New York.

Rosin, A.J. (1965)
'After-care of elderly patients discharged from hospital', *The Medical Officer*, 29 January, 62-4.

Rosin, A.J. and Glatt, M.M. (1971)
'Alcohol excess in the elderly', *Quarterly Journal of Studies on Alcoholism*, 32, 53-9.

Roth, M. and Kay, D.W.K. (1956)
'Affective disorders arising in the senium: Part II physical disability as an aetiological factor', *Journal of Mental Science*, 102, 141-50.

Rowbottom, R., Hey, A. and Billis, D. (1974)
Social Services Departments: Developing Patterns of Work and Organisation, Heinemann, London.

Rowlings, C. (1981)
Social Work with Elderly People, Allen and Unwin, London.

Sainsbury, P. and Grad, J. (1971)
'The psychiatrist and the family of the geriatric patient', *Journal of Geriatric Psychiatry*, 4, 23-41.

Sanford, J. (1975)
'Tolerance of debility in elderly dependents at home: Its significance for hospital practice', *British Medical Journal*, 3, 471-3.

Schulz, R. and Brenner, G. (1977)
'Relocation of the aged: A review and theoretical analysis', *Journal of Gerontology*, 32, 323-3.

South East Thames Regional Health Authority (1978)
Strategies and Guidelines for the Care of Elderly People, SETRHA, London.
Sherwood, D.C., Morris, J.N. and Sherwood, S. (1975)
'A multivariate, nonrandomised matching technique for studying the impact of social interventions', in E. Struening and M. Guttentag (eds) *Handbook of Evaluation Research I*, Sage, London and Beverly Hills.
Simons, K. and Warburton, R.W. (1980)
A Sensible Service, Cambridgeshire Social Services Department, Cambridge.
Smale, G. (1983)
'Can we afford not to develop social work practice?', *British Journal of Social Work*, 13, 251-64.
Smits, H.L. (1981)
'The PSRO in perspective', *New England Journal of Medicine*, 305, 253-9.
Snyder, L.H., Rupprecht, P., Pyrek, J., Brekhus, S. and Moss, T. (1978)
'Wandering', *The Gerontologist*, 18:3, 272-80.
Steinberg, R.M. and Carter, G.W., (1983)
Case-Management and the Elderly, Heath, Lexington, Massachusetts.
Stevenson, O. (1981a)
'The frail elderly: A social worker's perspective', in T. Arie (ed.) *Health Care of the Elderly*, Croom Helm, London.
Stevenson, O. (1981b)
Specialisation in Social Service Teams, George Allen and Unwin, London.
Stevenson, O. (1981c)
'It's time to be all experts now', *Community Care*, 9 April, 18-20.
Stevenson, O. and Parsloe, P. (1978)
Social Services Teams: The Practitioners' View, HMSO, London.
Sugden, R. and Williams, A. (1978)
The Principles of Practical Cost-benefit Analysis, Oxford University Press, Oxford.
Sylph, J. and Kedward, H.B. (1974)
Social Adjustment and the Measurement of Social Dysfunction, unpublished paper, Epidemiology Research Unit, Clarke Institute of Psychiatry, Toronto.
Tobin, S.S. and Lieberman, M. (1976)
Last Home for the Aged, Jossey-Bass, San Francisco.
Townsend, P. (1962)
The Last Refuge, Routledge and Kegan Paul, London.
Tulloch, A.J. and Moore, V. (1979)
'A randomised controlled trial of geriatric screening and surveillance in general practice', *Journal of the Royal College of General Practitioners*, 29, 733-42.
Tunstall, J. (1966)
Old and Alone, Routledge and Kegan Paul, London.
Turner, B.F., Tobin, S.S. and Lieberman, M. (1972)
'Personality traits as predictors of institutionalisation in the aged', *Journal of Gerontology*, 27, 61-8.

Vaughn, C.P. and Leff, J.P. (1976)
'The influence of family and social factors on the course of psychiatric illness', *British Journal of Psychiatry*, 129, 125-37.
Vetter, N.J., Jones, D. and Victor, C. (1984)
'Effect of health visitors working with elderly patients in general practice: A randomised controlled trial', *British Medical Journal*, 288, 369-71.
Wager, R. (1972)
Care of the Elderly, Institute of Municipal Treasurers and Accountants, London.
Waltham Forest, London Borough of (1981)
Home Care Team: Position Statement, London Borough of Waltham Forest Social Services Department.
Wasser, E. (1971)
'Protective practice in serving the mentally impaired aged', *Social Casework*, 52, 510-22.
Wattis, J.P. (1981)
'Alcohol problems in the elderly', *Journal of the American Geriatrics Society*, 29, 131-4.
Wenger, G.C. (1984)
The Supportive Network: Coping with Old Age, Allen and Unwin, London.
Wheatley, V. (1980)
'Relative stress', *Community Care*, 28 August, 22-3.
Whittington, C. (1983)
'Social work in the welfare network: Negotiating daily practice', *British Journal of Social Work*, 13, 265-86.
Williamson, J. (1981)
'Screening, surveillance and case-finding', in T. Arie (ed.) *Health Care of the Elderly*, Croom Helm, London.
Williamson, J., Stokoe, I.M., Gray, S., Fisher, M. and Smith, A. (1964)
'Old people at home: Their unreported needs', *Lancet*, i, 1117-20.
Wing, J.K. (1978)
Reasoning About Madness, Oxford University Press, Oxford.
Woods, R.T. and Holden, U.P. (1981)
'Reality orientation', in B. Isaacs (ed.) *Recent Advances in Geriatric Medicine, 2*, Churchill-Livingstone, Edinburgh.
Wright, K.G., Cairns, J.A. and Snell, M.C. (1981)
Costing Care, Community Care/University of Sheffield, London.
Yarnell, J.W.G. and St Leger, A.S. (1979)
'The prevalence, severity and factors associated with urinary incontinence in a random sample of the elderly', *Age and Ageing*, 8, 81-5.
Yawney, B. and Slover, D.L. (1973)
'Relocation of the elderly', *Social Work*, 18 May, 86-93.
Zellner, A. (1962)
'An efficient method of estimating seemingly unrelated regressions and tests for aggregation bias', *Journal of the American Statistical Association*, 57, 348-68.

AUTHOR INDEX

Abrams, M., 234, 238
Abrams, P., 116, 164, 198, 216
Allen, I., 5, 51, 111, 115, 117, 162
Applebaum, R., 18
Audit Commission, 3, 4, 8

Bamford, T., 8
Barclay, P., 222
Barrowclough, C., 222, 224
Bayley, M., 5
Bebbington, A.C., 1
Bergmann, K., 6, 51, 85, 87, 96, 104 107, 115, 150, 160, 165, 204, 214, 218, 224, 238, 240
Berkmann, L. F., 150, 152
Berman, S., 99, 103
Biestek, F.P., 48
Black, J., 4, 6, 9, 22, 69, 104
Blazer, D., 150, 152
Bonnerjea, L., 164
Boyd, R.V., 79
Brearley, C.P., 49
Brenner, G., 151
Brent, London Borough of, 224
British Association of Social Workers (BASW), 43
Brocklehurst, J.C., 71, 76, 79
Brotherton, J., 3
Brown, G.W., 152, 226, 239
Butler, A., 229

Cahalen, D., 90
Cairns, V., 240
Campbell, D.T., 19
Carter, G.W., 222
Carter, K., 65
Carver, V., 60
Castledene, C.M., 78, 79,
Challis, D.J., xv, 2, 3, 10, 11, 14, 17, 19, 21, 22, 47, 62, 83, 107, 153, 167, 168, 189, 191, 211, 218, 225, 227, 228, 233
Charlesworth, A., 5, 11, 117, 186
Chartered Institute of Public Finance and Accountancy (CIPFA), 31
Chernesky, R.H., 60
Cheshire County Council, 2, 3
Chesterman, J., 10, 11, 22, 47, 62 187, 218, 219, 225
Clare, A., 240
Clinton, J.F., 227
Collins, A.H., 119
Connelly, N., 2, 3, 4, 6, 18, 68, 119, 144, 221, 233
Cormican, E.J., 49
Craig, J., 1
Culyer, A.J., 43

Davies, B.P., xv, 2, 11, 17, 19, 43, 47, 153, 167, 168, 189, 191, 211, 233, 237
Davies, J., 51
Davies, M., 129, 221
Davies, R.M., 42
Department of Health and Social Security (DHSS), 3, 174, 177
Department of the Environment, 169
Dexter, M., 2, 3, 4
Dimond, E., 14
Dowd, J.J., 144
Droller, M., 90
Duffin, H.M., 78, 79
Duncan, I.B. 42
Dunnachie, N., 18

Eason, D., 8
Edwards, C., 3
Edwards, J.L., 60
Epstein, L., 45, 48, 222
Evans, J.G., 103
Evans, T.N., 65

Family Policy Studies Centre, 5
Fean, L., 4

Fennell, G., 3
Ferlie, E., 3, 7, 228
Fleming, I., 222, 224
Foster, E.M., 85, 104, 197
Fuller, J., 96, 116

Garraway, W.M., 152
Gibbins, F.J., 18
Gilmore, A.J.J., 150
Gilroy, D., 5
Glatt, M.M., 90
Glendenning, C., 39
Glennerster, H., 228, 230
Goldberg, D.P., 85, 197, 229, 234, 238
Goldberg, E.M., 2, 3, 4, 5, 6, 7, 8, 9, 18, 22, 27, 33, 43, 45, 48, 51-2, 62, 68, 104, 119, 144, 157, 160, 197, 221, 222, 233, 237, 238, 239
Goldfarb, A., 49, 89
Grad, J., 5, 51, 117, 237
Gray, B., 87
Greengross, S., 5
Gwynedd Social Services Department, 4
Gwynne, D., 4

Hadley, R., 3, 62, 228
Hall, M.R.P., 73, 218
Hamdy, R.C., 76
Hamilton, M., 83, 234, 235, 237
Harbert, W., 2, 3, 4
Harris, T., 152, 239
Hedley, R., 3
Hemsi, L., 230
Henderson, S., 239
Hendriksen, C., 149, 152, 153, 165
Hey, A., 4, 6, 221, 224
Hillingdon, London Borough of, 4
Hirsch, F., 164
Hoenig, J., 235, 237
Holden, U.P., 103
Holme, A., 5
Howe, D., 5, 222
Howell, N., 2, 4
Hunt, A., 5, 32, 33
Huntington, J., 9
Hurley, B., 2, 3
Huxley, P., 85, 197, 229

Ingham, J.G., 152
Ingliata, J., 229
Isaacs, B., 27, 28, 76, 87, 96, 115 164, 201, 209, 238

Jacoby, R., 160, 165
James, O.F.W., 90
Johnson, M.L., 3
Jones, D.A., 37

Karn, V., 32, 64, 160
Kastenbaum, B.S., 90, 150
Kastenbaum, R., 150
Katz, S., 27, 33, 154, 160, 190, 236, 238
Kay, D.W.K., 33, 85, 150, 209
Kedward, H.B., 240
Knapp, M.R.J. 11, 17, 47, 168, 189

Lang, N.M., 227
Lask, B., 22
Lask, J., 22
Latto, S., 3, 4
Law, E., 60
Lawton, M.P., 190, 233, 234, 235
Leff, J.P., 224
Levin, E., 5, 22, 51, 55, 68, 79, 164
Lieberman, M.A., 150, 153, 224
Luker, K.A., 160, 165
Lurie, A., 60

Maizels, J., 5
Mayer-Gross, W., 191
McGrath, M., 3, 62, 227
Means, R., 3
Merry, J., 94
Merton, London Borough of, 4
Miller, P., 152
Mishara, B.L., 90
Moore, V., 160, 165
Moroney, R.M., 5
Morris, J.N., 233, 234

Morris, R., 222
Murphy, E., 152

Neugarten, B.L., 233
Neville, Y., 27, 28, 201, 209, 238
Nissel, M., 164
Norman, A., 3

Palmore, E., 150
Pancoast, D.L., 119
Parkes, C.M., 107
Parsloe, P., 2, 5, 6, 7, 9, 22, 68, 104
Plank, D., 1, 2, 3, 4, 6, 7, 221
Porter, R., 21
Post, F., 86, 95
Pritchard, C., 229

Qureshi, H., xv, 130, 133, 142, 152

Rappaport, M.B., 99, 103
Ratna, L., 51, 149, 152
Rees, S., 5
Reid, W., 45, 48, 222
Rosin, A.J., 64, 90
Roth, M., 85
Rowbottom, R., 3, 6
Rowlings, C., 48-9
Rutter, M., 239

Sainsbury, P., 5, 51, 117, 237
Sanford, J., 5, 77, 79
Schulz, R., 151
Sherwood, S., 233, 234
Shyne, A., 222
Simons, K., 54
Slover, D.L., 151
Smits, H.L., 227
Snyder, L.H., 102
St Leger, A.S., 79, 191
Stanley, J.C., 19
Steinberg, R.M., 222
Stevenson, O., 2, 5, 6, 7, 9, 22, 57, 68
104, 144
Sugden, R., 167
Sylph, J., 240
Syme, S.L., 150, 152

Tobin, S.S., 150, 153, 224
Townsend, P., 1
Tulloch, A.J., 160, 165
Tunstall, J., 237
Turner, B.F., 214

Vaughn, C.P. 224
Vetter, N.J., 149, 152, 165

SUBJECT INDEX

accountability in social care services, 7, 10, 131
accountability of case managers (see also responsibility of), 10, 131
Activities of Daily Living, Katz index of, 20, 27, 30, 33, 35, 96, 110, 154, 160, 201, 205, 209, 236, 238
admission to care in institutions, 18, 66, 145, 147, 148, 152, 164, 219
alcohol abuse and the elderly, 33, 54, 71, 83, 90-94, 104, 217, 222
ambivalence, 48
anxiety in the elderly, 6, 20, 24, 26, 33, 43, 51, 58, 66, 73, 83, 87, 89, 94, 95, 100, 107, 108, 126, 141, 154, 201, 204, 217
assessment in project, 43-6, 68
assessment instruments, project, 46, 61

bed-blocking and hospital back-up, 230
bereavement and other loss and project practice, 49, 50, 94, 108
boundaries to care, 24, 50, 78, 90, 116, 127, 129
breathlessness in elderly people, 85, 160, 190, 207, 213
budget limit, 10, 61, 228
budget, control over, 9, 228

Capacity to Cope variable defined, Clients' Felt, 153, 234
care planning and efficiency, 47
care planning in project, 47, 61
carers - see informal care
caring capacities of communities, 164
case finding in project, 39
case management, 2, 4, 5, 7, 8, 11, 13, 21, 39, 69, 144, 164, 199, 222, 223, 229
case management defined, core tasks of, 21, 39
case management in mental health, 223
case management tasks and aspects of efficiency, 2, 8, 13, 69
case review system - see also recording, 62, 250-60
centralisation and decentralisation, 62, 225, 227
'clinical generalisation', 21, 226-7
commercialisation effect and the project, 164, 219
community care approach, 8, 11, 14, 39, 43, 69, 222, 228, 229, 231
community care project records, 61-2, 121, 241-67
community care workers, use of time by, 78, 81, 82, 108
community care, health/social care models of, 13
community care, social care models of, 13
community nursing service and the project, 175-6
community psychiatric nursing, 175
confiding relationship, 152, 153, 154, 157, 165
confusion - see confusional states
confusional state, variable defined, 239

confusional states in elderly people, 26, 29, 43, 45, 64, 71, 76, 83, 95-6, 97, 136, 193, 201, 204, 222
contracts in community care, 22, 45, 50, 58, 83, 89, 126, 127, 128, 134, 135, 139, 140, 142, 173, 224, 261-4
coordination of services, 57
'cost-effectiveness issue', the, 17, 18, Chap. 9 passim, 219
cost effects, estimates of, 217
costs to clients and carers, 168, 177-80, 187, 211
costs to clients and carers estimated, opportunity, 168, 211
costs to national health service estimated, opportunity, 110, 168, 173-6, 186, 187, 190, 205, 217
costs to national health service variable defined, opportunity, 173, 186
costs to social services department estimated, opportunity, 168, 169-71, 186, 187, 190, 194, 220
costs to social services department estimated, revenue account, 169-71
costs to social services department variable defined, opportunity, 169, 186
costs to society estimated, opportunity, 180, 187, 190, 211, 216, 218, 220
costs to society variable defined, opportunity, 180, 187
costs, constituents of, 167-88
costs, research, development and running, 171-2

day care in community care project, 171
dementia - see confusional states
Department of Health and Social Security (DHSS), xvi, 168, 178
Dependency Groups defined, 28
depressed mood, variable defined, 83, 234
depression in elderly people, 20, 25, 26, 33, 42, 50, 53, 76, 77, 83-7, 92, 94, 95, 99, 141, 154, 197, 200, 201, 204, 215, 217

efficiency defined, horizontal target, 39
efficiency defined, input mix, 13, 222
efficiency defined, market or output mix, 221, 224
efficiency defined, technical, 13
efficiency defined, vertical target, 39
efficiency of project, input mix, 13, 43, 47, 222, 224
efficiency of the project, horizontal target, 13, 39, 40, 42, 224
efficiency of the project, vertical target, 13, 39, 40, 42
enabling - see making needed help acceptable
equivalence of experimental and comparison groups, 24, 26-30
experimental design, 18

falling, risk of - see risk of accidents
family practitioners and case management, 67, 100
family practitioners and the project, 67, 85, 86, 95, 96, 100, 153, 160, 205
family relationships, 114-5, 198, 226, 234, 237

functional psychoses, 93, 94

gaps in service, filling, 116
geriatricians, 9

health and social services, interdependence of, 1, 209-11
helpers' tasks - see also use of time by helpers, 134-41
helpers, motivations and rewards of project, 130
helpers, payment of project, 127-8, 130, 133, 173
helpers, recruitment, matching and management of project, 119-26
home help organisers, 3, 4, 25, 40
home help service, 3, 31, 42, 52, 53, 54, 64, 66, 76, 85, 96, 108, 116, 137, 173
home help service and the project, 31, 52-3, 66, 77
hospital discharge and the project, 43, 55, 61, 67, 73, 81, 94, 99, 104, 139, 145
hospital, acute wards in, 81, 209
hospital, psychiatric or psychiatric wards in, 87, 94, 96, 101, 174, 186, 229

incontinence in elderly person, 28, 61, 66, 67, 71, 72, 75, 76, 77, 78, 79, 96, 100, 104, 107, 108, 114, 122, 125, 129, 143, 160, 190, 197, 201, 205, 211, 213, 223
incontinence laundry services, 76, 77, 78, 79, 138
informal care and agency allocations, 2
informal carers and case managers, 52
informal support networks, strengthening, and helping informal carers, 5, 7, 14, 50, 58, 105, 110, 116, 117, 130, 139, 145, 204, 216, 223, 229
inter-agency collaboration - see also joint working, 4, 7, 59

joint working, 230

'letter of agreement' - see contracts
loneliness, 14, 20, 32, 50, 66, 92, 103, 105, 138, 154, 197, 213, 224, 234
loss and the elderly - see bereavment

making needed help acceptable, 43, 45, 48, 49, 135, 140, 198
management team, the project's, 39, 42
matching cases to improve equivalence, 28, 29, 150
matching helpers and clients, 20, 28, 30, 124-5
mental infirmity - see also dementia, 83, 128, 149, 150, 190, 219
monitoring in project, 61
Monument Trust, the, xvi
Morale - see Subjective Well-being
Morale variable defined, 233-4
mortality probabilities, 150, 151, 152, 153

night sitting service, 128

occupational therapists, 4, 42
organisational locus of project, 39
outcomes - see also outputs, 7, 17, 19, 20, 21, 46, 71, 115, 145, 155, 160 162, 189, 193, 233
outcomes, destinational, 71, 145-7
outputs, final, 19, 20, 233-7
outputs, intermediate, 19, 237-8

paranoid psychosis in elderly people, 33, 53, 222
'patch' organisation of field personnel, 228
peer review and community care, 10, 11, 14, 223
personality and attitudes to help, 43, 87-90, 191, 198, 208, 214, 239-40
physical illness in elderly people, 45, 85
private residential care, 56, 78, 94, 148-9
production of welfare approach, 17, 189
psychiatrists, 32, 86
psychologists, 223, 230
psychogeriatric service, 104, 230

Quality of Care variable defined, 235
'quasi-informal' carers, project development of, 142, 189, 193
'quasi-input' defined, 189, 191, 238-40

recording, case, 61, 62
referrals to project, 39-43
relocation effects, 151-2
residential care, 1, 4, 6, 8, 13, 14, 20, 21, 23, 24, 26, 33, 40, 41, 42, 56, 57, 58, 60, 65, 66, 67, 71, 75, 81, 85, 86, 96, 101, 107, 114, 139, 147, 148, 149, 150, 155, 157, 164, 167, 169, 176, 177, 179, 181, 186, 197, 198, 199, 204, 209, 214, 216, 217, 219, 224, 228, 230, 239
retirement, 30, 32, 63, 64, 65, 94, 105, 134, 162, 173
risk of accidents to clients, 36, 38, 71, 72, 73, 75, 104, 154, 160, 190 197, 200, 201, 204, 207, 217, 219

screening referrals for appropriateness and vertical target efficiency, 42
screening referrals for appropriateness in project, 39
Seebohm Committee on local authority and allied social services, the, 4, 229
selection of experimental and comparison cases, 22-36
sheltered housing and community care, 56, 58, 68, 173
short-term intervention - see also task-centred work, 21, 222
social isolation, 76, 85, 94, 105, 201, 204, 2l5, 217, 219
social networks - see also informal support, 1, 17, 65
social opportunity costs - see costs to society, opportunity
social support, 20, 65, 105, 150, 152, 191, 194, 198, 200, 208, 214
social work practice and the elderly, 226

social work roles and tasks, 221-2
Subjective Well-being, 20, 155, 156, 190, 193, 194, 201, 214, 215, 220, 224, 233, 235
Survival variable, length of, 145, 190
survival, effects on, 149, 186, 187, 190, 209

targeting, 8, 13, 23, 39, 40, 42, 208, 214, 215
task-centred work - see also short-term intervention, 45
technological determinacy in social care - see 'clinical generalisation'
time allocations of community care workers, 58-60

unit costs, 11, 169, 172-3, 175

voluntary organisations, 40, 63
volunteers and quasi-volunteers in community care - see helpers, community care
volunteers in social care, 57, 63, 85